Radical voices, radical ways

Manchester University Press

SEAA

Société d'études Anglo-Américaines
des XVII° et XVIII° siècles

XVII-XVIII

SEVENTEENTH- AND EIGHTEENTH-CENTURY STUDIES

General Editor

Anne Dunan-Page

Seventeenth- and Eighteenth-Century Studies is a series of the Société d'Études Anglo-Américaines des XVIIe et XVIIIe siècles promoting interdisciplinary work on the period *c.*1603–1815, covering all aspects of the literature, culture and history of the British Isles, colonial and post-colonial America, and other British colonies. The series welcomes academic monographs, as well as collective volumes of essays, that combine theoretical and methodological approaches from more than one discipline to further our understanding of the period and geographical areas.

Radical voices, radical ways

Articulating and disseminating radicalism in seventeenth- and eighteenth-century Britain

Edited by
Laurent Curelly and Nigel Smith

Manchester University Press

Published by Manchester University Press
Oxford Road, Manchester M13 9PL

www.manchesteruniversitypress.co.uk

British Library Cataloguing-in-Publication Data
A catalogue record for this book is available from the British Library

Library of Congress Cataloging-in-Publication Data applied for

ISBN 978 1 5261 0619 3 hardback
ISBN 978 1 5261 3432 5 paperback

First published 2016

Typeset in 10/12 Sabon by
Servis Filmsetting Ltd, Stockport, Cheshire

Contents

List of contributors   *page* vii

Introduction – *Laurent Curelly and Nigel Smith*   1

PART I Radical language and themes

1 Community of goods: an unacceptable radical theme at
   the time of the English revolution – *Jean-Pierre Cavaillé*   41
2 Thomas Paine's democratic linguistic radicalism: a
   political philosophy of language? – *Carine Lounissi*   60
3 English radicalism in the 1650s: the Quaker search for
   the true knowledge – *Catie Gill*   80

PART II Radical exchanges and networks

4 Secular millenarianism as a radical utopian project in
   Shaftesbury – *Patrick Müller*   103
5 The diffusion and impact of Baron d'Holbach's texts in
   Great Britain, 1765–1800 – *Nick Treuherz*   125

PART III Radical media and practices

6 The parliamentary context of political radicalism in the
   English revolution – *Jason Peacey*   151

v

7   Toasting and the diffusion of radical ideas, 1780–1832
    – *Rémy Duthille*   170

PART IV Radical fiction and representation

8   Contesting the press-oppressors of the age: the captivity
    narrative of William Okeley (1675) – *Catherine Vigier*   193
9   Ways of thinking, ways of writing: novelistic expression
    of radicalism in the works of Godwin, Holcroft and
    Bage – *Marion Leclair*   211
10 'The insane enthusiasm of the time': remembering the
    regicides in eighteenth- and nineteenth-century Britain
    and North America – *Edward Vallance*   229

Select bibliography   251
Index   270

List of contributors

Jean-Pierre Cavaillé is Senior Lecturer in History and Anthropology at École des Hautes Études en Sciences Sociales inToulouse. His interests include the cultural, intellectual and social history of early modern Europe as well as the history of early modern philosophy. He is a member of various European research groups and scholarly networks. He has published books, edited volumes and articles on seventeenth-century libertinism and religious dissent.

Laurent Curelly is Senior Lecturer in British Studies at Université de Haute Alsace in Mulhouse. He specialises in seventeenth-century history, politics and literature. He wrote his PhD on tears and weeping in the poetry of Crashaw, Donne, Herbert, Southwell and Vaughan. In addition to the Metaphysical poets, his interests include Civil War radicalism, early modern print culture and cultural trans-fers between the British Isles and the European continent. He has written widely on Civil War journalism and sectarian radicalism and contributed essays to scholarly reviews as well as chapters to edited volumes on these topics. He has published a translation into French of the editorials of the radical newsbook *The Moderate* (2011). He is currently working on a monograph in English on *The Moderate*.

Rémy Duthille is Senior Lecturer in British Studies at Université Bordeaux Montaigne. He wrote his PhD on the patriotism of British radicals in the twenty years preceding the French Revolution, and has published various articles on Richard Price. He is now broadening the scope of his research on political discourse, including toasting, in the long eighteenth century.

Catie Gill is Lecturer in Early Modern Writing in the Department of English and Drama, School of the Arts, Loughborough University. She has published on Quakerism, and specifically on the collective values of the movement with respect to gender. Her second book was an edited collection: *Theatre and Culture: From Leviathan to the Licensing Act.* She is currently working on William Chillingworth's religious rationalism.

Marion Leclair is an École Normale Supérieure graduate and a doctoral student at Université Paris 3 Sorbonne Nouvelle. She specialises in the English radical novel. She has published a translation into French of *A Dream of John Ball* by William Morris.

Carine Lounissi is Senior Lecturer in American Studies at Université de Rouen and a member of the LARCA research group at Université Paris Diderot. She wrote her PhD on Paine's political thought. She published it in November 2012 as *La Pensée politique de Thomas Paine en contexte: théorie et pratique.* Her research focuses on the history of political ideas, the American Revolution, republicanism and political language.

Patrick Müller, PhD in British Studies, is a teacher of English for the German Federal Office of Languages. His doctoral thesis *Latitudinarianism and Didacticism* was published in 2009. He organised a symposium on the social and political impact of the first and third Earls of Shaftesbury at the Ashley-Cooper's family seat, St Giles's House, Dorset, in 2015. He has lectured and published widely on Shaftesbury, other issues related to the eighteenth century and on contemporary British and American literature.

Jason Peacey is Professor of Early Modern British History at UCL. He edited *The Regicides and the Execution of Charles I* (2001) and *The Print Culture of Parliament, 1600–1800* (2007), co-edited *Parliament at Work* (2002), and is the author of *Politicians and Pamphleteers. Propaganda in the Civil Wars and Interregnum* (2004) and *Print and Public Politics in the English Revolution*

(2013). Recent articles include 'Print, publicity and popularity: the projecting of Sir Balthazar Gerbier, 1640–1662', *Journal of British Studies* (2012) and 'Sir Edward Dering, popularity and the public, 1640–1644', *Historical Journal* (2011). He is currently working on a project relating to overlapping and interlocking publics in seventeenth-century Europe.

Nigel Smith is William and Annie S. Paton Foundation Professor of Ancient and Modern Literature at Princeton University. He has published mostly on early modern literature, especially the seventeenth century; his work is interdisciplinary by inclination and training. He has edited the Longman Annotated English Poets edition of *Andrew Marvell's Poems* (2003, pbk 2007), is the author of *Andrew Marvell: The Chameleon* (Yale University Press, 2010; pbk 2012), and many articles on Marvell. His other major works are *Is Milton better than Shakespeare?* (2008), *Literature and Revolution in England, 1640–1660* (1994) and *Perfection Proclaimed: Language and Literature in English Radical Religion 1640–1660* (1989). He has also edited the *Journal of George Fox* (1998), and the *Ranter Pamphlets* (1983; revised edn. 2014), and co-edited with Nicholas McDowell the *Oxford Handbook to Milton* (Oxford University Press, 2009, pbk 2011). A new book concerned with the state and literary production in early modern Europe is forthcoming, and he has co-edited a forthcoming collection with Jan Bloemendal, *Politics and Aesthetics in European Baroque Tragedy* (Brill, 2016).

Nick Treuherz is Lecturer at the University of Liverpool. His PhD thesis examined the writings of French materialists Diderot, La Mettrie, Helvétius and d'Holbach, and more particularly their diffusion and impact on the German Enlightenment.

Ted Vallance is Professor in Early Modern British Political Culture at the University of Roehampton and has previously taught at the universities of Sheffield, Manchester and Liverpool. He is the author of *A Radical History of Britain* (Little, Brown and Co., 2009), *The Glorious Revolution* (Little, Brown and Co., 2006) and *Revolutionary England and the National Covenant* (Boydell, 2005). With Harald Braun he has edited two volumes on conscience and casuistry in early modern Europe: *Contexts of Conscience* (Palgrave, 2004) and *The Renaissance Conscience* (Wiley Blackwell, 2011).

His articles have featured in *Albion, English Historical Review, Historical Journal, Historical Research, History Workshop Journal, The Huntington Library Quarterly, Journal of British Studies, Renaissance Studies* and *The Seventeenth Century*.

Catherine Vigier is Senior Lecturer in British Studies at Université de Rouen. She specialises in British captivity narratives from the Mediterranean on which she has published various articles.

Introduction

Laurent Curelly and Nigel Smith

The chapters in this volume study the presence of radical ideas in Britain from the period of the English Civil Wars in the mid-seventeenth century to the Romantic revolution in the nineteenth century. They explore the modes of articulation and dissemination of radical ideas in the period by focusing on actors ('radical voices') and a variety of written texts and cultural practices ('radical ways'), ranging from fiction, correspondence, pamphlets and treatises to petitions presented to Parliament and toasts raised in public. They analyse the way these media interact with their political, religious, social and literary contexts.

Radicalism is an evasive concept that does not lend itself to easy categorisation. The word itself, which is used to mean a thorough transformation of a system from the root upwards according to its Latin etymology, is a fairly recent coinage. *The Oxford English Dictionary* records the first usage of the substantive 'radical' in a political sense as 1802, and has 1819 as the first recorded use of the term 'radicalism'. The French, German, Italian and Spanish languages seem to have borrowed their respective *radicalisme, Radikalismus* and *radicalismo* from the English word 'radicalism' and gradually extracted it from of its British context to describe domestic political and social realities. While the term accompanied the revolutions and emancipation movements of nineteenth-century Europe, its usage in the British context of late eighteenth-century political agitation, notably during the French Revolution, is conveniently accepted; however, applying it

1

to religious, political, social and cultural phenomena that emerged in mid seventeenth-century England in defiance of the existing order of things is certainly problematic and raises questions that will be addressed in this chapter.

Historians and literary scholars over the last forty years, in fact since the publication of Christopher Hill's article 'From Lollards to Levellers' in 1978,[1] have taken renewed interest in the word and the realities it encapsulates, debating whether radicalism is a heuristically innocuous and methodologically feasible historical concept. Some of them have expressed their doubts that such a notion is effective in any way.[2] They ask whether it makes sense at all to use the word before it was coined and whether its usage really helps early modern scholars to have a clearer understanding of the British Isles during the Civil Wars. There is a fair chance, they argue, that students of the period may run the risk of grafting their own ideological constructs, interpretations, even prejudices, onto a society in which the majority of the people had no apparent desire for groundbreaking change, one in which even those who later came to be labelled as 'radicals' had no intention of turning the world upside down[3] but only wanted England to go back to what they assumed were its religious and/or political roots.

The contributions to this volume challenge the 'nominalist' view that writing about radicals before the word even came into existence is dangerously anachronistic. However, the linguistic debate should not be evaded altogether; one should arguably go beyond merely claiming that the absence of a word to describe phenomena does not mean that these phenomena are nothing but a figment of the observer's imagination. Instead, one should concentrate on the linguistic evidence pointing to the existence of radicals and radical movements in seventeenth-century England. These individuals and groups were clearly identified by their contemporaries, not least by their opponents, as when heresiographers reviled the 'sectaries', 'heretics' and 'schismatics' of their time,[4] or when the term 'Levellers' was bandied around in pamphlets and newsbooks to cast opprobrium on political objectors. The fact that these labels were intrinsic to propagandistic scare stories aimed at preserving the religious or political *status quo* at a time when it was under serious attack need not lessen the scope of such assaults or preclude our name-tagging sectaries and Levellers 'radicals'. Despite their desire to return to an ideal or imagined *status quo ante*, many radical

2

groups did have a programme of reform – Levellers, Diggers, Fifth Monarchists and Quakers, to mention but a few.

Implied by the fortunes of the word 'Leveller' in the late 1640s is the fact that this very term became an apposite label as well as a convenient benchmark of radicalism. While Lilburne and his friends denied being Levellers, Winstanley and his Digger acolytes insisted on being named 'True Levellers' and the Ranter Abiezer Coppe dismissed 'sword levelling, or digging levelling' as thoroughly inconsistent with what he considered to be 'the prime levelling', by which he meant 'spiritual, inward levelling'.[5] Thus, Coppe was anxious to distance himself from Leveller levelling, as symbolised by the 'power of the sword' motif of Leveller tracts, and from Digger levelling; instead he meant to promote his Antinomian brand of levelling, an obvious sign that members of these groups were in fact self-conscious actors of change, be it of a political, social or religious nature, and that they sought to outperform one another in terms of attracting public attention, even if this entailed bearing the brunt of repression. They were involved, it seems, in some sort of self-fashioning that allowed them to promote their programme of reform.

There may have been more than one signifier to refer to radicals in seventeenth-century England, possibly indicating various strands of radicalism coming from individuals who were no longer happy with the political, social, religious or cultural norms that prevailed in a certain place and at a certain time. The 'nominalist' hypothesis is not sustainable, in that it is shaped by a static approach to historical phenomena and ignores the fluctuating and dialogic essence of these phenomena. Radicalism is a labile concept, and the prominence that it achieves depends on historical circumstances, in the same way as those whom we label radicals may change over time. This goes some way towards explaining why the Leveller leader William Walwyn, for example, adopted a radical stance in the 1640s before moving into the more settled field of medicine in the 1650s and penning medical treatises, which were published well into the restoration of the Stuart monarchy.[6]

The terms of the scholarly debate about the appropriateness of using the 'radical' label in an early modern context should be briefly stated before a tentative definition of the word 'radicalism' is suggested. In his 'Introduction' to *English Radicalism 1550–1850*, Glenn Burgess identifies three distinct approaches that he argues have characterised scholarly work on radical groups in early modern England since the 1970s: the 'nominalist', the 'substantive' and the 'functional' approaches.[7] The 'substantive' approach gained currency in academic circles as a result of Marxist historians in post-war Britain, especially under the influence of the Communist Party Historians' Group, developing an interest in the lives and ideas of the plebeians that Whig grand historical narratives had somewhat left out of their descriptions of Britain's march forward towards full democracy. Marxist teleology constructed radicalism as a continuous ideological tradition stretching back to the peasants' revolts of the Middle Ages and construed mid seventeenth-century radicals as fully-fledged, if disempowered, actors in a narrative that linked them to their radical predecessors and successors.[8]

The study of radicalism from a Marxist perspective was given fresh impetus in the ideologically fraught climate of post-war Europe, in the same way as the Cold War political context affected the historiography of the English revolution at large. So-called 'revisionist' historians rejected that perspective, which resulted in marginalising those that Christopher Hill and other Marxist scholars had brought centre stage in an attempt to write 'history from below' by recovering the voices of mid seventeenth-century plebeians. Revisionists criticised Marxist historians' overdependence on printed materials and favoured some manuscript sources instead in an effort to portray English society as it truly was during the revolution, not as it was perceived to be by those who had access to print.[9] The existence of Ranters was even dismissed as a propagandistic fabrication.[10] Revisionist scholars especially rehabilitated religion as a key explanation for what led individuals to embrace a particular cause, and kept a keen eye out for contingencies as factors of change instead of the overpowering structural dynamics of Marxist historians' theories. Revisionist historiography rejected the radical canon as being unrepresentative of a society that was by no means animated by any sense of class war but rather by a desire for consensus. 'Post-revisionist' historians challenged these theories and made use of Christopher Hill's influential appreciation of the events affecting England in the mid-seventeenth century as a wide-ranging cultural revolution. They turned their attention to new areas of enquiry, such as print culture and book history, to make sense of the English revolution, which they came to regard as a historical object with a literary expression of its own. They borrowed from the work of literary scholars in the process, thus making a strong case for interdisciplinary research.

This relatively recent historiographical trend has affected studies of radicalism and influenced scholars who are willing to take a broad view of historical phenomena without falling back into the highly readable but somewhat too systematic grand narratives of yesteryear. This volume makes a case for adopting a 'functional' approach to seventeenth- and eighteenth-century radicalism, as opposed to the over-restrictive 'nominalist' approach and the all-embracing 'substantive' construct, and recognises that radicalism is a situational category best understood in its historical context.[11] What is lacking, though, is a conceptual framework associated with the 'functional' approach to make it effective, one that will allow a definition of radicalism to emerge. We suggest four distinguishing features.

First, radicalism is of an oppositional quality and, as a result, evolves through time. Ariel Hessayon is right to argue that it is a relative concept and that what is perceived to be radical at one time may be the norm at another time.[12] Radicalism may thus be defined from an axiological perspective as a process that consists in individuals or groups challenging existing political, social, religious or cultural norms. It represents a minority position, whether it is real or only perceived to be so, while by the majority we mean those who occupy positions of authority and defend the normative status quo, as well as the vast body of the population who accept the established order and manifest no need for change. Radicalism has 'mainstream' rather than 'moderate' as an antonym. It is precisely its oppositional character that makes it volatile and susceptible to change over time. The Independents in the English Civil Wars, for instance, emblematise the radicalisation of English politics in the 1640s, both at Westminster and in the New Model Army. Their demands for religious toleration based on the coexistence of autonomous congregations were certainly anathema to the proponents of a religious settlement, members of the Church of England and of the Presbyterian church alike, who defended the idea of a national church as a bulwark against sectarianism. In the autumn of 1648, the Independents' radicalism expressed itself mainly in political terms. The Independents opposed the Treaty of Newport as a mere diversion on the part of the King to outmanoeuvre Parliament, and their criticisms both of Charles's procrastination and of the

Presbyterians' irresoluteness reflected their defiance of the constitutional *status quo*, as in Ireton's *Remonstrance of the Army* of 16 November,[13] a radical stance that resulted in Pride's purge of Parliament and the subsequent trial of the King. The Independents' growing impatience with the King and the New Model Army officers' fear of being robbed of their victory over the royalist army possibly explain why their concerns and those of the Levellers as well as of the Army rank and file seemed to coincide in the later months of 1648. This short-lived community of purpose, however, need not blur the lines between Independent leaders and Army officers, on the one hand, who came to embody the political *status quo* in the wake of the regicide, and the Levellers and the Army soldiers, on the other, who continued to challenge the political norms imposed on the nation, an opposition conducive to Army mutinies in the spring of 1649. Nor need the relative consensus between Army officers and the soldiers in the autumn of 1648 obscure the confrontation between those who had accepted political traditions at Putney in October and November 1647, and those who had railed against the political disenfranchisement of the masses and argued for an alternative to the constitutional settlement. The New Model Army soldiers and their supporters in the Leveller movement were radical voices. So were Independent leaders and Army officers, at least at a particular time of the Civil Wars, in that they opposed the existing religious and political norms, even if a degree of self-serving expediency may account for their posture in the autumn of 1648. After the execution of Charles I and the abolition of monarchy, their authority as guardians of the new norms – some of which did not entirely differ from the previous ones – came under growing criticism from those who felt excluded from the post-regicide political settlement and thus adopted an oppositional stance.[14]

Closely related to the oppositional nature of radicalism is its second distinguishing feature, namely the fact that radicalism is temporary in essence. One should think of it as consisting of a series of short-lived manifestations rather than as being woven into some long-lasting radical tradition.[15] These manifestations, however, need not be isolated phenomena. Hessayon goes some way towards accepting the recurrent nature of radicalism as he calls for the adoption of a 'functional' approach with some of the 'substantive' put back in, albeit 'in emasculated form',[16] thus cautioning against hastily associating seemingly disparate historical phenomena. He and Burgess[17] reject the radical tradition of British Marxist historians and the radical canon that comes out of it as part of an ideological construct based on causation and dismissive of historical contingencies and coincidences. Burgess argues for a comparative history of radical moments rather than a continuous history of a broad radical tradition. We wish to go one step further than Burgess's tracing of an intellectual lineage between radical voices as well as remove the caveat from Hessayon's methodological perspective. The very volatility of radicalism and its temporariness, we argue, do not make resurgences impossible. Nor do they make investigating them an unacceptable and impractical scholarly enterprise. Some of the contributions to this volume find the parallels between a number of eighteenth-century radical manifestations and the radical writings and practices of the English Civil Wars to be more than fortuitous echoes and distant reminiscences of a past that had been laid to rest.[18] Mapping continuities makes sense, if only because this can help us to determine how far eighteenth-century radicals modelled their own identities on those of their seventeenth-century predecessors and, thus, have a clearer picture of both the eighteenth- and the seventeenth-century radical scene. Admittedly, the appropriation of seventeenth-century radical figures and ideas by later radicals may have resulted in somewhat romanticised or fantasised reconstructions of the past. However, the study of the influence of Civil War radicalism on eighteenth-century radical thought and discourse as well as of its presence in later radicals' memories need not be dismissed as a historical fabrication, although of course it is by no means the only content of that later radicalism. We concur with Edward Vallance that one should reassess the 'degree of intellectual sympathy and continuity between the radicalism of the seventeenth century and that of the eighteenth'.[19] We wish to build on the work of Timothy Morton and Nigel Smith who, in their *Radicalism in British Literary Culture 1650–1830*, insist that the scholarly concern with the transmission and re-emergence of radical texts does not entail reviving the Marxist vision of a radical tradition but leads to a better understanding of late eighteenth-century radicalism's reinvention of seventeenth-century radical issues.[20] Through the example of Richard 'Citizen' Lee and his radical publishing circle, Jon Mee, for example, discusses the influence of Ranterism and seventeenth-century heterodoxy on late eighteenth-century enthusiasts, thus highlighting the professed familiarity of the latter with the former.[21] Continuities can clearly be traced from the appropriation by eighteenth-century radicalism of the energies unleashed by religious dissent in the English Civil Wars. Thus, it is possible to talk about some degree of the transmission of radical materials through time and across generations, but always within a broader context where there were also far more discontinuous phenomena. It is no surprise that contemporaries turned to the metaphor of metempsychosis to explain something that appeared to leap from place to place, from time to time, but with no obvious direct connection between each occurrence:

> The first broacher of the Presbyterian Religion, and made it differ from that of *Rome* and *Luther* was *Calvin,* who being once banished *Geneva,* was revok'd, at which time he no less petulantly than prophanely applyed to himself that Text of the Holy Prophet which was meant of Christ, *The Stone which the Builders refused is made the head stone of the corner, &c.* Thus *Geneva* Lake swallowed up the Episcopall *See,* and Church Lands wer made secular, which was the white they levell'd at. This *Geneva* Bird flew thence to *France* and hatch'd the *Huguenots,* which make about the tenth part of that people; it took wing also to *Bohemia* and *Germany* high and low, as the *Palatinate,* the land of *Hesse,* and the Confederat Provinces of the States of *Holland,* whence it took flight to *Scotland* and *England;* It took first footing in *Scotland,* when King *Iames* was a child in his Cradle, but when he came to understand himself, and was manumitted from *Buchanan,* he grew cold in it, and being com to *England* hee utterly disclaim'd it, terming it in a public Speech of his to the Parliament a *Sect* rather than a *Religion:* To this Sect may bee imputed all the scissures that have happen'd in Christianity, with most of the Wars that have lacerated poor *Europe* ever since, and it may be call'd the source of the civill distractions that now afflict this poor Island.[22]

From the idea that radicalism is oppositional and temporary, if potentially resurgent, stems the notion of radicalism as a polymorphous category – this being its third distinguishing feature. In the same way as there is no such thing as a radical tradition, a monolithic conception of radicalism is clearly not an effective hypothesis as it fails to account for the various modes of radical expression. It is worth identifying them and proposing an acceptable analytical framework, however daunting the challenge. Jonathan Scott views the development of mid seventeenth-century radicalism as a three-phase process: religious, republican and Restoration radicalism, which burgeoned respectively in the 1640s, the 1650s and the 1670s.[23] The problem with this linear pattern is that it lacks flexibility, making little allowance for any amount of interaction or relatedness between the contiguous phases that it describes. We prefer a paradigmatic perspective that identifies different brands of radicalism rather than stages and which accepts the possibility of overlap between them. Nicholas McDowell thus distinguishes between prophetic radicalism – as exemplified by the Ranters or the Quakers – stemming from the Puritan tradition, and rational radicalism – as typified by the Levellers – deriving from the humanist belief in man's capacity for self-improvement; although not all Levellers fit this category, and Winstanley was both prophetic and in his terms 'rational'.[24] Burgess names three strands of radicalism: religious, constitutional and republican radicalism, the last two brands corresponding closely to McDowell's 'rational' label;[25] these can be simultaneous or successive, isolated or connected. We would like to add a fourth category to Burgess's typology, which offers an apt definition of Leveller radicalism, Harringtonian radicalism and Ranter radicalism, but appears to overlook Digger radicalism. The fact that the Diggers styled themselves 'True Levellers' unmistakeably reflected their desire to level social differences, tamper with private property and redistribute wealth – a far cry from the Levellers' constitutional radicalism – but their communistic agenda had much in common with the Ranters' vindication of communalism against private property as an overbearing symbol of domination.[26] Social radicalism may smack of Marxist class struggle rhetoric, but it is certainly a useful category to describe Digger attitudes – and also Ranter attitudes, for that matter – and may overlap with the other modes of radicalism, such as religious radicalism, which apply to the Diggers as well. By suggesting a workable taxonomy of radicalism we run the risk of exposing ourselves to charges of oversimplification and sweeping systematisation. On the other hand, it would not help much to maintain that there were as many radicalisms as there were radicals or groups of radicals and thus eschew any attempt at definition, for, in that case, the radical label would become so fissiparous as to lose almost all of its relevance. We thus identify four varieties of early modern radicalism – constitutional, religious, republican and social – while acknowledging that some individuals or groups fit equally into several of these categories, each of which accommodates nuances and singularities.

The fourth distinguishing feature of radicalism is that it allows idiosyncratic voices to express themselves. Individuals should be given as much attention as groups; personal trajectories matter as much as collective posturing. For all their achievements in terms of political organisation and communication, the Levellers, for example, did not speak with just one voice. The distinctive identities and modes of thought of Lilburne, Overton and Walwyn need not be diluted in or subsumed under their collective enterprise as they continued to express themselves in their writings.[27] Studying their lives and their texts separately certainly helps us to have a better grasp of the Leveller movement as a whole.[28] Similarly, the New Model Army is known to have been a hotbed of radicalism, with radical figures in some places appearing as part of a group, as in the petitions or in the engagements they penned, in others expressing themselves singularly, as when Edward Sexby or Thomas Rainborough stood up to their officers during the Putney Debates. This is not to say that theirs were isolated voices; after all, as representatives of their regiments, they spoke on behalf of the soldiers who had chosen them and voiced their concerns. Yet, the fact that historians still debate whether Sexby was a Leveller or not indicates that his radical identity still evades us and that it was probably more of a personal than of a collective nature.[29] We argue that these seventeenth-century radical figures should be recovered or rediscovered separately, much as their late eighteenth-century radical successors have been; they should be regarded not as participants in a grand narrative in which the plural prevails over the singular or the collective dominates over the personal, but as personal voices – even if not disconnected from significant historical events and movements involving many actors – that truly give us an insight into the complex essence of early modern radicalism.

Owing to its polymorphic nature, radicalism allows for multifaceted scholarly approaches that draw upon a variety of methodological tools. This volume makes a strong case for an interdisciplinary approach to the study of radicalism. Building upon the work of Nigel Smith on mid seventeenth-century religious enthusiasts, *Perfection Proclaimed*, literary scholars have shown special interest recently in recovering radical voices.[30] The variegated conceptual approaches that we propose in this volume fit into the global scholarly picture of mutual enrichment and cross-fertilisation as promoted by wideranging publications like *The Cambridge Companion to Writing of the English Revolution, The Oxford Handbook of Literature and the English Revolution* and *The Cambridge Companion to British Literature of the French Revolution in the 1790s.*[31] We believe that a literary discussion of seventeenth- and eighteenth-century materials, one that brings texts and contexts together, can shed new light on the history of the period and thus revitalise its historiography. Most literary students of the seventeenth and eighteenth centuries have now challenged the post-structuralist paradigm regarding the instability of meaning and have benefited a great deal from historians' work as they endeavour to revive contextual studies.

It seems to us that literary approaches too can enhance the study of radicalism in two ways. First, they help to bring printed texts back into focus in this post-revisionist age of ours. Modes of radical expression may thus be analysed as literary productions *per se* that interact with their historical context. A fruitful approach is to examine how motifs, imagery and rhetoric are used in texts pertaining to different literary genres or transposed from one type of text to another type of text in the same context or in a different context. It does not make much sense, for instance, to isolate Marvell the oppositional pamphleteer of the 1670s from the earlier Marvell, the poet of the 1640s and 1650s, whose verse is today much more celebrated than his prose, even if recent editions of his polemical writings opportunely add to the knowledge we have of the man and the poet.[32] Similarly, John Milton's and George Wither's polemical pamphlets should not be divorced from their poetry. Studying textual resonances between Marvell's, Milton's and Wither's poetry and their prose may help not only to identify rhetorical and stylistic idiosyncrasies but also to determine how these authors engaged with their political and cultural environment. Another potentially successful approach consists in assessing how much radical texts were affected by canonical literary genres and how much they deviated from them, thus making it possible for radical voices to be recovered in terms of their interaction with the cultural norms of their time. We agree with McDowell that the literary evidence that can be garnered from a close study of texts may point to the existence of an English radical imagination, which developed from the interface between elite and popular language.[33] McDowell defines seventeenth-century radicals as 'sophisticated writers and readers who were not excluded from mainstream culture but rather appropriated aspects of that culture in a moment of historical crisis to

11

develop languages of subversion, opposition and reform'.[34] This observation tallies with our characterisation of radicalism as an oppositional, polymorphic and idiosyncratic category. It is the object of this volume to map the English radical imagination of the seventeenth and eighteenth centuries, partly at least, by focusing on the media used by radicals.

The second way in which literary approaches contribute to the study of radicalism is that they provide tools with which to examine radical discourse. We reject the notion that there exists a radical language that transcends historical epochs and territorial boundaries as a fantasy which tends, if not to obliterate time and space categories, at least to downplay their significance. However, it would be just as preposterous to deny that radical ideas are conveyed through language; thus, early modern radical speech acts need to be revisited as providing insights into how radicals accommodated, travestied or subverted linguistic conventions in an attempt to challenge cultural and political norms.[35] Language is the most tangible part of the communicative practices that make up radical discourse. We support an interdisciplinary approach that studies early modern radical discourse in context and interrogates the media through which it communicated itself to its audience. We argue that seventeenth- and eighteenth-century radical discourse was shaped by the interaction of three factors, each of which is best understood in relation to the other two, namely intention, language and reception. These factors apply both to oral and textual manifestations of radical expression, although the only evidence we have of oral interaction in an age which did not leave behind any sound archives is bound to be skewed and partial as it necessarily relies upon written sources. An effective examination of radical discourse thus requires a conceptual framework that borrows methodological tools from various scholarly approaches: biographical and contextual studies; linguistic and semiotic analysis; book history. Analysing how various media, such as pamphlets, newspapers and petitions, became the loci of radical expression in early modern Britain, and how radical texts were disseminated and read, matters as much as the ideas they promoted.

Print culture as a scholarly object opens new avenues for the study of early modern radicalism. The print explosion of the 1640s is not exactly uncharted territory; it has inspired a fair amount of academic work in recent years, with a number of historians and literary scholars variously probing into cheap and ephemeral materials such as pamphlets and newsbooks.[36] They have drawn upon the Habermasian theory of the emergence of a public sphere in seventeenth-century Europe while largely divesting it of its Whiggish systematisation.[37] Print culture in seventeenth-century England is now commonly seen as a dynamic process, informed both by historical circumstances and by factors that are intrinsic to its very nature as popular and accessible literature. We wish to extend these findings to our appreciation of radical texts. First, radical literature catered to specific readers who may not be readily identifiable to contemporary eyes but whose concerns and expectations were clearly reflected through the printed medium. Just like writing, reading was a political act whereby disenfranchised individuals symbolically became empowered citizens. Second, radical print was influenced by two major constraints: topicality and regulation. Printing and disseminating material swiftly was a necessity; evading pre-publication censorship was a prerequisite for such material to be circulated.[38] Third, the materiality of texts should not be overlooked as printing and transmitting them involved several actors, sometimes whole networks, participating in the economy of the book trade. Printers, like Giles Calvert in the 1640s and Nathaniel Ponder in the 1670s, played a crucial role in diffusing radical texts.[39] Therefore, understanding the dynamics of radical communication cannot be divorced from the study of radical discourse.

We think this is best achieved through the meticulous study of cases, which may allow us to draw far-reaching conclusions regarding radical ideas and practices. The following reflections on the mid seventeenth-century newsbook the *Moderate* will serve to demonstrate how, by paying close attention to a printed medium, we may form a clearer picture of radicalism in the English Civil Wars. The *Moderate* is commonly associated with the Leveller movement as it included Leveller pamphlets and Leveller-inspired petitions. Our contention is that it was not a Leveller newspaper from the outset but developed into one as it seemed to adjust to evolving political circumstances.

Although the birth of the *Moderate* appears to be shrouded in mystery, examining facts regarding publication as well as external and internal textual evidence raises interesting possibilities. There is scant material evidence as to who first took it upon himself to produce this new weekly, and just as little evidence of the editor's motives for it. What is known for certain is that – in June 1648 – this person appropriated the title and the features, such as numeration and layout, of a long-running news-sheet, the *Moderate Intelligencer*, together with the date of publication; both he and the printer, Robert White, thus collaborated in producing the first issue of this alternative newsbook. The *Moderate* was the first counterfeit Civil War newspaper to develop into a full-blown publication with a distinct identity.[40] Thus, on Thursday 22 June, there came out two newsbooks entitled the *Moderate Intelligencer* and numbered 170, the logical numeration for the original. Unfortunately, the forged issue has not been found, and the original was just its own true self, with no apparent sign that its editor, John Dillingham, was aware that he was being robbed of his title. Had the forged copy survived, would it have made the conundrum of its origins easier to solve? After all, the first issues of many Civil War weeklies included pro-grammatic statements that spelled out their editors' objectives and, sometimes, made their political bias clear. The first number of the *Moderate Intelligencer*, for example, contained one such expository editorial comment.[41]

Is the forger of the *Moderate Intelligencer* likely to have imparted his editorial intentions to his readers, assuming he had some inten-tions to impart, just as Dillingham had done in the first number of his own newsbook? Only wild guesses can be made: if he did state his purpose in the first issue, this would lend further credence to the political manoeuvre hypothesis whereby its alleged editor, the state censor Gilbert Mabbott, refused to license the newsbook in order to teach Dillingham a lesson in political behaviour. However, the odds are high that the author of the forgery may have wished to operate undercover, keeping as low a profile as possible, and, should this have been the case, he is unlikely to have provided his readers with a programmatic statement. This assumption would certainly sub-stantiate the claim that the *Moderate* was born out of a commercial intrigue as there was good money to be made from journalism, but need not invalidate the political option since both theories are not mutually exclusive.

There is a fair chance that readers were confused by a forgery that was only partly redressed. The editor of the *Moderate* went to great lengths to authenticate his newsbook, first claiming that it was genuine, not counterfeit,[42] and then giving it a somewhat different shape that would make it more than one of two peas in a pod: it had a new numeration and pagination, its size was reduced from twelve to eight pages made out of one sheet of paper instead of two, and its day of publication changed from Thursdays to Tuesdays. The editor justified the last two changes with this introductory address: 'Reader, I am desired by many to change my day from Thursday to Tuesday, because the Kingdom hath much wanted a satisfactory sheet to send that day by the Post into the severall parts thereof; which I have consented unto, for the better Information of all. And because it should not be too voluminous, I have reduced it into one sheet.'[43] Taking advantage of the Tuesday postal service indeed made it possible for him to cater for provincial readers at a time when the market for news in the metropolis was especially tight, even if the demand was high. Lack of fortune with insufficient funding and poor sales probably accounted for the emergence of a leaner Tuesday *Moderate*, together with the need for it to show itself as a viable alternative to the *Moderate Intelligencer*, similar enough in outlook for it to claim authenticity but slightly different, all the same, so that it could not be mistaken for its twin publication.

It was only late in August 1648 that the *Moderate* began to diverge from its *alter ego* as a significant innovation was introduced – editorials – which were to crown virtually every issue and give the newsbook its distinct flavour. This innovation was probably part of the editor's strategy to gain a competitive edge over his business rival Dillingham since the *Moderate Intelligencer* had been running short editorials for two weeks, implicitly calling for compromise and the appeasement of passions as a way out of the civil war. There is clearly some irony in the fact that by trying to emulate his competitor and carving out a niche for himself in the news market the editor of the *Moderate* ended up cutting a thoroughly different political figure, a far cry from its sibling the *Moderate Intelligencer*. The reasons why the *Moderate* evolved into a radical weekly which came to support hard-line parliamentarians against the Presbyterian majority and began to speak for the Levellers may only be guessed at. Possibly the need to penetrate a new market, at a time when sales may not have allowed the newsbook to outperform its rival the *Moderate Intelligencer*, justified a renewed editorial line. Maybe political developments in the summer of 1648, when a negotiated settlement with the King was high on the agenda, made for a different approach to news. Perhaps one should think of the *Moderate* as having acquired its radical character instead of having been born with it.

A close examination of how the editorials of the *Moderate* – for which the publication has received posthumous acclaim – are integrated into the cheap print economy reveals a more inclusive political stance than is commonly accepted. The leading articles in the autumn of 1648 voiced concerns over the Presbyterians' compromising attitude with the King and enunciated principles that were common to both leading Independents and Levellers. They were not only shaped by Leveller identification, for most of them were fiercely anti-royalist, to a greater degree perhaps than Leveller leaders would have acknowledged for themselves, and resolutely defended popular sovereignty in much the same terms as the *Remonstrance of the Army*, inspired by the Independent officer Ireton. Some of the October editorials provide examples of texts that were circulated in the New Model Army as pamphlets or collections of news.[44] Only after the regicide and the establishment of the republic did the *Moderate* tread an exclusively Leveller path and throw all its weight behind those who found fault with the ruling oligarchy. In addition to editorials which criticised the Commonwealth elite it included seditious Leveller pamphlets. It also proved to be sensitive to the plight of the poorer part of the population, who especially suffered from the severe economic crisis besetting England, and was the only newsbook to show some sympathy for the Diggers, whose occupation of communal land on St George's Hill in Surrey in April 1649 gave Commonwealth authorities cause for concern.[45] The Levellers, it should be recalled, expressed reservations about the Diggers' social radicalism[46] and, as a result, might have disapproved of the *Moderate*'s reasonably benign treatment of Winstanley's digging community.

All these remarks on the birth of the *Moderate* as well as some of its content imply that it was not a 'Leveller organ',[47] in that it was not the official, institutional publication of the Levellers as an organised group, but of course this does not mean that it was not radical. Its radical identity, precisely, contributed to the denigration of the *Moderate* as 'the most infamous periodical that had yet appeared', unlike the *Moderate Intelligencer*, authored by Dillingham, 'a moderate Presbyterian to whom the idea of any personal attack on the King was abhorrent'.[48] The *Moderate* thus reflected the views of a composite radical scene during and immediately after the second Civil War, one that was occupied by the Levellers and the New Model Army, including its officers in the autumn of 1648, and shaped by the course of events. The *Moderate* was a vehicle for radical discourse: studying the medium as integral to the popular print culture of seventeenth-century England cannot be separated from a thorough examination of the content conveyed by this medium.

It is essential to discover how radical voices, whether they were individual or collective, were mediated through print; in other words, in what ways they engaged with their political, religious, social and cultural environment. It is just as important to appreciate what made specific media, chiefly pertaining to the cheap print economy, effective means of diffusing radical ideas. Our efforts at defining radical communicative practices should be directed towards a better understanding of how widely ideas travelled. The historiography of seventeenth-century English radicalism has been mostly Anglocentric so far and has tended to overlook transnational contiguities, with the possible exception of transatlantic exchanges with New England.[49] The influence of the French Revolution on eighteenth-century British radicalism is well documented, although some work still needs to be done on how ideas and men circulated before a full picture of radical networks, however fluid, emerges. Seventeenth-century radicals lacked the unity of purpose and the organisation to operate Europe-wide networks. There was no public endorsement of the English revolution in Europe, probably because the English revolution was originally a civil war that degenerated into a regicide accompanied by a change of state. There was no founding popular event in England on the scale of the storming of the Bastille in Paris to encourage copycat actions elsewhere on the continent. This is not to say, however, that what we have described as radical ideas and texts did not cross the Channel at all. Exchanges of radical ideas between Britain and the European continent did take place, but in a low-key fashion which makes European radical influences and connections rather difficult to detect.

We argue that British radicalism is best appreciated in its transnational context, and that this principle applies as much to the British Isles in the seventeenth century as to eighteenth-century Britain. The need to trace cultural transfers between Britain and Europe in the early modern period has given rise to an expanding field of research which studies the mutual recuperation of ideas as well as the role played by *passeurs* or transmitters, for example Quirinus Kuhlmann – a Silesian millenarian with an influence in England and right across northern Europe. We still need to explore how radical ideas were intermediated, that is to say who passed them on, what media were used for their diffusion and how these media were employed. We should look into the dissemination, reception and modes of radical communication between Britain and the continent; this includes the study of translations of radical texts into English or European languages and the adaptation of these texts to contexts for which they were not intended.[50]

We wish to build on such recent scholarly works as Gaby Mahlberg and Dirk Wiemann's *European Contexts for English Republicanism* and Ariel Hessayon and Sarah Apetrei's *An Introduction to Jacob Boehme: Four Centuries of Thought and Reception*.[51] The former collection of essays offers a two-dimensional perspective on the circulation of republican ideas as it brings to the fore how English republican ideas were shaped by contemporary European republican thought and how they impacted on it. It notably studies cultural transfers between the English Commonwealth and the Dutch Republic.[52] The latter book seeks to map European heterodox networks by focusing on the publication, dissemination and influence of the writings of Jacob Boehme, the illiterate shoemaker turned millenarian prophet who is shown to have had a significant impact and enjoyed a long afterlife across Europe. In his own contribution to his edited volume, Hessayon studies the translation of Boehme's writings into English and discusses their influence on English radicals, notably the Diggers and the Ranters, only to conclude that there were relatively few English Behmenists and that Boehme's texts made no major contribution to political and religious debates in revolutionary England and had a muted impact on heterodox thinkers, save for a handful of individual figures. Nigel Smith offers a contrasting view and has different conclusions on the influence of Boehme on English radical sects.[53] Boehme's thought possibly contaminated English heterodox cosmologies indirectly more than it informed them, and undoubtedly came to have a lasting influence in England.

England did not just accommodate teachings from the continent but also exported its own radical ideas, whether they were home-bred or reworked from continental writings. It is certainly of interest to look beyond the official diplomatic high game to retrieve underground connections from oblivion. The influence of the English revolution on France during the Fronde, for example, and the impact of radical transfers in particular, ought to be measured with greater accuracy. We wish to stress the pivotal role played by Edward Sexby, the New Model Army radical, as a vector of ideas, one who helped to promote English radical ideas in France.

The Council of State as the executive body of the Commonwealth commissioned Sexby to visit France in the autumn of 1651 in order to secure precise information about the political situation there and capitalise on the revolt against chief minister Cardinal Mazarin, a highly unpopular and contested figure, to destabilise the country even further.[54] The Fronde spread to regions other than Paris, notably Bordeaux and the province of Guyenne, where several rebellious factions were at play. One of them was the radical Ormée, named after a square planted with elm trees and described in a condescending manner by the French nineteenth-century historian Victor Cousin in his *Madame de Longueville* as 'sortie du bas people, ou du moins de la très petite bourgeoisie, quoiqu'elle eût aussi des adhérents dans les rangs les plus élevés' ('grown out of the masses or, at least, out of the very lowest orders of the bourgeoisie, although some of its members came from the upper ranks of society'), as opposed to the 'petite Fronde', which included 'ce qu'il y avait de mieux dans le parlement, l'hôtel de ville et la bourgeoisie, par la naissance, les lumières, la fortune' ('the best men among Parliament members, town officials and the bourgeoisie, in terms of birth, education and wealth').[55] Both the Ormée and the Prince de Condé, the leader of the Fronde of the Princes, sent emissaries to England so as to secure the support of Cromwell. All they got in the end was some timid public backing which fell far short of their expectations but had the advantage of not alienating French authorities and leaving diplomatic options open.[56] Meanwhile, Sexby advertised English republican ideas with Ormée members as he encouraged them to adopt a translated version of the Leveller manifesto *The Agreement of the People* whose style Cousin disparaged as betraying the work of a foreign hand.[57]

A comparison of the translated version, poor and sloppy though it may be, with the original text yields interesting results. The most obvious observation is that Sexby translated the third and last version of *The Agreement of the People*, which the Leveller leaders drafted while they were in gaol in the Tower of London and rolled off the radical printer Giles Calvert's press on 1 May 1649.[58] Its publication accompanied a spate of radical agitation within the

New Model Army, caused by growing dissatisfaction with the new republic as unheeded grievances were left to simmer, and was instrumental in fostering Army mutinies in the spring of 1649. A close examination of both the original and the translated texts reveals that the French translation generally follows the English version, except for a few unimportant emendations meant to accommodate local linguistic and political realities.

Two seemingly minor changes were made to the specifics of the text, but these are revealing of Sexby's intentions and political positioning. First, article XXVI in the English manifesto, which calls for liberty of conscience and provides that none shall be disabled from 'bearing any office in the Common-wealth, for any opinion or practice in Religion, excepting such as maintain, the Popes (or other forraign) Supremacy',[59] is absent from the French translation, reproduced by Cousin in *Madame de Longueville*. Article X, which defends religious toleration in the most general terms as a constitutional right and makes it illegal for Parliament to interfere with matters of conscience, duly appears in the French text. This shows that the principle of religious toleration as defended by the Independents and the Levellers alike is enshrined in this constitutional document, which in a French context probably meant that Huguenots should be guaranteed the right to practise their faith and be protected from persecution. In addition to that, the French translation of the Agreement provides a sound example of *realpolitik* or practical adaptation to contingencies as it does not explicitly exclude Catholics from any political settlement, if only because the Ormée faction was a motley assortment of Catholics and Protestants. It is very likely, therefore, that Sexby was a keen political observer. Either he was given significant leeway by Commonwealth authorities for the compiling of his translation, assuming that he had not taken it upon himself to produce the text, or religious concerns were only second to political priorities.

The second major change that Sexby introduced in his translation concerned political institutions, and more specifically the distribution of power between the executive body of the Commonwealth and the Representative of the People, as the legislative assembly was named in the text. Article VIII in the original version establishes the absolute supremacy of Parliament and rejects the Council of State as an illegitimate body: 'in times of adjournment [the next & al future Representatives] shall not erect a Councel of State but refer the managing of affairs in the intervals to a Committee of their own members, giving such instructions, and publish them, as shall in no measure contradict this agreement'.[60] The wording of the French translation is ambiguous: 'durant le temps d'adjournement ils [les représentatives] erigeront un conseil d'Estat, ou comitté, de ceux de leurs corps, leur donnant telles instructions qui ne contreviendront point à cest accord et le feront publier'[61] ('in times of adjournment [representatives] shall erect a council of state, or committee, of their own members, giving such instructions, and publish them, as shall in no measure contradict this agreement'). The phrase 'council of state' may have been intended as a convenient synonym for the word 'committee' or as a straightforward reference to the Council of State as it was in 1653 when Sexby translated the *Agreement of the People*. We will never know whether, by supplying an imprecise translation of the Levellers' text, Sexby, the former opponent of the Army Grandees in the Putney debates, was doing his utmost to ingratiate himself with the Council of State, at a troubled time when Cromwell had dismissed the Rump Parliament, or whether he was simply eluding the ire of Commonwealth authorities who might have resented an attack on their prerogatives, even in translated form, had the caveat regarding the Council of State in the original Leveller text remained untouched.

In any case, Sexby's attempt to import the English revolution into France by fanning the flames of rebellion in Bordeaux and encouraging popular revolt was unsuccessful, for the Frondeurs, with the exception of the members of the Ormée faction, had no intention of subverting political or social norms. As Philip Knachel claimed, 'the English example aborted rather than stimulated the growth of republican sentiment among most Frondeurs'.[62] According to Wilbur Abbott, the impact of the translated *Agreement of the People* on the Bordeaux rebels was minimal: 'This [translation of the *Agreement of the People*] found little acceptance among those in charge of the Fronde, and though Sexby and his colleagues remained in the south of France for more than a year, they did not accomplish much in the way of an agreement between the Commonwealth and the opponents of French monarchy.'[63] They may have had a lasting subterranean influence, though, which would need further analysis.

Yet, on the other side of the Channel, there was hope that the English model would be copied in France and that the Fronde would end in an all-out revolution, if the reports on French events given in the official Commonwealth and Protectorate newsbook *Mercurius Politicus* are anything to go by. While the contributors to the newspaper consistently voiced prejudices against the French, whom they vilified as 'those Monkies of Mankind',[64] and seemed to find amusement in the Fronde, which they compared to a mere game of tennis, they expressed admiration for the 'brave Bourdelois'[65] and especially praised their tireless resistance to royal power, as embodied by Mazarin, combined with an unflinching resolve to secure liberty.[66] The encouragements Marchamont Nedham, the principal author of *Mercurius Politicus*, gave to the rebels in Bordeaux were possibly a ploy to fashion a positive image of the Commonwealth by striking a patriotic chord with readers and, thus, to ward off any risk of political instability at home. They may also have reflected the English Government's satisfaction with the idea of having a weakened France at its door, considering that France harboured English royalist exiles and that they still posed a threat to the Commonwealth.

The French translation of the *Agreement of the People* illustrates the fortunes of this Leveller text, which was adapted to a different context from the one for which it was intended. It shows that there was a breeding ground for radical activity in south-western France in the early 1650s, but Sexby's ultimate failure to generate support for it indicates that the form of radicalism associated with the Levellers could not find its way into French society as a whole; it remained epiphenomenal and peripheral. It also shows that such a radical text could be recuperated by the unofficial agent of a government that had gone to great lengths to suppress radical groups of all stripes. The fact is that the English Government is unlikely to have been unaware of Sexby's doings in Guyenne, given that, some time after his return to England, the ex-Agitator received payment to cover the expenses he had incurred during his mission in France. It cannot be ruled out that the Commonwealth intended to get rid of Sexby in the first place by sending him abroad. Perhaps it should be accepted that, of all radicals, Sexby was the most capable of achieving two different aims at the same time: standing by the Commonwealth, whose leaders he had once opposed, while not renouncing his radical ideas altogether, hence his translation of the *Agreement of the People* into French. A plausible option is that Sexby was in fact involved in double-dealing, pretending to be serving his government while pursuing his own political agenda.

His case is a fitting illustration of what popular radicalism is all about. His personal trajectory offers an insight into the global picture that caused radical energies to circulate from one context to another at the time of the English revolution. As an Army Agitator in the Putney debates, Sexby took an active part in promoting the principles of equal representation and quasi-universal suffrage as enshrined in the 1647 Leveller constitutional text *The Agreement of the People*, thus challenging the political norms of his time. He was instrumental in diffusing these principles, albeit on a limited scale in Bordeaux, by translating the *Agreement* into French. The Leveller manifesto was part and parcel of the cheap print economy that was shaping up in mid seventeenth-century England and made it possible for radical ideas to travel, including across borders.

In 1657 Sexby drew up an apology for tyrannicide, *Killing No Murder*, explicitly targeted at Cromwell and evidently influenced by anti-monarchical writings of the sixteenth century, as well as by Machiavelli's thought. This pamphlet is a particularly apt example of cultural transfer between England and France. It was translated into French almost immediately after its publication by Jacques Carpentier de Marigny.[67] It survived the Restoration in England as a new edition of it came out in Edinburgh in 1745, which may have been commissioned and circulated by Jacobites. Another French edition of the original text was published in revolutionary France and a new translation into French, with a dedication to Napoleon instead of Cromwell, was completed in 1804, the very year Napoleon was crowned Emperor.[68] Following the peregrinations of Sexby's tract on both sides of the Channel helps to measure the fluidity and porosity of English radicalism, as well as its adaptability to other contexts than the one which produced it. Looking out for continuities and resurgences need not imply that we are losing track of original contexts, but it does help to cast new light on them. A study of radicalism in early modern England should therefore not ignore transnational continuities.

It has been shown that the study of seventeenth- and eighteenth-century English radicalism will benefit from multifarious approaches. Transnational and transhistorical explorations which avoid the pitfalls of systematisation have been duly lauded. It has been argued that methodological approaches developed by literary scholars are well suited to this study as they offer renewed perspectives that are fully compatible with and complement historical analysis. We have insisted that radical communicative practices need to be investigated further, which is precisely what this volume purports to do, by focusing on the expression of radical voices and their interaction with various media. Contributors were given leeway to use their own methodological tools and approaches with a view to studying various aspects of radical communication in seventeenth- and eighteenth-century Britain.

Part I of this volume explores the language and motifs used by some seventeenth- and eighteenth-century radicals. Jean-Pierre Cavaillé in Chapter 1 discusses the 'community of goods' motif permeating Digger and Ranter writings, a theme he studies from an axiological perspective which draws upon the notions of acceptability and unacceptability. While borrowing from Christopher Hill's analysis of seventeenth-century radical plebeians the idea that the 'community of goods' theme is rooted in English history, he acknowledges that this motif owes as much to literary culture as to popular culture and argues that the context in which it developed should not be overlooked. According to Jean-Pierre Cavaillé, the fact that community of goods as a political motif was publicised through print in the late 1640s and early 1650s reflected the attempt of hitherto marginal radical voices to enter the public sphere. The motif was taken up by some early Quakers but they soon developed a more acceptable form of public discourse.

In her Chapter 2, Carine Lounissi studies Thomas Paine's 'democratic style' as being part and parcel of his inherently republican and democratic radicalism. She argues that in his writings Paine sought to deconstruct the discourse of the political elite of his time, associated with the trappings of royalty, and promoted the language of common sense instead as an instrument of resistance premised on the universality of human nature. She shows that Paine's relentless attack on monarchy borrowed from different anti-monarchical motifs and forms of language, including the 'Norman Conquest' and 'Norman Yoke' motifs as used by the Levellers and the Diggers. Paine thus tried to uncover the earlier language that he thought monarchy by conquest had erased and replaced by a usurped form of language that did not produce any sensible discourse. One should be careful not to overplay the linguistic parallels between Paine and seventeenth-century radicals, but one cannot ignore them either. It is fair to argue that linguistic norms as symbols of political and social domination posed a challenge to a number of radicals, as

exemplified by the Levellers' and the Diggers' unflagging denun-
ciation of the language of lawyers, which they associated with the
Norman Conquest. Political usurpation cannot be divorced from its
linguistic manifestations.

Catie Gill in Chapter 3 discusses early Quakers' unease with language and the written word as expressed by their attitudes towards
unlearnedness. She contends that the Quakers' position on learning
is not as clear and monolithic as appears at first glance. The way
Quakers described inward learning changed from writer to writer
and was expressed in a variety of writings, such as conversion narratives, poetry and polemical tracts. Various case studies underpin her
analysis: she analyses Edward Burrough's and William Dewsbury's
conversion narratives, and examines other Quaker writings, such
as a poem by Susanna Bateman which stages the ontological divide
between reason and faith, to establish how Quakers responded to
the debate about whether the Bible encouraged learning and knowledge. She contrasts this poem with Quaker writings that are not so
averse to outward learning and that hint at the limits of experiential
knowledge. From Catie Gill's analysis it becomes clear that a study
of seventeenth-century heterodoxy, and early modern radicalism
at large, cannot dispense with a close examination of the modes of
expression used by individual voices, apprehended in their sheer
diversity. Her chapter is an illustration of the practical and demotic
nature of radicalism.

Part II of this volume examines radical exchanges and networks,
as well as transfers between Britain and Europe, essentially France.
Patrick Müller in Chapter 4 examines a personal trajectory, that
of the third Earl of Shaftesbury, against the backdrop of post-
Restoration politics. He asks whether a new interpretation of
Shaftesbury as a radical political theorist is justifiable and whether
the term 'radical' can be applied to a man who has traditionally
been regarded as an aesthete and a moralist rather than a political writer, and whose political identity has been thought to be
Whig. To answer this question he proposes a chronological survey
of Shaftesbury's development as an actor on the political scene.
He first reviews Shaftesbury's early political career and shows the
influence of his grandfather, who helped to forge a distinctively
Whig ideology in Shaftesbury's political stance. He then discusses
Shaftesbury's early years as a parliamentarian who conversed with
a number of radical figures, especially Toland, with whom he wrote

The Danger of Mercenary Parliaments, a detailed reckoning with Charles II. Shaftesbury's correspondence provides evidence that he had a hand in new editions of classical English republicans, including the writings of James Harrington, John Milton and Algernon Sidney. Patrick Müller studies Shaftesbury's *Characteristicks* as a utopian text which makes a case for dispensing with the political influence of the Church and all established forms of religion and promotes religious toleration. It is likely that Shaftesbury's radicalism was the result of his rubbing shoulders with radical thinkers but, as Patrick Müller argues, it was counterbalanced by his pragmatism, so that the radical implications of his thought are constantly held in check by a contrary impulse.

Nicholas Treuherz in Chapter 5 explores radical networks and investigates transnational continuities as he appraises the impact of the French *philosophe* Baron d'Holbach's works on eighteenth-century British radicals. Drawing upon the resources offered by the digital humanities he analyses bibliographical data regarding d'Holbach in terms of translations, sales and circulation of his works in Britain as well as press reactions to them. He finds evidence of the diffusion of d'Holbach's texts in the library holdings of canonical figures, such as David Hume and John Wilkes, as well as in private correspondence. He concludes that multiple intellectual networks and friendships could have potentially allowed d'Holbach's texts to penetrate British markets. Finally, Nicholas Treuherz examines how d'Holbach's texts were read by describing four case studies of British radicals whose reading of the French philosopher's works was instrumental in circulating his ideas in Britain: William Godwin, Dr John Jebb, Joseph Priestley and William Hodgson. His review of these radical voices allows him to not only to map transnational networks of radical thought but also to consider how French notions of radicalism were made to adjust to a British context. Both Patrick Müller's and Nicholas Treuherz's chapters establish that any effective study of radicalism will benefit from a careful examination of exchanges made possible by coteries and social circles as well as national and transnational networks.

Part III of this volume discusses media and practices used by seventeenth- and eighteenth-century radicals. Civil War petitions and eighteenth-century toasts as vehicles for radical expression receive attention in two chapters. In Chapter 6, Jason Peacey studies the relationships between Parliament, print and petitioning in revolutionary England. He explores the tension between the potential for political participation at Westminster and the problems related to this practice, and argues that this tension allows for a better understanding of political radicalism in the English revolution. His chapter rests on two foundations: first, the idea that an information revolution relating to Parliament developed in the seventeenth century, which made political information affordable; second, a sense that Parliament was extremely useful, hence citizens' increased participation in its proceedings, not least through petitioning. Jason Peacey highlights the radicalisation of petitioners' rhetoric stemming from their frustration with Parliament's handling of their petitions and concludes his chapter with the contention that radicalism was forged by forces that brought together individuals who became disappointed with participatory politics.

Rémy Duthille in Chapter 7 studies how another cultural practice, the raising of toasts, was adopted by eighteenth-century English radicals as a political act in its own right, one that was integral to the repertoire of practices deployed during ritualised dinners. He argues that it is possible to reconstruct the thought pattern of those present at these dinners from the toasts they raised and that the toasts could fail, thus provoking strife instead of unifying reformers. Drawing upon archival evidence, in particular the minute books of the Society for Constitutional Information, he analyses toasts as speech acts and as rituals of interaction, for toasting performed an integrative function in radical societies, fostering solidarity and mobilisation. He shows that toasts were often used as rituals of remembrance that helped to build a sense of historical continuity with seventeenth-century England and, through an analysis of their linguistic structure, proves that toasts reflected evolving thoughts rather than set ideas, and consequently helped to redefine political vocabulary. Rémy Duthille finally looks into responses to controversial toasting, from prosecution to fighting, and proves that toasting was often used by radicals to test one another's loyalties, sometimes begetting violence.

The final Part IV of this volume studies fiction as a mode of radical expression, thus illustrating the interdisciplinary approach that has been advanced in this Introduction. Catherine Vigier in Chapter 8 discusses the diffusion of radical ideas from the perspective of a captivity narrative, *Ebenezer; or, A Small Monument of Great Mercy, Appearing in the Miraculous Deliverance of William Okeley*, published by the radical printer Nathaniel Ponder. Her premise is that the captivity narrative is best apprehended as a literary text constructed in the light of the political and ideological debates of its age since it offers a veiled criticism of domestic events under the guise of a remote setting and plot. The publication of Okeley's narrative is to be interpreted as an act of militant Protestantism in a culture of dissent at a time – the post-Restoration era – which witnessed increased repression against dissenters. Catherine Vigier argues that Okeley's narrative should be understood as part of a corpus of work published by Ponder in defence of nonconformist ideas and, by examining the themes and imagery running through the narrative, she establishes links with some of Andrew Marvell's poems and prose works, in particular *The Rehearsal Transpros'd*. She analyses biblical and mythological references in both Okeley's narrative and Marvell's pamphlets to support her claim that the Okeley text carried the polemical debate surrounding *The Rehearsal Transpros'd* to a wider public, and that publishing this captivity narrative, a popular literary genre, allowed Ponder and his collaborators to make a further case for freedom of speech.

Marion Leclair's Chapter 9 studies the novels of Godwin, Holcroft and Bage from the perspective of novelistic conventions. She argues that these eighteenth-century British radical novelists subverted the prevailing novelistic order – style, plot and narration – and that their radical challenge to established authority is reflected in the form of their novels. They found fault with contemporary novels glossing over truth and using ornament as a truth-distorting device, this being associated with Burke and conservative politics. In return, they had an embryonic stylistic programme for their novels which rejected the conventional style of such highly popular and marketable publications as sentimental novels and gothic romances. Marion Leclair then examines the three novelists' treatment of plot and shows them to challenge the conventional types of plot – romantic, picaresque and gothic – which they levelled from a social perspective, from a structural point of view, and from a moral angle. She then discusses narration and mentions the disappearance of a clearly identifiable moral voice, the narrator's authority being challenged as the dividing line between character and narrator became blurred. She concludes that novelistic conventions underwent more substantial changes at the hands of these radical writers than is usually acknowledged.

The last chapter of this volume, Chapter 10, provides an inter-disciplinary analysis that reaches across historical and national boundaries. Its author, Edward Vallance, studies the representation of three English regicides, John Dixwell, William Goffe and Edward Whalley, in early nineteenth-century British fiction via the treatment made of them in late eighteenth-century histories and biographies. The three of them escaped to New England in the 1660s and their fate remained largely unknown until the late eighteenth century, as dissenting historians were not comfortable about tackling this topic because of the connections made between nonconformity and republicanism by High Church critics. Edward Vallance examines the histories of Thomas Hutchinson and Ezra Stiles, whose story of the 'Angel of Hudley', thought to be the ghost of Willam Goffe, was a fruitful source for authors of fiction, ranging from Sir Walter Scott to James Fenimore Cooper and Nathaniel Hawthorne, as well as poets like Robert Southey. Edward Vallance then raises the question of what provoked this flurry of literary interest in the three regicides and suggests that the story of Dixwell, Goffe and Whalley had a wide appeal in the Romantic period. Edward Vallance then explores the impact of historians' accounts of the three regicides on the Romantic imagination. By presenting the regicide as an act of madness, early nineteenth-century writers of fiction – such as Ebenezer Elliott and Robert Southey – ultimately diminished its political threat.

From the Diggers to the Ranters and the Quakers, from Shaftesbury to d'Holbach and Paine, from Okeley to Godwin, Holcroft and Bage, from seventeenth-century English regicides to eighteenth-century British radicals, a diversity of seventeenth- and eighteenth-century radical voices beckon to us. From pamphlets to correspondence and fiction, from ritual toasts to petitions to Parliament, these voices expressed themselves in a variety of media, thus interacting with their contemporaries and communicating themselves to those who came after them; they still speak from bygone ages. By exploring the ways in which radical voices engaged with forms and means of expression the chapters collected in this volume offer a sense of the complexity of radical communication in seventeenth- and eighteenth-century England.

The editors of this volume make a case for a broad definition of radicalism, one that eschews prescriptive categorisation and includes descriptive accounts of what it actually was. We wish to end this Introduction with a suggestion that, we hope, will foster further debate. Our definition of radicalism may apply to groups that are not, and have not been, commonly described as radicals, for example Roman Catholics after 1588, royalists after the 1649 regicide or Jacobites after 1688. It is certainly no coincidence that part of the English Jesuit Robert Persons's tract *A Conference about the Next Succession to the Crown of Ingland* (1596), written in support of tyrannicide, found its way into the *Moderate* in the winter of 1648–49 after it had been reprinted by the radical printer Robert Ibbitson.[69] This example ties in with our definition of radicalism as an oppositional and temporary phenomenon as well as expressing a minority position. We trust that this volume will open up new avenues of research and lay the foundations for successful explorations and fresh discoveries.

Notes

1 C. Hill, 'From Lollards to Levellers', in M. Cornforth (ed.), *Rebels and their Causes: Essays in Honour of A. L. Morton* (London: Lawrence and Wishart, 1978), pp. 49–68.

2 C. Condren, 'Radicals, Conservatives and Moderates in early modern political thought: a case of the Sandwich Islands Syndrome?', *History of Political Thought*, 10 (1989), 525–42; C. Condren, *The Language of Politics in Seventeenth-Century England* (Basingstoke: Macmillan, 1994); C. Condren, 'Afterword: Radicalism revisited', in G. Burgess and M. Festenstein (eds), *English Radicalism 1550–1850* (Cambridge: Cambridge University Press, 2007), pp. 311–37; J. C. D. Clark, *Our Shadowed Present: Modernism, Postmodernism and History* (London: Atlantic, 2003); J. C. D. Clark, 'Religion and the origins of radicalism in nineteenth-century Britain', in Burgess and Festenstein (eds), *English Radicalism*, pp. 241–84.

3 This phrase refers to the Marxist historian C. Hill's seminal work *The World Turned Upside Down: Radical Ideas during the English Revolution* (London: Maurice Temple Smith, 1972). Hill took the term from a contemporary pamphlet of a hostile kind.

4 For example, Thomas Edwards, *Gangræna: Or A Catalogue and Discovery of many of the Errours, Heresies, Blasphemies and pernicious Practices of the Sectaries of this time, vented and acted in England in these four last years* (London, 1646).

5 *The True Levellers Standard Advanced* (London, 1649); Abiezer Coppe, *A Fiery Flying Roll: A Word from the Lord to all the great Ones of the Earth, whom this may concerne: Being the Best Warning*

Piece at the dreadfull day of Judgement (London, 1650), p. 4. On the issue of naming radical sects, see Nigel Smith's introduction to his new edition of Ranter writings: *A Collection of Ranter Writings – Spiritual Liberty and Sexual Freedom in the English Revolution*, ed. Nigel Smith (London: Pluto Press, 2014), pp. 1–31. See also Jean-Pierre Cavaillé's Chapter 1 in this volume.

6 This does not mean that Walwyn had renounced his ideas altogether but that he did not publicise them in polemical pamphlets the way he had in the 1640s. On Walwyn's later career as a physician, see Derek Hirst, 'A happier man: the refashioning of William Walwyn', *The Seventeenth Century*, 27:1 (2012), 54–78.

7 G. Burgess, 'Introduction', in Burgess and Festenstein (eds), *English Radicalism*, pp. 1–16; G. Burgess, 'A matter of context: "Radicalism" and the English Revolution', in M. Caricchio and G. Tarantino (eds), *Cromohs Virtual Seminars: Recent Historiographical Trends of British Studies (17th–18th Centuries)* (2006–7). www.cromohs.unifi.it/seminari/burgess_radicalism.html (accessed 29 August 2015).

8 H. Kaye, *The Education of Desire: Marxists and the Writing of History* (New York, N.Y.; London: Routledge, 1992), pp. 98–115.

9 For a survey of revisionist approaches to the English revolution, see G. Burgess, 'On revisionism: an analysis of early Stuart historiography in the 1970s and 1980s', *Historical Journal*, 33 (1990), 609–27.

10 J. C. Davis, *Fear, Myth, and History: The Ranters and the Historians* (Cambridge: Cambridge University Press, 1986).

11 For a defence of the 'functional' approach, see J. C. Davis, 'Radicalism in a traditional society: the evaluation of radical thought in the English Commonwealth 1649–1660', *History of Political Thought*, 3 (1982), 193–213; J. C. Davis, 'Afterword: reassessing radicalism in a traditional society: two questions', in Burgess and Festenstein (eds), *English Radicalism*, pp. 338–72.

12 A. Hessayon, 'Reappraising early modern radicals and radicalisms', in A. Hessayon and D. Finnegan (eds), *Varieties of Seventeenth- and Early Eighteenth-Century English Radicalism in Context* (Farnham: Ashgate, 2011), pp. 6–7.

13 *A Remonstrance of His Excellency Thomas Lord Fairfax, Lord Generall of the Parliaments Forces and of the Generall Councell of Officers Held at St Albans the 16. of November, 1648. Presented to the Commons assembled in Parliament, the 20. instant and tendred to the Consideration of the whole Kingdome* (London, 1648).

14 As expressed in their later tracts, the Levellers would have been happy with a monarchy rather than the Commonwealth oligarchy, but a mixed, not an absolutist, monarchy which accommodated democratic principles.

15 See J. C. Davis, 'Afterword: reassessing radicalism', p. 364.
16 A. Hessayon, 'Fabricating radical traditions', in Caricchio and Tarantino (eds), *Cromohs Virtual Seminars*.
17 G. Burgess, 'A matter of context', in Caricchio and Tarantino (eds), *Cromohs Virtual Seminars*.
18 See, for example, chapters 2 and 7.
19 E. Vallance, 'Reborn John? The Eighteenth-Century Afterlife of John Lilburne', *Historical Workshop Journal*, 74:1 (2012), 21. Also see his Chapter 10 in this volume.
20 T. Morton and N. Smith, 'Introduction', in T. Morton and N. Smith (eds), *Radicalism in British Literary Culture, 1650–1830 – From Revolution to Revolution* (Cambridge: Cambridge University Press, 2002), p. 10.
21 J. Mee, 'The strange career of Richard "Citizen" Lee: poetry, popular radicalism and enthusiasm in the 1790s', in T. Morton and N. Smith (eds), *Radicalism in British Literary Culture*, p. 155.
22 James Howell, *Additionall Letters Of a fresher Date, Never Publish'd before, And Composed by the same Author*, in *Epistolae Ho-Elianae. Familiar Letters Domestic and Forren; Divided into sundry Sections, Partly Historicall, Politicall, Philosophicall, Vpon Emergent Occasions* (1650), pp. 5–6.
23 J. Scott, *England's Troubles – Seventeenth-Century English Political Instability in European Context* (Cambridge: Cambridge University Press, 2000), pp. 37–8.
24 N. McDowell, 'Writing the literary and cultural history of radicalism in the English revolution', in Caricchio and Tarantino (eds), *Cromohs Virtual Seminars*.
25 Burgess, 'A matter of context', in Caricchio and Tarantino (eds), *Cromohs Virtual Seminars*.
26 Coppe, *A Fiery Flying Roll*, p. 21. See L. Curelly, 'The Diggers and the Ranters: eccentric bedfellows?', in S. Aymes-Stokes and L. Mellet (eds), *In and Out: Eccentricity in Britain* (Newcastle upon Tyne: Cambridge Scholars Publishing, 2012), p. 99.
27 R. Foxley, 'The Levellers: John Lilburne, Richard Overton, and William Walwyn', in L. L. Knoppers (ed.), *The Oxford Handbook of Literature and the English Revolution* (Oxford: Oxford University Press, 2012), pp. 272–86; R. Foxley, *The Levellers: Radical Political Thought in the English Revolution* (Manchester: Manchester University Press, 2013).
28 L. Borot, 'Richard Overton and radicalism: the new intertext of the civic ethos in mid seventeenth-century England', in Burgess and Festenstein (eds), *English Radicalism*, pp. 37–86; R. Foxley, 'John Lilburne and the Citizenship of "Free-Born Englishmen"', *Historical Journal*, 47:4 (2004), 849–74; A. Sharp, 'John Lilburne and the Long Parliament's

Book of Declarations: a radical's exploitation of the words of authorities', *History of Political Thought*, 9:1 (1988), 19–44; William Walwyn, *The Writings of William Walwyn*, ed. Jack R. McMichael and Barbara Taft (Athens, G.A.: University of Georgia Press, 1989), pp. 1–51.

29 A. Woolrych, 'The debates from the perspective of the army', in M. Mendle (ed.), *The Putney Debates of 1647– the Army, the Levellers and the English State* (Cambridge: Cambridge University Press, 2001), pp. 53–78; J. Morrill and P. Baker, 'The case of the armie truly re-stated', in Mendle (ed.), *The Putney Debates of 1647*, pp. 103–24; J. Holstun, *Ehud's Dagger: Class Struggle in the English Revolution* (London; New York, N.Y.: Verso, 2000), pp. 305–66.

30 N. Smith, *Perfection Proclaimed: Language and Literature in English Radical Religion, 1640–1660* (Oxford: Clarendon, 1989).

31 N. H. Keeble (ed.), *The Cambridge Companion to Writing of the English Revolution* (Cambridge: Cambridge University Press, 2001); L. L. Knoppers (ed.), *The Oxford Handbook of Literature and the English Revolution*; P. Clemit (ed.), *The Cambridge Companion to British Literature of the French Revolution in the 1790s* (Cambridge: Cambridge University Press, 2011).

32 *The Prose Works of Andrew Marvell*, eds A. Patterson *et al.*, 2 vols (New Haven, C.T.; London: Yale University Press, 2003).

33 McDowell, *The English Radical Imagination*, pp. 19–20.

34 McDowell, 'Writing the literary and cultural history of radicalism in the English revolution', in Caricchio and Tarantino (eds), *Cromohs Virtual Seminars*.

35 For examples of radical language and radical speech acts, see chapters 2 and 7.

36 J. McElligott. *Royalism, Print and Censorship in Revolutionary England* (Woolbridge: Boydell, 2007); J. Peacey, *Politicians and Pamphleteers: Propaganda during the English Civil Wars and Interregnum* (Aldershot: Ashagte, 2004); J. Peacey, 'News, Pamphlets, and Public Opinion', in Knoppers (ed.) *The Oxford Handbook of Literature and the English Revolution*, pp. 173–89; J. Raymond, *The Invention of the Newspaper: English Newsbooks, 1641–1649* (Oxford: Clarendon Press, 1996); J. Raymond, 'The newspaper, public opinion and the public sphere in the seventeenth century', in J. Raymond (ed.), *News, Newspapers and Society in Early Modern Britain* (London: Frank Cass, 1999), pp. 109–40; J. Raymond, *Pamphlets and Pamphleteering in Early Modern Britain* (Cambridge: Cambridge University Press, 2003); J. Raymond (ed.), *The Oxford History of Popular Print Culture – Volume One: Cheap Print in Britain and Ireland to 1660* (Oxford: Oxford University Press, 2011).

37 J. Habermas, *The Structural Transformation of the Public Sphere*,

trans. T. Burger (Cambridge, M.A.: Massachusetts Institute of Technology, 1991). See S. Pincus, 'The State and civil society in early modern England: capitalism, causation and Habermas's bourgeois public sphere', in P. Lake and S. Pincus (eds), *The Politics of the Public Sphere in Early Modern England* (Manchester: Manchester University Press, 2007), pp. 213–31; D. Zaret, *Origins of Democratic Culture: Printing, Petitions and the Public Sphere in Early Modern England* (Princeton, N.J.: Princeton University Press, 2000).

38 J. McElligott, *Censorship and the Press, 1640–1660* (London: Pickering & Chatto, 2009); J. McElligott, 'The book trade, licensing, and censorship', in Knoppers (ed.), *The Oxford Handbook of Literature and the English Revolution*, pp. 135–53.

39 A. Hessayon, 'Calvert, Giles (bap. 1616, d. 1663), bookseller', in *Oxford Dictionary of National Biography* (Oxford: Oxford University Press, 2004); M. Caricchio, 'News for the new Jerusalem: Giles Calvert and the radical experience', in Hessayon (ed.), *Varieties of Seventeenth- and Early Eighteenth-Century Radicalism*; pp. 69–86; F. Mott Harrison, 'Nathaniel Ponder', *The Library*, 15:3 (1934), 257–94; B. Lynch, 'Ponder, Nathaniel (1640–1699)', bookseller, in *Oxford Dictionary of National Biography*. Catherine Vigier in Chapter 9 studies a captivity narrative published by Nathaniel Ponder.

40 Many newsbooks had established distinct identities, both Parliamentarian and royalist but, unlike the *Moderate*, they were not counterfeit publications to begin with.

41 *Moderate Intelligencer*, no 1 (27 February – 6 March 1645), p. 1.

42 He inserted the inscription 'This is the true *Moderate Intelligencer*' at the end of number 173, possibly leaving readers in greater confusion than before. *Moderate Intelligencer*, aka *Moderate*, no 173 (6–13 July 1648), p. 1444.

43 *Moderate*, no 1 (11–18 July 1648), p. 1. This comment was reproduced in the next six issues of the newsbook, ending with number 7 (22–29 August 1648), p. 41.

44 Jürgen Diethe identifies three versions of the editorial in number 14: *New Articles for Peace*, dated 18 October 1648, which is closest to the *Moderate* text, except for the fact that it leaves out the first seventeen lines and a whole paragraph; *New Propositions of the Army*, dated 24 October by Thomason, and *A Bloudy Fight at Pontefract Castle in York-shire*, a collection of news dated 27 October. See J. Diethe, 'The *Moderate*: politics and allegiances of a revolutionary newspaper', in *History of Political Thought*, 4 (1988), 247–94. For a study of the *Remonstrance of the Army* in comparison with the Levellers' political agenda, see I. Gentles, *The New Model Army in England, Ireland, and Scotland, 1645–1653* (Oxford; Cambridge, M.A.:

Blackwell Publishers, 1992), pp. 272–6, and G. Burgess, 'Radicalism and the English Revolution', in Burgess and Festenstein (eds), *English Radicalism*, pp. 72–3.

45 *Moderate*, no 41 (17–24 April 1649), p. 425.

46 See, for example, their vindication of private property and rejection of communalism in *A manifestation from Lieutenant-Colonel John Lilburne, Mr William Walwyn, Mr Thomas Prince, and Mr Richard Overton (now prisoners in the Tower of London), and others, commonly (though unjustly) styled Levellers* (London, 1949), pp. 4–5.

47 H. Brailsford, *The Levellers and the English Revolution* (Nottingham: Spokesman, 2nd edn, 1983), p. 402.

48 J. B. William, *A History of English Journalism to the Foundation of the Gazette* (London; New York, N.Y.: Longmans, Green, & Co, 1908), pp. 104–5. Also see A. N. B. Cotton, 'John Dillingham, journalist of the Middle Group', *The English Historical Review*, 93 (1978), 817–34. Brailsford calls the *Moderate Intelligencer* a 'commonplace' newsbook: Brailsford, *The Levellers and the English Revolution*, p. 403.

49 See for example D. Lovejoy, *The Glorious Revolution in America* (Hanover, N.H.: University Press of New England, 1972); M. and J. Jacob (eds), *The Origins of Anglo-American Radicalism* (London: Allen & Unwin, 1984). Chapter 10 is a further contribution to the study of transatlantic exchanges.

50 See, for example, Gaby Mahlberg's study of the transmission of English republican ideas in French-speaking Europe through the translation into French of a pamphlet that included miscellaneous texts of the English regicides: G. Mahlberg, '*Les Juges Jugez, Se Justifians* (1663) and Edmund Ludlow's protestant network in seventeenth-century Switzerland', *Historical Journal*, 57:2 (2014), 369–96.

51 G. Mahlberg and D. Wiemann (eds), *European Contexts for English Republicanism – Politics and Culture in Europe, 1650–1750* (Farnham: Ashgate, 2013); A. Hessayon and S. Apetrei (eds), *An Introduction to Jacob Boehme: Four Centuries of Thought and Reception* (New York, N.Y.; Abingdon: Routledge, 2014). For an overview of cultural transfers at the time of the English Revolution, see N. Smith, 'England, Europe, and the English Revolution', in Knoppers (ed.) *The Oxford Handbook of Literature and the English Revolution*, pp. 29–43.

52 A. Weststeijn, 'Why the Dutch didn't read Harrington: Anglo-Dutch republican exchanges, c. 1650–1670', in Mahlberg and Wiemann (eds), *European Contexts for English Republicanism*, pp. 105–20; H. W. Blom, 'Popularising government: democratic tendencies in Anglo-Dutch republicanism', in Mahlberg and Wiemann (eds), *European Contexts for English Republicanism*, pp. 121–37. See also also Charles-Édouard Levillain's study of the reception of Tacitus as a guide to differences

between Dutch and English republicans: C.-E. Levillain, 'William III's military and political career in neo-roman context, 1672–1702', *Historical Journal*, 48:2 (2005), 321–50.

53 A. Hessayon, 'Jacob Boehme's writings during the English Revolution', in Hessayon and Apetrei (eds), *An Introduction to Jacob Boehme*, pp. 77–97. For Nigel Smith's argument, see J. F. McGregor, B. Capp, N. Smith, B. J. Gibbons, 'Fear, myth and furore: reappraising the "Ranters"', *Past and Present*, 140 (1993), 171–8.

54 On Sexby's involvement in France, see L. Curelly, '"Do look on the other side of the water": de la politique étrangère de Cromwell à l'égard de la France', *E-rea*, 11:2 (2014), https://erea.revues.org/3751 (accessed 29 August 2015).

55 V. Cousin, *Madame de Longueville: études sur les femmes illustres et la société au XVIIe siècle: Madame de Longueville pendant la Fronde: 1651–1653* (Paris: Didier, 1859), p. 266.

56 T. Venning, *Cromwellian Foreign Policy* (London: Macmillan; New York, N.Y.: St Martin's Press, 1999), p. 5.

57 Cousin, *Madame de Longueville*, p. 282.

58 For further details on the various drafts of the text, see I. Gentle, 'The *Agreements of the People* and their political contexts, 1647–1649', in Mendle (ed.), *The Putney Debates of 1647*, p. 148–74.

59 John Lilburne, William Walwyn, Thomas Prince and Richard Overton, *An Agreement of the Free People of England. Tendered as a Peace-Offering to this distressed Nation* (London, 1649), p. 7.

60 Lilburne *et al.*, *An Agreement of the Free People of England*, p. 4.

61 V. Cousin, *Madame de Longueville*, p. 467.

62 P. Knachel, *England and the Fronde – The Impact of the English Civil War and Revolution on France* (Ithaca, N.Y.: Cornell University Press, 1967), p. 106. This opinion is shared by a number of Fronde historians. For example, see C. Vicherd, 'La "République" dans les mazarinades: à propos des événements anglais contemporains de la Fronde', in Y.-C. Zarka (ed.), *Monarchie et république au XVIIe siècle* (Paris: Presses Universitaires de France, 2007), p. 228; P. Goubert, *Mazarin* (Paris: Fayard, 1990), p. 306; and C. Giry-Deloison, 'Le rôle de l'Angleterre dans les événements de la Fronde bordelaise 1649–1653', in A.-M. Cocula and M. Boisson-Gabarron (eds), *Adhésions et résistances à l'État en France et en Espagne 1620–1660* (Bordeaux: Presses Universitaires de Bordeaux, 2001), pp. 132–5. For Sexby's involvement in the Ormée, see also H. Kötting, *Die Ormée 1651–1653* (Münster: Aschendorff, 1983), pp. 159–65, 194–225, 230–43; S. Westrich, *The Ormée of Bordeaux: a Revolution during the Fronde* (Baltimore, M.D.: Johns Hopkins University Press, 1972), p. 56.

63 W. C. Abbott, *The Writings and Speeches of Oliver Cromwell*

(Cambridge, M.A.: Harvard University Press; New York, N.Y.: Russell & Russell, 1937–1947), vol. 2, pp. 524–5.

64 *Mercurius Politicus* (hereafter *MP*), no 1 (6–13 June 1650), p. 10. For a discussion of the way the French Fronde was represented in this newsbook, see L. Curelly, '"The French, those monkies of mankind": the Fronde as seen by the newsbook *Mercurius Politicus*', *Revue de la Société d'Études Anglo-Américaines des XVIIe et XVIIIe siècles*, 69 (2012), 29–50.

65 For example *MP*, no 2 (13–20 June 1650), p. 29; no 12 (22–29 August 1650), p. 187.

66 *MP*, no 6 (11–18 July 1650), p. 89.

67 *Traité politique, composé par William Allen Anglois, Et traduit nouvellement en François, où il est prouvé par l'exemple de Moyse, et par d'autres, tirés hors de l'escriture, que tuer un tyran, Titulo vel exercitio, n'est pas un meurtre* (Lugduni, 1658), reproduced in O. Lutaud, *Des révolutions d'Angleterre à la Révolution française – Le tyrannicide et Killing No Murder* (The Hague: Martinus Nijhoff, 1973), pp. 411–42. *Killing No Murder* was in fact published by Sexby in Holland under the name of his former fellow Agitator William Allen.

68 Lutaud, *Des révolutions d'Angleterre à la Révolution française*, pp. 367–70.

69 For a discussion of how some of the winter editorials of the *Moderate* plagiarised and recycled this pamphlet, see L. Borot, '"Vive le Roi!" ou "Mort au tyran!"? Le procès et l'exécution de Charles Ier dans la presse d'information de novembre 1648 à février 1649', in F. Laroque and F. Lessay (eds), *Figures de la royauté en Angleterre de Shakespeare à la Glorieuse Révolution* (Paris: Presses de la Sorbonne Nouvelle, 1999), pp. 143–64. Although authorship of this tract is still disputed, it is generally attributed to Persons (or Parsons). Its first part was reprinted by Ibbitson in 1648 under the title *Severall Speeches Delivered at a Conference concerning the Power of Parliament, to proceed against their King for Misgovernment.*

PART I

Radical language and themes

1

~

Community of goods: an unacceptable radical theme at the time of the English revolution

Jean-Pierre Cavaillé

The puropose of this chapter is not to provide a thorough explora-
tion of the condemnation of private property and the promotion of
common property as feature in the works of English radical writers
of the seventeenth century, such as those of Gerrard Winstanley or
Abiezer Coppe. Instead, a reflection is proposed upon the conditions underpinning the use in public debate of the community of
goods theory, one of the most provocative and dangerous ideas that
appeared in the literature of many radical writers of the time.

This idea and the political ideal it expressed were perceived as so
much of a threat that, by condemning them, contemporary critics
seem to have been pursuing imaginary enemies and have often been
said to have produced the community of goods theory the better to
combat it. The few sources that provide evidence of the existence of
this theory are of little value. Marxist historians, chief among whom
Christopher Hill,[1] have been charged with imparting a political
dimension to what were primarily spiritualist and millenarian religious positions.[2] Thus, as they rely on texts which condemned the
community of goods theory, these historians are often regarded as
the inventors of 'radicalism', understood here as a political doctrine
foreshadowing communism. They are accused of overinterpreting
Leveller pamphlets and the writings of 'visionaries' and 'deranged
minds' such as Winstanley and Coppe. The revisionist approach to
early modern radicalism will be challenged through an examination
of the conditions of production, distribution and transmission of
what is one of the most radical social ideas in seventeenth-century

England. A useful conceptual tool in attempting to account for the persistence of radical ideas in European culture is the notion of acceptability, as opposed to unacceptability. Here it is not a matter of ideas floating in the Platonic Empyrean, but rather ideas that were publicised by individuals and groups operating clandestinely and the diffusion of which, as a result, mostly relied on oral transmission. These ideas are typically only known from the repeated condemnations they provoked, though at certain times they did seem to have enjoyed positive expression and public visibility.

In such instances, they may have shaped collective practices and possibly penetrated the space of public controversy and political action. The concepts of acceptability and unacceptability are helpful tools to offer a practical description of a certain amount of underground popular culture whose public expression was judged unacceptable. The very presence of such cultural factors points to the existence of what may be called 'restricted acceptability' – that is to say a form or acceptability limited to certain social groups, whether they be fringe groups or not. In addition, these are useful concepts to analyse the constant shifting of boundaries that allowed, in certain circumstances, ideas previously considered wholly unacceptable to be uttered in public and to become acceptable without being necessarily accepted; at most, it became acceptable – at least for a time – to discuss them publicly. This approach challenges the so-called revisionist readings that tend to deny real relevance or even a historical existence to radical phenomena, but also criticises the historical determinism of the Marxist tradition, which understands radical self-fashioning as foreshadowing revolution and advanced modernity. That ideas should be given publicity and hence become, to some degree, publicly acceptable in particular historical circumstances does not imply that they are accepted, that is to say, recognised as generators of change beyond the small groups that produce them. On the other hand, their effective removal from the public sphere, the fact that they become unacceptable again, does not exclude their persistence and their transmission in restricted spaces of acceptability where they operate 'under the radar'.

In this chapter, the approach to radical egalitarianism and common property in England between 1648 and 1652 is based on three assumptions: the first being that the common property theme was of a radical nature, as it was used by some individuals and radical groups from a political and an eschatological perspective in

England in the late 1640s and early 1650s within the context of the rise and fall of the Leveller movement; the second, that this radical egalitarian and libertarian theme did not come out of thin air, nor was it a figment of critics' imaginations, but had been circulating in England and throughout Europe for a long time, in the oral culture of the lower classes as well as in the most elitist of written culture; the third, post-regicide England witnessed changing attitudes towards the community of goods theme, from the Levellers' denial of the charges that they intended to level private property and that they pursued a communistic agenda to the emergence of groups who embraced 'levelling' practices openly, especially the Diggers, the Ranters and some of the first Quakers – a sect that is known to have attracted former Levellers, Diggers and Ranters. All these names initially carried denunciatory overtones and caused whole groups of people to be stigmatised, but such categorisation should be taken with a pinch of salt, if only because it was the doing of adversaries.[3] The aim of this chapter is to reflect upon the polemical names of groups identified as unacceptable 'sects', and on how these groups responded to accusations in an attempt to defend themselves, but also appropriated and redefined the names and picked up on the accusations linked to these names, thus promoting as acceptable principles ideas that had previously been held to be unacceptable, at least in the domain of public expression, a strategy which presupposed the existence of spaces of restricted and clandestine acceptability.

One of the striking features of the writings of such radicals as Gerrard Winstanley and Abiezer Coppe is the extreme strength, consistency and, arguably, theoretical maturity of their authors' positions regarding the issue of property. The use of the term 'radicals' is justified here by the presence of a radical challenge – understood as the desire to return to the ontological and historical root of things – to social and economic inequalities as well as to power relations based on the appropriation of land and goods by a few to the detriment of the many. Property as appropriation – the concept of property carries significant meaning in the literature of the time, as will be discussed below – is most clearly identified by Winstanley as the major source of domination, together with all the excuses given by clerical and political authorities to legitimise their seizing of goods and their oppression of the people. Winstanley's criticism is grounded in a vision of the state of nature – identified with the paradisiacal state of Adam and Eve[4] – in which freedom, equality and community of goods are one and the same.

The topic of property understood as the appropriation of land ranks first in Winstanley's writings because property creates inequality and destroys freedom. For the Digger leader, freedom was incompatible with property, for the very notion of property implies that landowners necessarily dominate the landless who are made to serve their landed masters. By seizing the earth and its fruits for their own benefits, owners establish a *de facto* power relation with those who are excluded from property. This is what Winstanley calls the 'government of highwaymen', because all that owners actually possess is stolen property and they endlessly rob the community of those who now depend on them for their survival. Winstanley describes the historical process of alienation thus: 'In the beginning of time the great Creator Reason made the earth to be a common treasury.' But as they are abused by a 'selfish imagination' and by 'covetousness', men choose one among themselves to teach them and to supply them with rules; therefore, 'man was brought into bondage, and became a greater Slave to such of his own kind, then the Beasts of the field were to him. And hereupon, the earth ... was hedged into enclosures by the teachers and rulers, and the others were made servants and slaves.'[5]

This theory is similar to the one produced contemporaneously by 'libertine' naturalists, whose eclectic philosophical background included Epicurean, Stoic and Cynical ideas.[6] Winstanley was undoubtedly influenced by some form of Stoicism, notably through the identification of God with reason and nature.[7] But his millenarian beliefs show that he viewed the political struggle for a restoration of freedom and community as an ethical and spiritual necessity, inseparable from a process of regeneration of the individual and of all mankind.

The goal was freedom, but 'there cannot be a universal liberty till this universal community be established'.[8] Only the universal community of goods, as expressed in this phrase 'the earth shall be made a common treasury of livelihood to whole mankind, without respect of persons',[9] allows the establishment of freedom for all. It is the only escape from the endless struggle of individuals for possession and power, which Winstanley viewed as the degeneration of humanity. Contemporaneous with Winstanley's writings was Hobbes's theory that possessive individualism was part of the natural condition of man, and his view that the state of nature led to the war of all against all. Hobbes therefore highlighted the need to establish a contract-based sovereign power capable of maintaining civil peace, that is to say neutralising the harmful effects of individual competition, or rather taking advantage of it for the benefit of all.[10] For Winstanley, the restoration of the state of community, freedom and equality guaranteed the sovereignty of reason and freed humanity from the yoke of domination. Establishing equality, indeed, implied giving power to reason – indissolubly divine, natural and human – in a world where covetousness, competition and the unbridled desire for possession still prevailed.

Winstanley's pamphlets and the ephemeral experience of collective land occupation and common digging in which he himself was the leading light undoubtedly left a mark on an unquantifiable but probably not insignificant number of Levellers or their followers who were especially sensitive to the issue of property. It may even be argued that some of them had reached similar conclusions by themselves.

This at least can be inferred from the unique testimony of Lawrence Clarkson who, recalling his years as a Ranter when he was nicknamed the 'Captain of the rant', tells about the interaction between his Antinomian theological speculations and their expression in his own life, as he was confronted with the Diggers' active challenging of property:

> The ground of this my judgment was, God made all things good, so nothing evil but a man judged it; for I apprehended there was no such thing as theft, cheat, or a lie, but as man made it so; for if the creature had brought this world into [no] propriety, as Mine and Thine, there had been no such title as theft, cheat, or lie; for the prevention hereof Everard and Gerrard Winstanley did dig up the Commons, that so all might have to live of themselves, then there had been no need of defrauding, but unity one with another.[11]

This extract is followed by a criticism of Winstanley based on a rejection of the empire of reason promoted by the Digger leader, in accordance with Clarkson's monist theory which he advertised in *A Single Eye*, in which reason and unreason, like good and bad actions, pure and impure acts, holiness and sin, dissolve and fuse in the unity of God. However, he agreed with the Diggers when they claimed that God had neither created nor wanted property, and that property was inseparable from theft, fraud and deceit, which he confessed to having practised in a purely innocent manner. Such an attitude, of course, had nothing to do with the Diggers' sense of community.

As for Coppe, he denounced private property, social inequality and the enslavement of the poor, using the scandalous word and notion of 'levelling', distinguishing his own practice of levelling from the 'sword levelling' of the Leveller soldiers and the 'digging levelling' of Winstanley.[12] He wielded only the sword of the spirit, which led him day and night to protest publicly on the streets of London against the rich in their carriages, shaking his fist and gritting his teeth. He argued that the Levellers – 'Men-Levellers' – crushed at Bradford – 'the last Levellers that were shot to death' – were nothing but the 'shadowes of most terrible, yeat great, glorious good things to come'.[13] Coppe thus heralded the great levelling of God in the inner man, but necessarily in society too, by means of the transgressive practices of the Ranters: 'I come (saith the Lord) with a vengeance, to levell also your Honour, Riches, etc.'[14] Coppe's God bursts into the night like a thief, a ruthless purse-cutter: 'Thou hast many baggs of money, and behold I [the Lord] come as a thief in the night, with my sword drawn in my hand, and like a thief as I am – I say deliver your purse, deliver sirrah! deliver or I'l cut thy throat!'[15] As often in Coppe's pamphlets, the biblical metaphor is to be taken literally. The chapter in which it appears, indeed, is entitled 'How the Lord will recover his outward things (things of this life) as Money, Corn, etc. and for whom, and how they shall be plagued who detaine them as their owne',[16] and ends with a command, or rather a straightforward threat: 'Give up your houses, horses, goods, gold, Lands, give up, account nothing your own, have ALL THINGS common, or els the plague of God will rot and consume all that you have.'[17] Thus, the great levelling consists in the abolition of 'Honour, Nobility, Gentility, Propriety, Superfluity, etc.', all things being reduced to 'parity, equality, community'.[18] As for Winstanley, one should add 'perfect freedom', the perfect liberty for which Coppe claimed he had renounced everything else.

The 'levelling' Ranter practice of community, as opposed to the 'sword levelling', is described by Coppe in a most provocative and outrageous way: 'We had as live be dead drunk every day of the weeke, and lye with whores i'th market place; and account these as good actions as taking the poor abused, enslaved ploughmans money from him ... we had rather starve, I say, then take away his money from him, for killing men.'[19]

The original unity between liberty, equality and community professed by Winstanley and, in his own manner, by Coppe, comes remarkably close to the way in which the lost state of nature is apprehended by philosophers who, in the sixteenth and the seventeenth centuries, exploited Hesiod's myth of the Golden Age both in its Lucretian and Ovidian versions. But what these philosophers understood as a bygone age of humanity, whose very remote return was only conceivable within the framework of a cyclical representation of time – as in *Theophrastus Redivivus*, a philosophical treatise and compendium of libertine naturalism completed in 1659 – was seen by English radicals, as heirs to a long spiritualistic tradition involving in particular the ideas and the communal experience of some Anabaptists,[20] from the perspective of impending millenarianism giving sense and strength to present action and speech, however transgressive they might seem.

It is useful here to bring together the theories of two markedly opposed philosophical schools. The first is extremely elitist and features the figure of a wise man who stays away from any political reformism, persuaded as he is that unacceptability is irreducible and that philosophical truth is socially dangerous, and who considers that life should be ruled only by the law of nature; that is to say, according to the state of nature which knew neither property nor domination or religion. The second movement is deeply rooted in the culture of the underclass in European societies; for its followers, the establishment or rather the restoration of community of goods and of both natural and spiritual freedom, as an expression of God's will, can be achieved immediately, and they believe in an immediate reversal and levelling of states and conditions, which means that what still seems absolutely unacceptable and leads to fierce repression is about to reveal and impose itself as Truth. The millennial eschatology here is inseparable from a political interpretation of the Fall: Mine and Thine, inequality and enslavement, are not produced by original sin but *are* sin, understood as a divorce between man and God and between man and man through property, domination and the power of the clergy. The remedy, however, is at hand; it has an inextricably political and religious nature, in that it is a spiritual and moral revolution whose actors are regenerated man in God and God Himself manifesting His love and His levelling power within man.

47

Community of goods as a political motif has a distinct shape in England as it cannot be divorced from the franchise and property issue. Nor can it be separated from the double myth of the original freedom of the Anglo-Saxons and of the Norman Yoke and, perhaps most importantly, from the appropriation of the commons by the nobility through the raising of enclosures. The Diggers and the Ranters, then, are heirs to a long-standing tradition, only partly recovered through the controversies of the mid-seventeenth century. There is no need to go back to the claims of some Lollards[21] or to the peasant revolt of 1381 – as exemplified in the proverbial phrase attributed to John Ball 'When Adam delved and Eve span,/ Who was then the gentleman?', which was often quoted during the revolutionary period[22] – to argue that the topic of social equality and the community of goods motif drew upon aspects of both popular and high culture. This reference was common during the English revolution. Thomas Fuller, for example, remarked that 'the dangerous rebellion of Wat Tyler and Jack Straw [in 1581], with thousands of their cursed company' was the act of 'pure Levellers':

> These all were pure Levellers, (inflamed by the abused eloquence of one John Ball, an excommunicated priest) who, maintaining that no gentry was *Jure Divino*, and all equal by nature, 'When Adam delved, and Eve span,/ Who was then the gentleman?', endeavoured the abolishing of all civil and spiritual degrees and distinctions. Yea, they desired to level men's parts, as well as their purses.[23]

This recalls Thomas More's *Utopia*: 'Though, to speak plainly my real sentiments, I must freely own that as long as there is any property, and while money is the standard of all other things, I cannot think that a nation can be governed either justly or happily: not justly, because the best things will fall to the share of the worst men; nor happily, because all things will be divided among a few (and even these are not in all respects happy), the rest being left to be absolutely miserable.'[24] The community of goods motif also inspired those who were involved in the Midlands riots in 1607 to protest against the appropriation of the commons and call themselves 'Levellers' and 'Diggers'.[25]

It is no coincidence that the repeated charge that radical groups in the revolutionary years intended to destroy private property and establish social and economic equality should have found an expression in the words 'Levellers' and 'levelling' to signify the levelling of men's wealth, states and conditions. As is well known, the Levellers were labelled as 'Levellers' by their enemies, who thus attempted both to identify and to discredit them by presenting them as the underground champions of the destruction of private property and of all forms of social hierarchy. We know how vigorously Leveller leaders rejected these accusations as downright slanderous and refused to be called 'Levellers', as when the authors of the 11 September 1648 petition to Parliament wrongly claimed that the Long Parliament intended to abolish private property: 'We have long expected things of another nature from you, and such as we are confident would have given satisfaction to all serious people of all parties [...]. That you would have bound yourselves and all future parliaments from abolishing propriety, levelling men's estates or making all things common.'[26] Equality of rights and universal suffrage as advocated by the Levellers were not attacks on private property.[27] Calling for a better redistribution of land and wealth did not in itself lead to questioning the very principle of private property; it may be argued, instead, that the Levellers promoted access to property, trade and business. As Laura Brace puts it, 'Levellers would not have advocated a community of goods, but they were opposed to the extreme concentration of wealth in the hands of an elite which was determined to prevent a broader acquisition of property. Levellers (and later Quakers) were defending a specific sort of property in labour which has been constantly under attack by the rich, whose own property acquired by appropriation had been treated as sacrosanct.'[28] It is certainly not incongruous to see in the writings and the collective actions of the Levellers one of the first sources of political liberalism, or at least one of its strands, which resolutely raises the individual above any type of property, even self-property.

Despite the doubt raised by the definition of individual freedom as 'self-property', the Levellers did not support any conception of the individual as being quintessentially an owner, or any form of possessive individualism. This is expressed, for example, by Richard Overton in his *An arrow against all tyrants and tyranny*:

> To every individual, in nature, is given an individual property by nature not to be invaded or usurped by any. For every one, as he is himself, so he hath a self-propriety, else could he not *be* himself, and on this no second may presume to deprive any of without manifest violation and affront to the very principles of nature and of the Rules

of equity and justice between man and man. Mine and thine cannot be, except this be. No man has power over my rights and liberties, and I over no man's. I may be but an individual, enjoy my self and my self-propriety and may right myself no more than my self.[29]

The Levellers' rejection of possessive individualism was demonstrated in Hampsher-Monk's seminal paper against Macpherson in 1976.[30] For the Levellers, as for many of their English contemporaries, the word 'property' retained much of its medieval sense, with its inclusion of the individual usufruct of collective property:

> What this approach implies is that essentially ownership is not vested in a single 'lord', but in a group; nor need physical objects, especially land, be subject to the exclusive use or ownership of any one such individual or group, but may be divided up amongst a number of them according to the various rights or 'properties' which may be exercised over it: sheep grazing, wood gathering, hunting, etc. 'Property' stands in stark contrast to the modern notion of an all-encompassing right to the use and disposal of an object by individual owners.[31]

Thus, in seventeenth-century England the word 'property' was still naturally applied to constitutional freedoms which were not based on the model of private ownership of land or goods. By insisting on the property that each individual had over his own natural faculties – reason, in particular – the Levellers challenged the definition of property as limited to private property. This is particularly clear in the Putney debates of 1647, in which Thomas Rainsborough and his friends opposed Ireton over the property issue. In this respect, Hampsher-Monk pointed out that even in *A Manifestation*, a pamphlet written from the Tower of London in 1649 in which they once again attempted to defend themselves against the accusation that they wanted to abolish private property, the four Leveller leaders did not assert the inviolability of property but insisted that a consensus was required for its abolition, making it clear that community of goods among early Christians was 'voluntary not coactive', so that 'an inducing the same is most injurious, unless there did precede an universal assent thereunto from all and every one of the People'.[32]

The existence in seventeenth-century England of a theory of the religious, philosophical and moral superiority of community of goods over private property, on the one hand, and the belief that property was a fundamental right, on the other, probably explains why the opponents of the Levellers believed that universal suffrage inevitably led to the destruction of private property, which was said to be part of the Levellers' hidden agenda. This is, for example, the unequivocal point that Ireton made about the *Agreement of the People* in the Putney debates: 'First, the thing itself [universal suffrage] were dangerous if it were settled to destroy property. But I say that the principle that leads to this is destructive to property; for by the same reason that you will alter this Constitution merely that there's a greater Constitution by nature – by the same reason, by the law of nature, there is a greater liberty to the use of other men's goods which that property bars you.'[33]

It is precisely in this context that the notion of acceptability proves to be useful. There are many clues indeed pointing to some Levellers challenging not only property, with a minimum annual capital of 200 pounds as a condition for Englishmen to be granted the franchise, and thus full citizenship, but also the very principle of private property in the name of an ideal vision of common property, although it was by no means the official doctrine and probably – even if this cannot be proved with absolute certainty – remained a minority opinion.

This is what comes in particular from William Walwyn's searing attacks on property in *Tyranipocrit Discovered*, if indeed he was the one who authored it,[34] and in other statements that he is alleged to have made, as reported for example in *Walwins wiles*:

This Mr *Walwyn,* to work upon the indigent and poorer sort of people, and to raise up their spirits in discontents and clamours, &c. did one time profess, *he could wish with all his heart that there was neither Pale, Hedge nor Ditch in the whole Nation, and that it was an unconscionable thing that one man should have ten thousand pounds, and another, more deserving and useful to the Common-wealth, should not be worth two pence;* or to that purpose. At another time discoursing of the inequality and disproportion of the estates and conditions of men in the world, had words to this purpose, That *it was a sad and miserable thing that it should so continue, and that it would never be well until all things were common;* and it being replyed, *Will that ever be?* Answered, *We must endeavor it:* It being said, That this would destroy all Government; Answered, That then *there would be less need of Government, for then there would be no theeves, no covetous persons, no deceiving and abusing of one another, and so no need of government, &c. but if in such a case they have a form and rule of government to determine cases, as may fall out, yet there will be no need of standing Officers in a Common-wealth, no need of Judges, &c but if any difference doe fall out, or any criminall fact be committed, take a Cobler from his Seat, or a Butcher from his Shop, or any other Tradesman that is an honest and just man, and let him heare the case, and determine the same, and then betake himself to his work again.*[35]

While they represented a distinct minority, such radical critics of property as Walwyn existed within the Leveller movement, but the extreme violence of attacks against the Levellers on this issue and the great care their leaders took to refute them, while rejecting the dogma that private property was sacred, bring to light how unacceptable the expression of these ideas was in mid seventeenth-century England.

A Buckinghamshire group claiming to be Levellers in 1648 – even before Winstanley had started publishing his writings – called for equal property for all men: 'All men being alike privileged by birth, so all men were to enjoy the creatures alike without property one more than the other, all men by the grant of God are free, and every man individual, that is to say no man was to lord over his own kind; neither to enclose the creatures to his own use, to impoverishing of his neighbours.'[36] The ideas that shaped Winstanley's egalitarian theory were already there. It has been suggested that he could himself have contributed to the two Buckinghamshire pamphlets, but Christopher Hill uncovered other links in 1648–49 between ideas defended by the so-called Levellers and by the 'true Levellers', a name which Winstanley and his friends claimed for themselves in the title of their pamphlet *The True Levellers Standard Advanced*, and which was taken up by some of those accused of being Ranters.

When the political defeat of the Levellers was a certain fact, ideas that were attributed to the Levellers in order to criminalise them and which, in fact, were attached to the very name that they had been given, were publicly appropriated, in a positive way, in printed writings. It is no easy thing to explain why these ideas were given access, precisely at a time which coincided with the regicide, to the publicity of print. The fact that book censorship was virtually abolished in that period only makes for a partial explanation, attractive though it may be. It can also be assumed that the difficulties and the failure of the Levellers released, within the movement itself, a more radical discourse, which had hitherto been kept away from the public sphere. This trend may be seen as an attempt to allow the community of goods motif to penetrate public debate – be it through provocation, as Coppe did – and to make the political, economic and spiritual system of thought that went with it acceptable.

The Digger experiment, though fiercely contested, was only short-lived. The print production of Winstanley stopped in 1652 with the publication of *The Law of Freedom*. The Ranters were repressed, especially with the passing of the *Blasphemy Act* of 1650, though this piece of legislation did not include any explicit mention of the doctrine of community of goods. They were repeatedly accused of planning to establish a 'community of all things': 'They taught, that it was quite contrary to the end of Creation, to Appropriate anything to any Man or Woman; but that there ought to be a Community of all things.'[37] Like most of his friends, Coppe was forced to recant his writings and ideas. However, he managed to stick to his egalitarian precepts without too much ambiguity:

> As for community, I own but that Apostolical, saint-like community, spoken of in the Scriptures. So far I either do, or should own community, that if flesh of my flesh, be ready to perish; I either will, or should call nothing that I have, mine own. If I have bread, it shall, or should be his, else all my religion is in vain. I am for dealing bread to the hungry, for cloathing the naked, for the breaking of every yoak, for the letting of the oppressed go free ... I am utterly against that community which is sinful, or destructive to soul or body, or the being of a Common-wealth. I own no other, long for none other; but that glorious liberty of the sons of God [Rom. 8].[38]

Coppe only condemned the 'community of women', which the Ranters were accused of promoting and practising. It seems that, far from merely repeating the old theme of the 'community of women', some Ranters, who were invariably associated in hostile pamphlets with community of goods, proposed a universal sexual community. Edward Hyde hints at Ranters' sexual practices in these terms: 'All the women in the world are but one woman's husband in unity; so that one man may lie with all the women in the world in unity, and one woman may lie with all men in the world, for they are all her husband in unity.'[39]

As Alan Cole has shown, the community of goods motif may still be found in the Quaker movement, which rallied numerous

Levellers, Diggers and Ranters, at least in its early stages and in a rather covert way: 'Some Quakers advocated the use of ecclesiastical and royalist lands for the relief of poverty, and others even looked with favour on the community of goods which they believed had been practised by the early Christians.'[40] Quakers soon developed a more acceptable public discourse, as they rejected any identification with the 'Levellers' and denied supporting the abolition of property and the advent of a classless society. Yet they bore the brunt of persistent accusations.[41] They limited themselves to a more conventional praise of assistance for the poor and defined themselves as a community of believers with no political, social or economic agenda. In Alan Cole's words, 'they consistently repudiated the charge that they sought the wholesale levelling of men's estates by political means'.[42]

Even though most of the writings discussed in this chapter soon slipped into oblivion, the rejection of private property and the desire to see the advent of community of goods come true continued their underground progress, in England and elsewhere in Europe, following paths which still remain largely unexplored. To conduct this exploratory survey, as has been attempted here, is no easy matter: it requires that historians should develop a specific method of interpreting sources, try out speculative extrapolations and, at every step along the way, be on the lookout for any perceptible indication of a paradigm shift between what is regarded as acceptable or unacceptable in public debate. This certainly supports a nuanced, even tentative, approach that interrogates the silences of history and interprets weak, tenuous and contradictory signs. However, if research is limited to positivist methods which imply that all that does not find a straightforward expression in historical sources is not relevant to the reading of history, it will never be possible to account for the emergence in the nineteenth century – that is to say, it may be argued, the coming into full visibility – of theories making a case for social and economic equality between all citizens.

Notes

1 C. Hill, *Intellectual Origins of the English Revolution Revisited* (Oxford: Clarendon Press, 1997); C. Hill, *The World Turned Upside Down: Radical Ideas During the English Revolution* (London: Temple Smith, 1972); L. Morton, *The World of the Ranters: Religious*

Radicalism in the English Revolution (London: Lawrence & Wishart, 1970).

2 See the works of so-called 'revisionist' historians, in particular: J. C. Davis, 'Radicalism in a traditional society: the evaluation of radical thought in the English Commonwealth 1649–1660', *History of Political Thought*, 3 (1982), 193–213; C. Condren, *The Language of Politics in Seventeenth-Century England* (Basingstoke: Macmillan, 1994); and more recently the study of G. Burgess, 'Radicalism and the English Revolution', in G. Burgess and M. Festenstein (eds), *English Radicalism, 1550–1850* (Cambridge: Cambridge University Press, 2007), pp. 62–86.

3 On the issue of labelling radical sects, also see the Introduction in this volume.

4 See also, for example, the royalist Thomas Aston: 'The old seditious argument will be obvious to them, that we are all the sons of Adam, born free; some of them say the gospel hath made them free ... They will plead Scripture for it, that we should live by the sweat of our brows', *A Remonstrance, against Presbitery, exhibited by divers of the nobilitie, gentrie, ministers and inhabitants of the county palatine of Chester, together with a short survey of the Presbyterian discipline* (London, 1641). A few years later, Lilburne wrote: 'Adam and Eve are the earthly original foundation as begetters and bringers forth of all and every particular individual man and woman ... who are therefore all equal and alike in power dignity and only exercise power by mutual agreement for the good and benefit of each other', *The Free-mans freedom vindicated. Or A true relation of the cause and manner of Lievt. Col. Iohn Lilburns present imprisonment in Newgate* (London, 1646).

5 G. Winstanley, *The True Levellers Standard Advanced*, in *The Works of Gerrard Winstanley. With an Appendix of Documents Relating to the Digger Movement*, ed. George H. Sabine (hereafter *Works*) (Ithaca, N.Y.: Cornell University Press, 1941), pp. 77–8.

6 See, for example, *Theophrastus Redivivus*, eds G. Canziani and G.Paganini (Firenze: La Nuova Italia, 1981–2). This treatise, apparently written by a French author in 1659, brings together elements of a long-standing philosophical tradition.

7 A thorough study of the profane sources of Winstanley is still needed.

8 Winstanley, *The Saints Paradice*, in *Works*, p. 199.

9 *A Watch-Word to the city of London, and the Armie* (London, 1649), fol. A3.

10 On Winstanley and Hobbes, see C. Hill, 'Winstanley and freedom', in R. Richardson and G. Ridden (eds), *Freedom and the English Revolution* (Manchester: Manchester University Press, 1986), pp. 151–68.

11 L. Clarkson, *Lost Sheep Found,* in *A Collection of Ranter Writings from the Seventeenth Century,* ed. Nigel Smith (London: Junction Books, 1983), pp. 181–2.

12 A. Coppe, *A Fiery Flying Roll,* in Smith, *A Collection of Ranter Writings,* p. 86.

13 *A Fiery Flying Roll,* pp. 87–8.

14 *A Fiery Flying Roll,* p. 88.

15 A. Coppe, *A Second Fiery Flying Roule* [sic], in Smith, *A Collection of Ranter Writings,* p. 100.

16 *A Second Fiery Flying Roule,* p. 100.

17 *A Second Fiery Flying Roule,* p. 101.

18 *A Fiery Flying Roll,* p. 88–9.

19 *A Fiery Flying Roll,* p. 89.

20 On the relationships between the Diggers and the Anabaptists and on the spiritual inspiration of the writings and the actions of the Diggers, see A. Hessayon's seminal article 'Early modern communism: The Diggers and community of goods', *Journal for the Study of Radicalism,* 3:2 (2009), 1–50.

21 C. Hill, 'From Lollards to Levellers', in J. M. Bak and G. Benecke (eds), *Religion and Rural Revolt: Papers Presented to the Fourth Interdisciplinary Workshop on Peasant Studies* (Dover, N.H.: Manchester University Press, 1982), p. 94.

22 See the sermon of John Ball in J. Froissart, *Chronicles* (Harmondsworth: Penguin, 1968), p. 212.

23 T. Fuller, *The Church History of Britain: From the Birth of Jesus Christ Until the Year M.DC.XLVIII* (Oxford: Oxford University Press, 1845), vol. IV, p. 451.

24 Thomas More, *Utopia,* ed. George M. Logans and Robert M. Adams (Cambridge: Cambridge University Press, 2002), p. 37.

25 The chronicle of England written by Edmund Howes to complement Stow's *Annales* mentions riotous persons who 'bent al their strength to level and lay open enclosures, without exercising any manner of theft or violence upon any man's person, goods or chattels'. E. Howes, *Annales, Or, A Generall Chronicle of England. Begun by Iohn Stow: Continued and Augmented with matters Forraigne and Domestique, Ancient and Modern, vnto the end of this present yeere, 1631* (London, 1631), p. 890. Apparently, these first Levellers and Diggers did not call for the collectivisation of private land but, as E. C. Pettet points out, it is not known whether some of them did not voice the same opinion as the carpenter Bartholomew Stere who, in 1596 during the Oxfordshire disturbances, said: 'His outward pretence was to overthrow enclosures, and to help the poor commonalty that were to famish for want of corn; but intended to kill the gentlemen of that country and to take

the spoil of them, affirming that the Commons long since in Spain did rise and kill all the gentlemen of Spain, and since that time have lived merrily there ?' E. C. Pettet, 'Coriolanus and the Midlands insurrection of 1607', in C. M. S. Alexander, S. Wells, T. Hawkes and P. Holland (eds), *The Cambridge Shakespeare Library. Vol I: Shakespeare's Times, Texts, and Stages* (Cambridge: Cambridge University Press, 2003), p. 324.

26 *To the right honourable, the Commons of England in parliament assembled. The humble petition of divers well-affected persons inhabiting the City of London, Westminster, the Borough of Southwark, Hamlets and places adjacent*, in *The English Levellers*, ed. Andrew Sharp (Cambridge: Cambridge University Press, 2007), p. 137.

27 On Levellers and property, see, for example, L. Brace, *The Idea of Property in Seventeenth-Century England: Tithes and the Individual* (Manchester: Manchester University Press, 1998), and C. Pierson, *Just Property: A History in the Latin West* (Oxford: Oxford University Press, 2013) vol. 1, p. 196 ff.

28 Brace, *The Idea of Property*, p. 49.

29 T. Overton, *An arrow against all tyrants and tyranny*, in Sharp, *The English Levellers*, p. 55.

30 I. Hampsher-Monk, 'The political theory of the Levellers: Putney, property and Professor Macpherson', *Political Studies*, 24 (1976), 397–422.

31 I. Hampsher-Monk, 'The political theory of the Levellers', p. 407. Hampsher-Monk also quotes an illuminating passage by E. Lewis: 'The individual owner could have no right to dispose of his property … There would be no essential difference between usufruct and property, and therefore no obstacle to a concept of multiple ownership. Ownership could not absorb the object; it was simply a right in regard to the object; and such rights might be numerous and widely distributed', *Medieval Political Ideas* (London: Routledge & Paul, 1954), p. 89.

32 *A manifestation from Lieutenant-Colonel John Lilburne, Mr William Walwyn, Mr Thomas Prince, and Mr Richard Overton … commonly (though unjustly) styled Levellers* (London, 1649), in Sharp, *The English Levellers*, p. 161.

33 'The Putney debates: the debate on the franchise', in *Divine Right and Democracy: An Anthology of Political Writing in Stuart England*, ed. David Wootton (Harmondsworth: Penguin, 1987), p. 311. On Ireton's position on property during the Putney debates, see I. Gentles, *The English Revolution and the Wars of the Three Kingdoms, 1638–1652* (Harlow: Pearson Education, 2007), p. 316.

34 *Tyranipocrit, discovered with his wiles, wherewith he vanquisheth. VVritten and printed, to animate better artists to pursue that monster*

(Rotterdam, 1649). On the scholarly debate regarding the authorship of *Tyranipocrit*, see *The Writings of William Walwyn*, ed. Jack R. McMichael and Barbara Taft (Athens, G.A.; London: University of Georgia Press, 1989), pp. 532–5.

35 John Price *et al.*, *Walwins wiles: or The manifestators manifested* (London, 1649), pp. 16–17.

36 *Light Shining in Buckinghamshire*, in Winstanley, *Works*, p. 611. The authors of this pamphlet were happy with being identified as Levellers: 'Mark this, poor people, what the Levellers would do for you.' See Hill, *World Turned Upside Down*, p. 94, and Hill's introduction to *Winstanley: 'The Law of Freedom' and other Writings*, ed. Christopher Hill (Cambridge: Cambridge University Press, 1983), p. 30.

37 *The Ranters Last Sermon. With the manner of their meetings, ceremonies, and actions; also their damnable, blasphemous and diabolicall tenents; delivered in an exercise neer Pissing-conduit* (London, 1654), p. 4. See Morton, *The World of the Ranters*, p. 90.

38 *Copp's return in the wayes of truth*, in Smith, *A Collection of Ranter Writings*, p. 155.

39 Edward Hyde, *A Wonder and yet no Wonder: a Great Red Dragon in Heaven* (London, 1651), p. 42.

40 A. Cole, 'The Quakers and the English Revolution', *Past & Present*, 10 (1956), 43.

41 See, for example, Francis Higginson: 'They hold all things ought to be common, and teach the Doctrine of Levelling privately to their Disciples ... Several of them have affirmed that there ought to be no distinction of Estates but an universal parity', *A Brief relation of the Irreligion of the Northern Quakers* (London, 1653), p. 20; Thomas Comber: 'That several Levellers settled into Quakers, incline to take them for *Winstanleys* Disciples, and a branch of the Levellers. And what this man writes of "*levelling men's estates, of taking in of Commons, that none should have more ground than he was able to Till and Husband by his own labour*" [*Fire in the Bush*, p. 64]. Proving unpracticable by reason of so many tough old laws which had fixed Propriety; yet it is pursued by the Quakers as near as they well can, in Thou'ing every one, in denying Titles, Civil Respects, and terms of Destinction among men, and at the first they were for Community, "*thinking it unreasonable that one man should have so much and another so little; and some of them were not free to be tenants to other men*" [*A Faithful Discovery of Mistical Antichrist &*, p. 39]. And George Fox said "*one man ought not to be above another*" [Informat. At *Lancaster Octob. 5. 1652*]', *Christianity no Enthusiasm: or, The Several Kinds of Inspirations and Revelations Pretended to by the Quakers, Tried and found Destructive to Holy Scripture and True Religion* (London, 1678), pp. 6–7.

42 Cole, 'The Quakers and the English Revolution', p. 43. On the Quakers'
denial of seeking the levelling of conditions and fortunes, see A. Davies,
'Levelling Quakers?', in A. Davies, *The Quakers in English Society,
1655–1725* (Oxford: Clarendon Press, 2000), pp. 64–74. The author,
who adopts a revisionist approach, acknowledges that 'identifying the
extent to which principles of equality and social justice underpinned
Quaker thoughts is no easy matter', p. 65.

2

~

Thomas Paine's democratic linguistic radicalism: a political philosophy of language?

Carine Lounissi

Thomas Paine's thought and writings have often been described as 'radical' with regard to various forms of 'radicalism'. They have been viewed as pertaining in turn or simultaneously to 'radical Lockeanism',[1] to a form of eighteenth-century 'new' British 'radicalism',[2] to a form of 'American radicalism' at the origin of the Declaration of Independence[3] and of a 'community of radical democrats'[4] in the United States of the 1790s, to 'transatlantic radicalism'[5] and to 'radical Enlightenment'.[6] This shows that characterising Paine's radicalism is not easy. It may be because his ideas can be seen as a blend of several patterns of thought which are often understood as independent or even as incompatible and also because his positions evolved from his first American writings in 1775 to his last ones in 1807, which sometimes led him to make statements that might be interpreted as contradictory. As Isaac Kramnick said about Paine, 'few liberals were so fervently committed to democracy and egalitarianism'.[7] Scholars who have recently worked on Paine's political thought have tended to emphasise that it combines 'liberalism' and either 'old' or 'new' forms of 'republicanism'.[8] Paine's radicalism may, in reality, be considered both as inherently 'republican' and 'democratic'[9] insofar as it is anti-monarchical and as it promotes a representative regime and universal suffrage[10] based on a fair political contract. His pamphlets can be viewed as democratic not only because they advocated democratic representative institutions, but also inasmuch as their pedagogic – some said 'demagogic' – form was meant to make his ideas available to the common man. At the same time Paine's works challenged established monarchical institutions and established ways of writing, as he himself stated explicitly in the preface to the second part of *Rights of Man*.[11]

It is well known that this writing triggered off a deluge of attacks in the 1790s on the part of conservative writers against his popular style which he had by then perfected since his first major writing, *Common Sense*. As early as 1776 one of the hallmarks of Paine's radicalism was his appeal to 'common sense', understood both as the faculty distinguished from reason and as the sense of the people as a nation. Not only did Paine defend representative government and write in an uncompromising way about hereditary regimes in pamphlets and articles that could be read by uneducated people, but he also wished to deconstruct the language – not to be understood here in a specific Derridian sense – used by those who held power in monarchical regimes by going back to the roots of words. He thus invented what may be considered as a radical linguistics. Language and politics were therefore closely related from the outset in Paine's works. The argument in this chapter is that his linguistic approach to political subjects, which implied writing for a popular readership and debunking the political language of monarchies, was based on a political approach to language or on a theoretical stand on the role of language in politics that he nonetheless never fully developed as such. Paine's political linguistics has not been given the attention it deserves, although it is essential to help define his radicalism. What has been looked into in critical studies is rather the way he applied this position on language through images or syntax.[12] This chapter explores the theoretical underpinnings of his style and focuses on his treatment of the political vocabulary as made up of what Olivia Smith has called 'identifiable object[s] which had been shaped by the historical process' or 'words' with 'disguised historical identities'.[13]

Paine's common sense language and philosophy

The pamphlet that inaugurated Paine's career as a political thinker, *Common Sense*, set the tone of his democratic language. It was based on the rhetoric of common sense, which proved to be a strategy of paradoxical persuasion. In the preface to the pamphlet, Paine warned the reader that 'the sentiments contained in the following pages are not yet sufficiently fashionable to procure them general favor',[14] these 'sentiments' being those in favour of the independence of the American colonies. Paine's first opponents, such as Charles Inglis and William Smith, quite expectedly made it clear that he expressed 'paradoxes'[15] and that the title of the pamphlet was a 'catachresis'[16] since its content went against what they viewed as the state of public opinion in the colonies. This negative interpretation may provide a critical approach to Paine's famous pamphlet if one understands the notion of 'paradox' in a less polemical context. Paine's text may be considered as a 'paradoxical pre-vision' in Bourdieu's words[17] or as a provocation insofar as he wished to give birth to a new sense of collective belonging and offer Americans a collective project after having convinced them that the current one, their participation in the structure of the British Empire through a political link with a hereditary regime, was archaic, illegitimate and ran against their most fundamental interests as a distinct people. Paine resorted to common sense ideas to promote the need for the colonies to declare their independence, and through this strategy of persuasion, which is the most well known aspect of the pamphlet,[18] he intended to create a national common sense. The two meanings of common sense thus appeared to be closely interrelated.

So Paine turned common sense into a weapon of massive persuasion in favour of the 'patriots'. He had understood that 'political subversion presupposes cognitive subversion' to quote Bourdieu again,[19] since he aimed at establishing a 'new method of thinking'.[20] Yet it went beyond merely taking sides, beyond a mere wish for his readers to agree with him and endorse a specific viewpoint. He rather wanted to make them think freely or, in Kantian terms, he wished them to 'have the courage to use their own understanding'. Paine's pedagogic intent was to teach people how to think and such a cognitive process meant listening to the voice of nature. To use Kant's phrase again, this time in the introduction to his own class of philosophy ten years before Paine's pamphlet was published, Paine's method may be considered as a kind of zetetic teaching[21] which did not take any theory for granted and which, in his own case, was based on common sense as a faculty and on common sense sayings. At the beginning of the third section of *Common Sense*, he asked his reader to 'divest himself of prejudice and prepossession and suffer his reason and his feelings to determine for themselves'. Paine's addressee was therefore the common man who is open-minded and who is neither 'interested', 'weak', 'prejudiced' nor too biased in favour of 'the European world'.[22]

In *Rights of Man*, Paine did not use 'common sense' as such an explicit motif. The phrase itself does not appear in either part. In the preface to the second part, he reasserted his belief in the universality of the capacity of people to use their understanding or their 'reason', or in his words to 'think for themselves', and he reminded his reader of the literal definition of prejudice which was the opposite of a genuine thinking process. In the same volume, he praised action thanks to 'the rational faculties' of men and 'general consent'. He appealed to 'reason' in that case, rather than to the faculty of 'common sense': 'reason and common interest' were the driving forces of political change.[23] Yet whether Paine clearly meant different faculties or seats of reflection when he used those terms is not established since he neither defined them precisely nor made it clear which theories on the subject he endorsed. In spite of this uncertainty, the use of their thinking faculty by people is what generates genuine revolutions and ensures their viability.

Such a process should happen on an individual basis but also collectively. Yet Paine never offered an in-depth reflection on this issue, though some of his statements may help to make up for this missing development. In *The Necessity of Taxation*, a pamphlet he published in the United States in 1782, he remarked: 'The furnishing ourselves with right ideas, and the accustoming ourselves to right habits of thinking, have a powerful effect in strengthening and cementing the mind of the country and freeing it from the danger of partial or mistaken notions.'[24] He defined a form of civic virtue that would use common sense, to be understood here as public opinion, as its main instrument. As he wrote in 1791 in the letter he sent to the authors of *Le Républicain*, the short-lived journal he published in France with Condorcet after the Varennes episode, a political revolution cannot be efficient 'before the sense of a nation is sufficiently enlightened, and before men have entered into a free communication with each other of their natural thoughts'.[25] He did not specify how this was supposed to take place, though. This certainly implied the use of written forms of 'communication', including newspapers and pamphlets, as well as oral communication, such as took place in clubs and coffee houses. Language as the medium of debate and thought is therefore essential in the political process of deliberation and participation.

Paine made the case for a forum or a 'public sphere', which should be institutionalised as an essential element of the community or of society. As Habermas underlined, appeals to the 'sense of the people' had become common in Great Britain from the beginning of the eighteenth century.[26] Yet this parallel between Paine's idea and Habermas' should be handled with caution, especially as the latter's concept concerns 'civil' but also 'bourgeois' society which, if understood in terms of social class, could not apply to Paine's vision as he wished to extend that sphere to every individual, including those in the lowest ranks of society.[27]

'Common sense' turns out to be a many-sided notion in Paine's radical rhetoric and theory. It can be both an individual faculty and the result of collective thinking or the deliberative process. It is the main component of revolutionary action, whereas thinkers like Burke, in contrast, invoked this idea in opposition to the French Revolution.[28] Therefore, common sense serves as an instrument of 'vigilance'[29] to help the governed watch their governors and possibly overthrow them if they betray the trust vested in them. Yet common sense can only lead men to adopt a democratic or representative government as the latter is based on what Paine believed to be an irresistible truth which is the equality of men's natural rights. It was 'self-evident', as the Declaration of Independence stated and as Paine confirmed in an article he published in 1778, because it did not need to be demonstrated and could be understood and sensed by everyone,[30] an idea premised on the universality of human nature whereby each individual naturally recognises the other as a fellow human being.

Whereas democracy was the most natural regime that would be and that might have been set up after the state of nature as Paine wished to show in *Common Sense*, monarchy was the product of a contract to which the people or the governed-to-be could not have committed if the real terms of it had not been hidden from them. As Paine wrote in his third 'Forester's Letter' in April 1776: 'No nation of people, in their true senses, when seriously reflecting on the rank God hath given them, and the reasoning faculties he hath blessed them with, would ever, in their own consent, give any *one man* a negative power over the whole',[31] an idea reminiscent of *Cato's Letters*.[32] Monarchy, which he equated with tyranny, was intrinsically flawed and inconsistent with common sense, which was itself closely connected with the idea of equal rights. In this regard, monarchy and aristocracy meant utmost political nonsense. Paine never stopped denouncing the illegitimacy of hereditary institutions which infantilised both the governed and their governors.

Paine's political age of reason and the criticism of monarchy

According to Paine, rejecting monarchy meant turning one's back on political childhood and childish institutions to enter what he viewed as adulthood or the political age of reason, which is a republican one since he believed that only representative democracy was founded on a rational way of thinking and on principles which were universally true. To a certain extent, it may be argued that Paine turned Kant's Enlightenment programme, coming out of nonage, into a political platform for progress, and in this regard Paine's project may be considered as pertaining to a form of 'radical Enlightenment'.

Establishing the illegitimate character of hereditary forms of government was part and parcel of Paine's strategy. He attacked the system as such, but neither merely existing forms of it nor only individual office holders. Whenever he did so, it was to exemplify the flaws of the regime in general.[33] Although Paine's anti-monarchical positions are well known, they have not been studied as closely and as systematically as may be expected, perhaps because they make up a complex web of both arguments and satire which needs to be unravelled. His demonstration is threefold as he assailed monarchy with evidence borrowed from the Bible – with the example of the book of Samuel in *Common Sense*[34] – and history – especially with the case of William the Conqueror[35] – in addition to philosophical proof based on the theory of the equality of natural rights and of the political contract.[36] Moreover, his diatribe did not come from nowhere and it seems that he took up and mixed at least three previously existing forms of anti-monarchical bashing, which are, in chronological order, that of monarchomachs, such as George Buchanan, possibly that of some Levellers and/or Diggers, like Gerrard Winstanley, and that of the country or radical Whig tradition, in particular that of Trenchard and Gordon.[37] Paine used the codes of each of these types of criticisms and transformed them, sometimes subverting them – in particular the myth of the Norman Yoke – often making them sound more extreme. The fact that he did not distinguish between tyranny and absolute monarchy from the limited form of it goes far to explain why his critique was harsher and went further than that of his predecessors.

Paine wished to prove that the principle of the hereditary transmission of power is illegitimate in all cases since it violates the equality of generations and cannot be included in a political contract, be it an 'original' one. The natural rights argument is Paine's most fundamental premise and it is the question on which he and Burke disagreed. Time and more particularly the importance and value of the past through legacy were central in their opposition.[38] Not only was heredity in politics fundamentally contrary to natural rights in Paine's thought, but such a way of transmitting political power was absurd because it did not guarantee the competence of governors[39] and because it often put children on the throne and obliged people to 'call a boy of one and twenty the father of his people'.[40] This way of exposing the absurdity of hereditary monarchy can be traced back to monarchomachs, especially to Buchanan, whom Paine had read although the date when he did so is not known,[41]who denounced the fact that 'the people are to be committed to their power who have no power over themselves'.[42] Beyond the nonsense of having children reign over a country, Paine more generally thought of monarchy and aristocracy as childish modes of government since they infantilised both the governors and the governed. He thus applied the motif of the supposed child–parent relationship between the colonies and the mother-country he had used during the American Revolution to what linked kings to their subjects in general. Again, it was an argument used by monarchomachs who, like Buchanan, likened the absolute monarch to 'a child's puppet'.[43]

The transmission of power through heredity therefore deprived individuals of their humanity and of their autonomy as thinking individuals. Aristocrats are dehumanised and objectified by the system. The idea of dehumanisation was present in eighteenth-century political literature against absolute monarchs, who were accused of transforming their subjects into cattle. Paine extended this charge to all types of monarchies which amounted to what he called the same 'animal-system'.[44] The beastly nature of monarchy was also conveyed in his writings through various images such as the comparison between George III and 'an ass',[45] a caricature often used to ridicule the King.[46] In addition, the bestial feature of monarchy was revealed by the menagerie of the Tower of London,[47] which Paine viewed as the zoomorphic sign of the genuine character of this regime.

The crux of the problem was the confusion between the physiological and the political aspects of monarchy which seemed dangerous and unnatural to Paine. Only in a representative democracy was government 'never young, never old ... subject neither to nonage, nor dotage ... never in the cradle, nor on crutches',[48] an idea which reversed the king's two bodies theory as expressed by medieval lawyers and later studied by Kantorowicz. Paine intended to invalidate the theory of the king's two bodies and establish that it was a fiction. This led him to desacralise both the king's real body and his mystical body. Paine's iconoclasm symbolically killed the king by showing his morbid and monstrous character. As Paine exclaimed in *Common Sense*, 'how impious is the title of *sacred majesty* applied to a worm, who in the midst of his splendor is crumbling into dust'.[49] Such provocative desacralisation is clearly reminiscent of the style of *Cato's Letters* in which Trenchard and Gordon write that royal pageantry consists in 'adorn[ing] an old skull with pearl and diamonds, and ... enrich[ing] a venerable rotten tooth with gold'.[50] Similarly, physical decay is to Paine the sign of the moral foulness of the regime. Paine thought that the whole constitutional system in Britain was 'rotten'.[51]

Paine also made use of history to support his conclusions. He notably turned William the Conqueror into the archetypal usurper, manipulating the myth of the Norman Yoke, in particular by refusing to consider Saxon times as the golden age of political history.[52] He never referred to it explicitly, although he hinted at it in *Rights of Man*.[53] He thus suppressed the background against which the Norman usurpation was supposed to have taken place as if 1066 was the beginning of all political history in England. Paine's revolution did not consist in going back to a specific moment in man's history, but in restoring what he defined as the equality of fundamental rights among men.

Links between Paine's thought and that of the Levellers and/or Diggers were made during the Price–Burke–Paine controversy, as Paine was often charged, for polemical purposes, with being a 'leveller'.[54] Recent scholarship has tentatively and insufficiently explored this possible legacy in a more objective way. David Wootton, for example, has argued that Paine's argument in *Common Sense* is reminiscent of John Lilburne's ideas.[55] Yet if such an influence can be traced, which is not sure, Paine should rather be viewed as being closer to Gerrard Winstanley, who presented the Conquest as the symbol of all usurpations and who used it as 'a polemical and rhetorical strategy' and 'not ... [as] a theory',[56] as Glenn Burgess argues. Like Paine, he thought that men should enjoy again the rights that they had been given by God through the Creation,[57] but Paine made it the starting point of a political revolution which was different from that envisioned by Winstanley, especially as he made a case for a return to the primitive communism he assumed humanity had experienced in ancient times.[58]

Still, even if their overall approaches to politics differed, in *The Law of Freedom in a Platform*, the Digger referred to 'kings alias conquerors',[59] a conception that was shared by Paine who developed a kind of monarchology that described the creation of monarchy as a standardised phenomenon. The process that led to the set-up of monarchy was always the same: 'Bands of brigands unite to subvert a country, place it under tribute, seize its lands, enslave its inhabitants. The expedition completed, the chieftain of the robbers adopts the title of monarch or king.'[60] This primal scene dramatised the anti-contract that was imposed on the people and that was at the root of monarchy. It can have been set up only through violence first and then by 'turning might into right' – as Rousseau wrote in the *Social Contract* – through the invention of a mythology that relied on what Paul Ricoeur called a 'falsification of language'.[61] The idea that monarchical regimes created myths and fictions in order to deceive the governed and make them accept the legitimacy of their origin underpins Paine's anti-monarchical edifice. He endeavoured to show that this regime was an absurdity in the literal acceptation of the word, that is, it neither made any sense nor produced any sensible discourse because it was based on the usurpation of *logos*, on the confiscation of reason and reasonable ways of expressing ideas and of dealing with politics and government.

Paine's radical linguistics and semiotics: from *mythos* to *logos*?

Paine's nominalist distrust of the usual political vocabulary of his time appeared as early as *Common Sense* in which he 'deconstructed' the British constitution, or rather the discourse of constitutionalists on it. He then said it was 'ambiguous' and 'applied to the description of something which cannot exist'. He even concluded that it was 'difficult to find a proper name for the government of England'. At the end of the pamphlet, he forced the colonists to face what he viewed as their own contradiction since they defended themselves against British troops while at the same time clinging to the 'name of subjects'. Their hesitation led to what he depicted as an absurd situation in which they had 'legislation without law' and 'a constitution without a name',[62] the latter phrase probably meaning an independent political system for the American colonies.

So matching signifiers and signified could help to make out the right course to take in the American Revolution. In his subsequent writings, he enlarged on this initial political use of language and he gradually focused on the word 'monarchy' itself. At the time of the French Revolution, he began to claim that the sign of the sinful origin of monarchy was visible in the term itself, or rather that the term was the sign or the symptom of it: 'The very word *monarchy* signifies, in its primary meaning, the despotic rule of one individual, though that individual be a madman, a tyrant or a hypocrite.'[63] Steven Blakemore considers this etymology as 'revisionist'.[64] It can be viewed as such in particular considering the way eighteenth-century dictionaries defined the word 'tyrant' as first encompassing all kings and then being restricted to despotic ones only.[65] The same explanation had also been provided by George Buchanan.[66] It seems that Paine reversed it to suggest that it was the word 'monarchy' which was originally a byword for 'tyranny' before it came to refer to a supposedly non-despotic ruler.

This paleography was only one feature of Paine's 'linguistic regicide'.[67] In the first part of *Rights of Man*, he made it clear that the 'Crown' was not a metonymy, as one of his opponents objected,[68] but a 'metaphor'.[69] Some of those who answered *Rights of Man* felt the need to remind Paine of the definition of the latter word as it appeared in Johnson's *Dictionary*[70] to demonstrate that Paine had made a mistake. Another author of an anti-Paine pamphlet resorted to a more common way of dismissing him, as an ignorant amateur who had 'probably picked up' this 'hard word' 'by chance'.[71] However, Paine's argument makes sense if one considers that a metaphor is a transfer of words through which 'sword' was substituted for 'sceptre', 'prerogatives' became 'assumptions', and 'robber' replaced 'monarch'.[72]

Therefore 'monarchy' and its vocabulary were palimpsests and Paine tried to uncover the earlier language that had been erased by them. In this regard, Paine's analysis of the word 'monarchy' was twofold: the superimposition of terms testified to the illegitimate origin of kings and the term itself was further evidence that this regime violated the rights and interests of the people. A third type of criticism concerned the function of monarchs, as Paine emphasised that 'when we speak of the crown now, it means nothing; it signifies neither a judge nor a general'.[73] The powers that the king used to have had been eroded and the signified of 'monarchy' had been gradually emptied out. Even the word 'executive' had no meaning any more since monarchs had lost their original judiciary function and had become useless as it was handed over to magistrates.[74] The signifiers designating the head of state in England, 'monarchy' and 'executive', were meaningless and reduced to 'merely a name in which acts of governments are done'.[75]

Paine argued that monarchy originated in conquest and he held that 'it is the nature of conquest to turn everything upside down',[76] including language, which was turned inside out. Such a reversal could also be perceived in words which referred to the aristocracy: 'nobility' could come from the modified pronunciation of 'no-ability', and 'robbery' might have evolved into 'foppery'.[77] Gentility thus consisted in giving 'a gentler name'[78] to illegitimate actions. In *The Decline and Fall of the English System of Finance*, Paine hammered in the inherent connection between aristocracy and robbery: 'These sort of folks change their names so often that it is as difficult to know them as it is to know a thief.'[79] More generally, as Paine wrote in *Rights of Man*, 'titles are but nick-names'. Aristocratic names are 'nicked': they are disfigured and disguised. They are at best 'equivocal' and at worst 'senseless'.[80]

In his writings Paine set about 'deconstructing' some of the King's speeches. In the appendix to *Common Sense*, which was added to the second edition of the pamphlet, he purported to 'execut[e]' the King's speech of 26 October 1775 'public[ly]'.[81] He called the speech an 'audacious libel against the truth, the common good and the existence of mankind', which was an emphatic way of turning monarchical censorship back on the King through moral and political censure. According to Paine, this speech was explicit enough and did not even need further explanation as 'brutality and tyranny appear on the face of it'. Monarchy was barbarism in the political and linguistic acceptations of the word. It displayed its scarlet letter to the world. In the fifth issue of *American Crisis*, Paine then compared the King's speech of 1777 to 'a soliloquy on ill luck',[82] thus undermining its credibility by turning it into a fictional kind of text. In *American Crisis X* he deciphered the King's speech of 1781 to unveil 'the cant of snivelling hypocrisy'.[83] A few years later, in his *Letter Addressed to the Addressers*, he reproduced extracts from Lord Stormont's and Baron (not George) Grenville's speeches with his own sarcastic comments inserted in brackets.[84] He then explicitly justified his method of speech analysis to dissect what he called their 'political cant'[85] by using the topic of revelation and secrecy: language was a 'cover' to 'hide' their ignominy and 'conceal the craft' they used to deceive the people, who should nonetheless be able to 'see through them'.

With reference to more recent terms of literary criticism one could say that Paine brought to light the subtext of such speeches. He viewed the words invented and delivered by hereditary governments as equivalents of 'Bastille[s]' which needed to be stormed.[86] The will to put monarchical language to the test of reason went as far back at least to Algernon Sidney, who had blamed those who 'allege the name of king, as if there was a charm in the word' and who remarked that it was 'usual with impostors to obtrude their deceits upon men by putting false names upon things, by which they may perplex men's minds'.[87] Paine applied such an approach to the words used by what he viewed as illegitimate governments.

Conversely, Paine's opponents, whether they were pro-Burkean or not, accused Paine of changing the meaning of words in an arbitrary way, one of them even comparing Paine to William the Conqueror who had imposed French in England.[88] They more generally reproached Paine and 'radicals' with using 'philosophical cant'.[89] Therefore, it may be said that they reversed Paine's radical linguistics. According to Charles Harrington Elliot, '"rights of man" … on a nearer approach … will change to a bloody scrawl, "*disappointment, – disaffection, – clubs, – conspiracy, – rebellion*"'. As a result, Paine's title, *Rights of Man*, was 'a most impudent *misnomer*',[90] quite a similar criticism to that levelled at Paine in 1776 by American 'loyalist' writers.

Many of those who took part in the great controversy of the 1790s attempted to dismiss Paine as an uneducated, unlettered and unread man, saying that 'he writes in defiance of grammar, as if syntax were an aristocratical [*sic*] invention'.[91] Some of them nonetheless conceded that Paine's plays on words were clever, such as the 'no-ability' pun[92] and the comparison of the crown to a 'meta-phor'.[93] The validity of Paine's linguistic or, more generally, semiological analysis was often questioned at the time. John St. John, for example, said that it proved Paine's incompetence as he thought it came 'in the place of arguments'.[94] He admitted that he failed to understand the relevance of the deictic phrase 'what is called', which is repeated more than sixty times in *Rights of Man*.[95] John St. John concluded that it evidenced Paine's deficient reasoning: 'His own inability to tell you *what they are* ... makes him content himself with *what they are called*.'[96]

Although this anti-Painite writer provided a polemical explanation for Paine's way of challenging the rules of political language, the questions he asked are not irrelevant and may be rephrased, in particular if one considers the fictional etymologies Paine invented for 'noblity' or 'monarchy'. Are they to be viewed as mere witticisms and therefore as expressions of a literary talent for satire, or can they be understood as cogent arguments in Paine's system of thought? In other words, should one distinguish between, on the one hand, what may be seen as his rational or philosophical demonstrations based on natural rights and, on the other, his more entertaining way of debunking monarchs and aristocrats providing pleasant but questionable illustrations of his more serious theory? There seem to be three kinds of arguments in Paine's system of thought: first, those based on the theory of natural rights, second the historical or pseudo-historical assumptions he made to account for the establishment of monarchical regimes – which in his works do not stem from a very rigorous study of history – and third his literary inventions in support of his indictment of hereditary regimes. It may be contended that the latter aspect and also the hypothetical chronologies explaining the origin of monarchy in reality tend to create another mythology, a radical or republican one, to replace that which Paine wished to denounce. Although he aimed at destroying what he thought were obstacles to a free use of *logos*, it may be argued that at the same time he fell back into *mythos*. Language turns out to be a *pharmakon*, that is to say both a remedy and a poison. It seems that he was not aware of this intrinsic ambivalence, maybe because he never fully theorised the role of language in his own way of dealing with politics.

Conclusion

Paine's democratic or pedagogic style appears as an essential part of his political theory. It is not a mere medium. Paine thought that monarchy was fictitious in two ways: it had invented fictions, or what he called 'superstitious tale[s]',[97] to account for its birth, and the term 'monarchy' itself was a sort of ghost word or a screen word that concealed another one – tyranny. So monarchy pertained to the realm of imagination and fantasy, and it devised means to prevent its subjects from investigating topics associated with it. It was an irrational regime based on the absurd principle of the hereditary transmission of power that did not guarantee competence and did not encourage the governed to use their reason and/or their common sense. Paine denounced it as an obscurantist regime which feared e/Enlightenment, and he relied on existing registers of satire, images and political arguments to work out his own critical approach to monarchy, which he used in a more 'radical' way as he rejected all forms of monarchy.

Yet some of the etymological instances quoted here were themselves fictional and thus raise the question of the soundness of Paine's arguments. Although his critics often ascribed them to wit or to ignorance, it may be argued that such etymologies do not undermine the overall validity of his anti-monarchical assault. Paine's radicalism was inherently based on *logos*, on reason and language. This conception of language informs his first major work, *Common Sense*, and his awareness of the role played by language, as very few writings by Paine before 1776 are known or extant, may explain why his career as a political writer really started in 1776. His relation to language, though he never formalised it in a specific piece of writing, can therefore be viewed as the keystone of his work, even if his failure to investigate this field further prevented him from potentially understanding or questioning the status of his own republican mythology.

Beyond his will to assert and illustrate his distrust of the language of monarchy, what may be considered as central in his writings is how he tried to teach everyone and particularly the lower class how to be vigilant, nay suspicious, of the various forms of usurpation devised by their governments, how to beware the language of governors beyond what he himself said of it. He viewed it as 'the right of every man' as he said in his *Letter Addressed to the Addressers*.[98]

However, it is somehow paradoxical that he did not work out a real theory of education, although he insisted on the importance of instruction, that of the poor in particular, in the second part of *Rights of Man*.[99]

Notes

1 R. J. Ellis, 'Radical Lockeanism in American political culture', *The Western Political Quarterly*, 45:4 (1992), 828–31.

2 H. T. Dickinson, *Liberty and Property: Political Ideology in Eighteenth-Century Britain* (Oxford: Blackwell, 1985), p. 240.

3 S. Lynd, *Intellectual Origins of American Radicalism* (Cambridge; New York, N.Y.: Cambridge University Press, new edn, 2009).

4 S. Cotlar, *Tom Paine's America: The Rise and Fall of Transatlantic Radicalism in the Early American Republic* (Charlottesville, V.A.: University of Virginia Press, 2011), p. 5.

5 M. Durey, *Transatlantic Radicals and the Early American Republic* (Lawrence, K.S.: University Press of Kansas, 1997), pp. 8, 225–8.

6 J. Israel, *A Revolution of the Mind: Radical Enlightenment and the Intellectual Origins of Modern Democracy* (Princeton, N.J.: Princeton University Press, 2010), p. 39.

7 I. Kramnick, *Republicanism and Bourgeois Radicalism: Political Ideology in Late Eighteenth-Century England and America* (Ithaca, N.Y.: Cornell University Press, 1990), p. 160.

8 J. Keane, *Tom Paine: A Political Life* (London: Bloomsbury, 1995), p. xx; G. Claeys, *Thomas Paine: Social and Political Thought* (Boston, M.A.: Unwin Hyman, 1989), p. 5; J. Fruchtman, *Thomas Paine: Apostle of Freedom* (New York, N.Y.: Four Walls Eight Windows, 1994), pp. 6–8; P. Pettit, *Republicanism: A Theory of Freedom and Government* (Oxford: Oxford University Press, 1997), p. 56; T. Paine, *Property, Welfare and Freedom in the Thought of Thomas Paine, A Critical Edition*, ed. Karen M. Ford (Lewiston, N.Y.: Edwin Mellen Press, 2001), p. 32.

9 Gregory Claeys describes Paine's position as 'democratic republicanism': G. Claeys, *The French Revolution Debate in Britain: The Origins of Modern Politics* (Basingstoke: Palgrave Macmillan, 2007), p. 38.

10 Paine defended quasi-universal suffrage as early as 1778 in 'A Serious Address to the People of Pennsylvania', *The Complete Writings of Thomas Paine*, ed. Philip S. Foner (New York, N.Y.: The Citadel Press, 1945) [hereafter *Complete Writings*], vol. 2, pp. 287–8. He also opposed the limitations that the French Constitution of 1795 set up on the franchise in *Dissertation on First Principles of Government*: T. Paine, *Rights of Man, Common Sense and Other Political Writings*,

ed. Mark Philp (Oxford: Oxford University Press, 1995) [hereafter *Political Writings*], p. 397.

11 *Dissertation*, in *Political Writings*, p. 203.

12 See among others: J. Hodson, *Language and Revolution in Burke, Wollstonecraft, Paine and Godwin* (Aldershot: Ashgate, 2007); S. Blakemore, *Intertextual War, Edmund Burke and the French Revolution in the Writings of Mary Mary Wollstonecraft, Thomas Paine, and James Mackintosh* (London: Associated University Presses, 1997); O. Smith, *The Politics of Language, 1791–1819* (Oxford: Clarendon Press, 1984); J. T. Boulton, *The Language of Politics in the Age of Wilkes and Burke* (Westport, C.T.: Greenwood Press, 1975); B. Woodcock, 'Writing the revolution: aspects of Thomas Paine's prose', *Prose Studies*, 15:2 (1992), 171–86.

13 Smith, *The Politics of Language*, pp. 44–5. The approach to the theoretical dimension of Paine's relation to language advanced in this chapter differs from John Turner who argues that Paine held the 'traditional Lockean belief that language ought to be transparent' but does not substantiate this claim. J. Turner, 'Burke, Paine, and the Nature of Language', *The Yearbook of English Studies: The French Revolution in English Literature and Art*, 19 (1989), 36–53.

14 *Political Writings*, p. 3.

15 C. Inglis, *The True Interest of America* (Philadelphia, P.A., 2nd edn, 1776), p. v; W. Smith. 'To the People of Pennsylvania', *American Archives: consisting of a collection of authentick records, state papers, debates, and letters and other notices of publick affairs, the whole forming a documentary history of the origin and progress of the North American colonies; of the causes and accomplishment of the American revolution; and of the Constitution of government for the United States, to the final ratification thereof*, ed. Peter Force (Washington, D.C., 1844), vol. 5, p. 851.

16 Inglis, *The True Interest*, p. vi.

17 P. Bourdieu, *Language and Symbolic Power*, trans. G. Raymond and M. Adamson (Cambridge: Polity Press, 1991), p. 128. This point was first made in C. Lounissi, 'La Notion de philosophie politique dans l'œuvre de Thomas Paine et son rapport à la pensée européenne et américaine dans la seconde moitié du XVIIIe siècle' (PhD dissertation, Université Paris III – Sorbonne Nouvelle, 2006), published in 2012 as C. Lounissi, *La Pensée politique de Thomas Paine en contexte: théorie et pratique.* (Paris: H. Champion, 2012), p. 239. This idea was taken up by S. Rosenfeld in 'Thomas Paine's common sense and ours', *William and Mary Quarterly*, 55:4 (2008), 633–68.

18 B. Bailyn, 'The Most Uncommon Pamphlet of the American Revolution: *Common Sense*', *American Heritage*, 25:1 (1973), 36–41, 91–3.

19 Bourdieu, *Language*, p. 127.

20 *Political Writings*, p. 20.

21 Immanuel Kant, *Annonce du programme des leçons de M. E. Kant durant le semestre d'hiver (1765–1766)*, trans. M. Fichant (Paris: Vrin, 1973), pp. 68–9.

22 *Political Writings*, pp. 19, 25.

23 *Political Writings*, pp. 208, 323, 318.

24 T. Paine, *Collected Writings*, ed. Eric Foner (New York, N.Y.: Literary Classics of the United States, 1995) [hereafter *Collected Writings*], p. 310.

25 *Collected Writings*, p. 378.

26 J. Habermas, *The Structural Transformation of the Public Sphere*, trans. T. Burger (Cambridge, M.A.: Massachusetts Institute of Technology, 1991), p. 64.

27 Habermas referred to Paine in *Theory and Practice*. He commented on the latter's interpretation of natural rights in relation to revolution but not on the issue dealt with here. J. Habermas, *Theory and Practice*, trans. J. Viertel (Boston, M.A.: Beacon Press, 1973), pp. 82–120.

28 E. Burke, *Reflections on the Revolution in France*, ed. Conor Cruise O'Brien (Harmondsworth: Penguin Classics, 1986), pp. 300, 328, 360.

29 L. Marcil-Lacoste, 'A propos de la philosophie de Thomas Paine: sens commun et droits fondamentaux', *Canadian Human Rights Yearbook*, 6 (1989–90), 258.

30 *Complete Writings*, vol. 2, p. 286.

31 *Complete Writings*, vol. 2, p. 79.

32 J. Trenchard and T. Gordon, *Cato's Letters: or, Essays on Liberty, Civil and Religious, and Other Important Subjects*, ed. Ronald Hamowy (Indianapolis, I.N.: Liberty Fund, 1995), no. 60, 6 January 1722, vol. 1, p. 415.

33 The only exception is the first part of *Rights of Man*, in which Paine momentarily refrained from criticising the fact that Louis XVI was maintained on the throne: *Political Writings*, p. 157.

34 *Political Writings*, pp. 12–14.

35 See *Political Writings*, p. 127: 'Conquest and tyranny transplanted themselves with William the Conqueror from Normandy into England ... May the example of all France contribute to regenerate the freedom which a province of it destroyed!', and *Dissertation*, p. 401.

36 Claeys, *Thomas Paine*, pp. 90–6.

37 Critical sources have mainly looked for common points between Paine and Junius: W. H. Burr, *Thomas Paine: Was He Junius?* (San Fransisco, C.A.: the Freethought Publishing Co., 1890), pp. 12–13; M. D. Conway, *The Life of Thomas Paine* (London: Routledge / Thoemmes Press, 1996), vol. 1, pp. 49–50; A. Williamson. *Thomas Paine: his Life,*

Work and Time (London: Allen and Unwin, 1973), p. 45; D. Henley, 'Thomas Paine: an emerging portrait', in J. Chumbley and L. Zonneveld (eds), *Thomas Paine in Search of the Common Good. Proceedings of a Colloquium Held at the United Nations in New York on December 10, 1987* (Nottingham: Spokesman Books, 2009), p. 103. Others have looked for similarities between Paine and Wilkes: J. Lessay. *Thomas Paine: professeur de révolutions, député du Pas-de-Calais* (Paris: Perrin, 1987), p. 39; Claeys, *Thomas Paine*, p. 22; Fruchtman, *Thomas Paine*, pp. 29, 31. Keane, *Tom Paine*, p. 67. It is likely that Paine read both Junius and Wilkes, but his anti-monarchy criticism went much further than theirs.

38 Claeys, *Thomas Paine*, pp. 66, 71.
39 *Political Writings*, p. 134.
40 *Complete Writings*, vol. 2, p. 290.
41 He quoted him late in his life in 'Farewell Reprimand to James Cheetham' (1807): see A. O. Aldridge, 'Thomas Paine and the *New York Public Advertiser*', *New York Historical Society Quarterly*, 37 (1953), 376–7.
42 G. Buchanan, *The History of Scotland* (Glasgow, 1799), vol. 1, p. 226. The quote comes from the seventh edition. Several editions of this book were published during the eighteenth century, so Paine may have read it in his early years.
43 G. Buchanan, *Appendix to the History of Scotland* (London, 1721), p. 193.
44 G. Buchanan, *Appendix*, p. 232.
45 G. Buchanan, *Appendix*, p. 15.
46 V. Carretta, *George III and the Satirists from Hogarth to Byron* (Athens, G.A..; London: University of Georgia Press, 1990), p. 150.
47 *Political Writings*, pp. 128, 248.
48 *Political Writings*, p. 233.
49 *Political Writings*, p. 11.
50 Trenchard and Gordon, *Cato's Letters*, no. 35, vol. 1, p. 250.
51 *Political Writings*, p. 10.
52 C. Hill, *Puritanism and Revolution, Studies in Interpretation of the English Revolution of the Seventeenth Century* (London: Secker and Warburg, 1958), pp. 99–103. E. Foner, 'Thomas Paine's republic: radical ideology and social change', in A. Young (ed.), *Explorations in the History of American Radicalism. The American Revolution* (DeKalb, I.L.: Northern Illinois University Press, 1976), p. 198.
53 See *Political Writings*, p. 127: 'Conquest and tyranny transplanted themselves with William the Conqueror from Normandy into England … May the example of all France contribute to regenerate the freedom which a province of it destroyed!', and *Dissertation*, p. 401.

54 Gregory Claeys (ed.), *Political Writings of the 1790s* (London: Pickering, 1995) [hereafter *Political Writings of the 1790s*], vol. 5, pp. 33, 36–7, 102, 131, 138, 153–5, 183, 199, 224, 280, 282, 315–16, 326, 361, 410; vol. 6, pp. 131, 142, 391.

55 D. Wootton, 'The republican tradition: from Commonwealth to *Common Sense*', in D. Wootton, *Republicanism, Liberty and Commercial Society, 1649–1776* (Stanford, C.A.: Stanford University Press, 1994), p. 28.

56 G. Burgess, 'Common Law, Norman Yoke and political "radicalism"', in P. Lurbe (ed.), *Le Joug normand, La Conquête normande et son interprétation dans l'historiographie et la pensée anglaises (XVIIe et XVIIIe siècles)* (Caen: Presses Universitaires de Caen, 2004), p. 26. On the appropriation of the Norman Yoke myth by seventeenth-century radicals, including Levellers and Diggers, see Chapter 1 and the Introduction to this volume.

57 G. Winstanley, *The Law of Freedom in a Platform* (London, 1652), p. 26.

58 Whether Paine had read Winstanley is quite problematic since there was no reprinting of the Digger's writings in the eighteenth century.

59 Winstanley, *Law of Freedom*, p. 26.

60 'Anti-monarchal essay. For the use of new republicans', in M. D. Conway (ed.), *The Writings of Thomas Paine* (New York, N.Y.: G. P. Putnam, 1894–6), vol. 3, p. 102.

61 'La tyrannie n'est pas possible sans une falsification de la parole' ('Tyranny is impossible but for the falsification of language'): P. Ricoeur, *Histoire et vérité* (Paris: Seuil, 1967), p. 305.

62 *Political Writings*, pp. 9, 19, 45, 50.

63 *Complete Writings*, vol. 2, p. 1316.

64 Blakemore, *Intertextual War*, p. 118.

65 '[Tyrant] at first was used for the king, or supreme magistrate; but when they began to use their power without limit or regard to justice, it was appropriated to a wicked, unjust, cruel, or illegal magistrate, and in that sense is now always used': William Pardon, *A New General English Dictionary* (London, 3rd edn, 1740); James Scott, *A General Dictionary of Arts and Sciences* (London, 1765–6), vol. 2; Abraham Rees. *Cyclopoedia, or an Universal Dictionary of Arts and Sciences* (London, 1781–6), vol. 4.

66 Buchanan, *Appendix*, p. 236.

67 Blakemore, *Intertextual War*, p. 117.

68 *The Republican Refuted*, in *Political Writings of the 1790s*, vol. 5, p. 339.

69 *Political Writings*, p. 175.

70 *Political Writings of the 1790s*, vol. 5, p. 191.

71 *Political Writings of the 1790s*, vol. 6, p. 29.
72 *Political Writings*, pp. 121, 257, 220.
73 *Political Writings*, p. 282.
74 *Political Writings*, p. 282.
75 *Political Writings*, p. 252.
76 *Political Writings*, p. 141.
77 *Political Writings*, pp. 158, 401.
78 *Complete Writings*, vol. 2, p. 53.
79 *Complete Writings*, vol. 2, p. 662. Among Paine's explicit sources were Defoe and Swift.
80 *Political Writings*, p. 132.
81 *Political Writings*, p. 47.
82 *Complete Writings*, vol. 1, p. 116.
83 *Complete Writings*, vol. 1, p. 192.
84 *Political Writings*, pp. 337–9.
85 *Political Writings*, p. 340.
86 *Political Writings*, p. 132.
87 A. Sidney, *Discourses Concerning Government*, ed. Thomas G. West (Indianapolis, I.N.: Liberty Fund, 1996), pp. 508, 383.
88 *Political Writings of the 1790s*, vol. 5, p. 127.
89 *A Defence of the Constitution of England*, in *Political Writings of the 1790s*, vol. 5, p. 23.
90 *The Republican Refuted*, in *Political Writings of the 1790s*, vol. 5, p. 315.
91 Quoted by Boulton, *The Language of Politics*, p. 147. On the issue of the existence of a 'radical style' in the late eighteenth century with regard to linguistic norms and literary conventions, see Chapter 10.
92 *Political Writings of the 1790s*, vol. 5, pp. 91, 194.
93 John Quincy Adams, in Benjamin Franklin Bache, *General Advertiser*, no. 251, 28 July 1791.
94 *Political Writings of the 1790s*, vol. 5, p. 191.
95 Hodson, *Language and Revolution*, p. 145.
96 *Political Writings of the 1790s*, vol. 5, p. 191.
97 *Political Writings*, p. 16.
98 *Political Writings*, p. 357.
99 *Political Writings*, pp. 294, 297.

3

~

English radicalism in the 1650s: the Quaker search for the true knowledge

Catie Gill

When the Quaker movement emerged in the 1650s, the converts to this branch of radical Protestantism were compelled to share with others, via print as well as in person, the 'true knowledge' of their God.[1] Quakers were no admirers of schoolmen, the educated clergy, or scholastically influenced dispute. They proposed that the habits of mind of those that had been university trained could be revealed to be at odds with the simple primitivism that was proper to Christianity. Learning was not 'a wholly virtuous activity', and was problematic in the seventeenth century in a way that it is not so today.[2] Hence, Quakers were, in fact, voicing a common concern that some of the educational methods adopted during this period were ornamental more than they were useful, layering what Richard Bauman in his overview of Quaker attitudes calls 'artificial refinement' on to the believer.[3] Quakers sought to set themselves in opposition to the increasingly professionalised clergy, insisting that true knowledge came from the believer's inner understanding of their God. Whereas other believers might look to their bibles for insight, Quakers proposed that they had only to look within themselves because God was perceived as a force or power that moved each person. It was common for many branches of religious belief in the seventeenth century to seek to marry the impulses of the heart with cerebral concerns, since faith was to be a felt experience and not just an abstract comprehension. In most instances, learning could be accommodated into the conception of religiosity, as was the case with Baptists, for instance.[4] Quakers often wanted to entirely replace formal learning with spiritual learning. As will be seen over the course of this chapter, which is a survey of first-generation Quaker attitudes, a consequence of this impulse was that their perspective on education was repeatedly discussed, and their own works elaborated a conception of their particular kind of wisdom.

If we consider them only through the eyes of their enemies, Quakers took an either–or position on learning. The peculiarities of the Quaker approach emerge in writing that views them askance precisely because their ideas were more focused on revelation than on exterior sources of religious understanding. The Independent minister Samuel Eaton paraphrases Quaker thought as follows: 'The Godhead ... supplies with all Wisdom, Knowledge, Graces of all kindes, strength, holiness, and with every thing, so that they need nothing that is external.'[5] Crudely put, Quakers (or 'Friends') proposed that a believer either spoke from the spirit and simultaneously rejected traditional humane learning, or wrongly imbibed formal education so aligning themselves in the process with fleshliness and deceit. Quakers, then, divided humanity into the godly and the ungodly through this demarcation. As will be shown, unlearnedness is paradigmatic to the extent that it underpins many sets of antitheses. Quakers contrasted spirit and flesh, inwardness and outwardness, knowledge and wisdom. They did this primarily to maintain the self-sufficiency of learning through the spirit, wherein they are developing from injunctions in the New Testament the Pauline insight that God favoured the foolish over the wise.[6] An insight that, as it was played out, could lead to the rejection of all forms of learning, culminated in a suspicion that language skewed all meaning, and spirituality was preferable to scripturalism. These conventions will emerge in many of the examples that will be explored here and, given their dominance in Quaker thought, it is little wonder that a 'teacher' like Eaton could paraphrase their approach so succinctly.[7] However, the Quaker position on learning is not quite so neat as it first appears, and this will be one of the contentions advanced in this chapter. Indeed, to return to Eaton again, it will be assessed how far terms like wisdom and knowledge have different connotations depending on the author and the circumstance. A survey of Quaker attitudes to knowledge must explore the degree to which they were different to co-religionists and non-Quakers, as well as their consistency on this theme.

Hugh Barbour has demonstrated that Quakers claimed that their inwardly felt learning 'linked [them] inseparably with the moral transformation of men by God's power'.[8] The claim that God was directing his instruments to do his work was one heard often during the 1650s, being part of the milieu of the era.[9] In exploring the contentiousness of this claim, as well as its appeal even to some outside of the movement, we see the potency of the prophetic persona. Writing as a sceptic intent on acquiring proof that he knew would be unforthcoming, Thomas Hobbes, for instance, maintained that there was no argument sufficient to 'oblige me to believe' anybody saying they were led by the direct call of God.[10] Such a position of incredulity contrasts with the opinion of the writer and sometime defender of the Quakers, Henry Stubbe, who, though not a Friend himself, understood the religious *episteme*, as well as the materialist perspective of Hobbes – the two entered into correspondence. Stubbe's *A Light Shining out of Darkness* (1659) is a text that Nicholas McDowell observes attacks the 'formal education' and 'spiritual authority' of clergymen in the established church.[11] In particular, the inwardness of the Quaker experience is the subject of Stubbe's discussion when he comments 'as for my part, since I am not sensible of the convictions or emotions of the Spirit under which another lyes, so I dare not condemn the *Quakers*'.[12] Indeed, Quaker leader George Fox's *An Epistle* (1657) contains a subtitle explaining the purpose of one of his works reading rather like a working definition of the approach that Stubbe was observing, namely 'the practice of many to wait in silence upon God, to hear his word, and know his voice'.[13] The fact that one believer cannot be 'sensible' as to another's relationship with his/her God opens out both the great strength of Quaker belief, and its chief limitation – at least to sceptics. Since Quakers had a more developed way of talking about the fusion of the individual with the divine than many other religionists of the time, they challenged contemporary attitudes.[14]

A basic principle to Friends, the sufficiency of inward learning was frequently detailed, but the way they described this in their pamphlets varied from writer to writer and, indeed, required some justification. This survey will bring in authors that expressed themselves through autobiography, through poetry and through polemical tracts. Though common factors in the Quaker approach to knowledge emerge, even in such varied genres of writing, the intention here is not to define a monochrome *episteme* but rather to demonstrate how nuanced was their position. We should be careful not to overstate the importance of a few examples of rationalist or sceptical thinking when assessing the Quaker *episteme*. The dominant paradigms in these writings are, certainly, that all knowledge, and especially that which comes from an inner understanding of God, should take one closer to the divine and not to a kind of individualistic rationalism. Even so, this chapter will refer, briefly, to seemingly atypical Quaker attitudes when discussing their ideas on the natural propensity of people to learn, and so incorporate some of the more recent insights into religiosity of the 1650s.[15] Owen Watkins has noted on this subject that many educated believers were reluctant to let go of 'analytical habits of mind', [16] and though his observation was of men broadly defined as Puritan, rather than Quaker, this impulse is evident in some work by Friends too.

As they engaged with the subject of humane knowledge and learning, defining their own approach as well as critiquing other people's, they also in the process showed the political import of their ideas, and hence Quaker attitudes to knowledge are part of the egalitarianism of the movement's theology. The debates over religious learning could, indeed, be said to go right to the heart of what was at issue, and therefore thoroughgoing, during the Commonwealth and Protectorate periods. Quaker attitudes to learning were one reason why the sufficiency of the spirit could lead many to speak with new assurance of their relationship to their God. That they did so whether male or female, rich or poor, was one of the effects of their egalitarian approach to knowledge.

Explanations about how the Quaker came to the understanding of the God within can be found in a key genre that many employed. Through conversion narratives, one glimpses attitudes that reveal the importance of education to the believer before s/he was a Quaker, prior to responding to the more experiential knowledge of the inward God whose presence they perceived as the Light within. As Luella M. Wright notes, 'practically every narrative contains a detailed account of the spiritual struggle involved in the surrender of the individual will to the leadings of the inner light'.[17] The aim of these writings is to express disenchantment and transformation in almost equal measure. Disenchantment with the practices of the established church brought about conversion, which Quakers called 'convincement' as a sign of the conviction they felt. The process of conversion is one of rejecting the teachings of a minister, often after hearing the more edifying preaching of a Quaker acting as a vessel for God's word. Following this first impression, contrast is made between the old and the new ministries in order to show how transformational the break from old ways is. Edward Burrough, for instance, called the ministry of the state church 'heavy, & high-minded', marking a moment of insight into the limitations of his former spiritual mentors.[18]

But one interesting feature of Quaker writings on the subject of education is that the criticism of the former minister's over-dependence on formal learning is not the whole story. Quakers are also hard on themselves. These acerbic self-reflections offer another insight into why the Quaker turned to the God within, and are a feature of the narratives of two Quaker leaders – the movement had a number in the early days – Francis Howgill's *The Inheritance of Jacob* (1656) and Richard Hubberthorn's *The Immediate Call* (1654), both of which document how these men took excessive pride in their erudition before joining the Quakers. Edward Burrough's conversion narrative will be considered rather than these, however, because so much hinges on his changed attitudes to learning. Margaret Ezell comments on the Quaker idea that 'relying on external forms' that are the 'products of man' is per-ceived to '[en]danger' the individual, and so it is with Burrough.[19]

A northern Quaker who joined the movement in the early 1650s, after having earlier rejected Presbyterianism, Burrough wrote *A Warning from the Lord to the Inhabitants of Underbarrow* (1654) in part as a conversion narrative. His early years, perhaps his middle teens, were spent pursuing the kind of religious high that could be achieved when focusing on the self-development, and especially learnedness, that he sees as integral to the Presbyterian faith. He represents his ways of worshipping as misguided, since during the time he was infatuated with having a reputation as an interpreter his 'delight was much in discoursing', he shamefacedly admits.[20] The image is of one possessed by a kind of kinetic energy that was mas-querading as faith. Hence 'I ran forth in my wisdom comprehending the mysteries of God, having a Light shined in me, and I grew up into a Notion, to talk of high things, for it was my delight to com-prehend in my busie mind, thus being ignorant of the Cross to keep low in it.' In time, Burrough viewed his activity as self-exaltation that was the more deceptive for seeming at first to be genuine. 'Pride grew up in me, for wisdom grew up in me', he writes. Burrough's conversion then occurred when he met with George Fox, the foremost of the Quaker leaders, and was compelled to recognise with him that his faith had no solid basis and was previously just 'airie notions and imaginations'.[21] The utility of conversion narratives as exemplar comes from the fact that they depict a process of transformation as one set of values is replaced by Quaker attitudes; and, in the case of learning, this means turning from formal worship to spiritual inwardness, while reflecting earnestly on this.

If Edward Burrough's account has a self-depreciatory tenor, and no small amount of bombastic criticism of ministerial shortcomings, William Dewsbury's conversion narrative has a different tone. Though Burrough and Dewsbury found Quakerism at roughly the same time, the latter's *Discovery of the Great Enmity of the Serpent* (1655) shows that spiritual epiphanies are personal to each writer. Dewsbury had a similar background to Burrough, being from the North of England, a Presbyterian, then possibly a Baptist, before converting to Quakerism. Of these factors, the documenting of overcoming sinfulness which had been so central to teachings Dewsbury would have likely heard while a Presbyterian and a Baptist seems most affecting. Dewsbury's autobiography contrasts the 'carnal' with what is 'within' and, in the process, suggests that the believer can strive for union with God making him begin wholly again as new. He writes as though throwing off the sinfulness that has been keeping him from God:

> Then the Lord discovered to me that his love could not be attained in any thing I could doe, in any of these outward observations; so in all these my turnings in my carnall wisdome, seeking the kingdom of God in observations without, thither the flaming sword turned which kept the way of the tree of life, and fenced me from it, and cut me down, and rent all my figlea[e]vs, coverings, and distroyed that minde that looked out to seek to hear the word of the Lord from man: then my minde was turned within by the power of the Lord, to waite in his counsel.[22]

The knotty problem of Quaker debt to continental religious movements cannot be drawn out here.[23] All the same, it is worth observing that this same trope, combining the flaming sword of Genesis (3:24) and comments on the Fall, also occurs in the *Journal* of George Fox, and that this echo led Rufus M. Jones to draw parallels between Fox and the German mystic Jacob Boehme.[24] If what Dewsbury found when he turned to the God within was a new way of understanding biblical symbolism that coincided with Boehme's use of the same imagery, then Dewsbury's experience can be categorised as mystical. The result is Antinomian, too. Dewsbury's motivation is to please the inward God, not the 'carnal'; in this context 'carnal' might be paraphrased to mean 'worldly'. Dewsbury shows a distrust of all messages other than those directly from his God.

This can be termed knowledge because its basis is experiential. As Fox puts it in *A Declaration* (1656), 'you need not that any man teach you'.[25] In religious writings, moreover, surrendering to God's love is often more highly regarded than comprehending God in the abstract. It is possible, then, that Dewsbury is not only establishing his new beginning through conversion to Quakerism, but also making this new way of knowing the world and himself seem vivid, as though inspired. Assessing these insights in the light of what Stubbe wrote about not being able to access the mindset, 'convictions or emotions', of another in the Spirit, cited earlier, it is clear that Dewsbury assumes differently. Arguably, he is trying to reconstruct the knowledge he now possesses through the emotional experience itself, hence attempting to capture for himself, but eventually for the reader, something of the intensity of his first epiphany. Quaker writings sought to move the reader through such methods.[26]

These explanations of how Quakers could learn from the God within were not only self-reflective; they used the contrast between the learned and the unlearned pointedly. Rather than formal education providing an extra level of helpful guidance, so wholly were the insights flowing from the spirit to be preferred, learning could be represented as a barrier to religiosity. It stirred the carnal mind with a desire for self-improvement and hence, for Quakers, the yearning for knowledge was most commonly a sign of being out of the ways of God. Sarah Blackborow, a Londoner who joined the movement in the early 1650s, writes in the genre of an admonition of the qualities that her God expects of ministers of the church. To be truly wise, the ministers would have to change their ways: 'That in your brain is what you have to boast of; be ashamed and put your mouthes in the dust, and never open them any more [...]. A Love there is which doth not cease, to the seed of God in you all; and therefore doth invite you everyone Priest and people to return in to it, that into Wisdoms house who may come.'[27] Sarah Blackborow's recommendation is evocative of the Bible. The charging of ministers with pride shows that what they regard as social advancement is not so, while the imagery used suggests that Blackborow is triggering a mystical experience. The encoding most typical of mystical symbolism can be seen in the phrase 'wisdom's house'. In the Bible, many who trust in God fully describe the security He provides as 'habitation'. Likewise, in mystical writings, 'wisdom' is represented as deeper and more fulfilling than conventional knowledge, hence 'wisdom's house'. Because of these elements in this acerbic address to ministers, Blackborow's account combines the approaches that have been identified in Burrough's and Dewsbury's texts.

In the Quaker diagnosis of the perils of education that have been examined so far, there has been no attempt to identify a root cause of the problem. However, one object of Quaker writing is tracing the emergence of carnal learning to social causes that does just that. Richard H. Greaves has noted that one of the most developed arguments on this theme is in relation to both the training and licensing of ministers, which shows why Quakers are the scourge of the universities and can be classified as anti-formalists.[28] Moreover, this was the intent of Hester Biddle's 'Woe to thee, City of Oxford' (1655), Margaret Greenway's A Lamentation (1657), Richard Hubberthorne's A True Testimony (1654), Jeremiah Haward et al., Here Followeth a True Relation (n. d.) and John Harwood's A Warning from the Lord (1655). By observing that Christ, his disciples and Apostles were wise but 'meek and lowlie' they maintained the simplicity of the Gospels.[29] More systematic accounts produced contemporaneously often cite Apollo as an exception, and the case of what Paul's trial as detailed in Acts reveals about his education was pored over in order to establish the source of his erudition, which was ambiguous.[30] But many Quakers, in line with the very early and collectively written False Prophets (1652), aver that the original ministers of God were not from seats of learning, but were 'plain men that laboured with their hands'.[31] The Quakers asked why ministers needed endorsement from the universities when formal learning was anathema to early Christianity. Hence, the Quaker attitudes were radical in that they overturned a hierarchy of learning that usually secured great status to university men: here, the unlearned were garlanded.

Quakers posed the following question: how could a humanist education equip men for the ministry? Even those non-Quakers who lauded education's benefits had to confess that some individuals were too suggestible: 'I have known some in my time in the University, that doted so long on Philosophy, that they proved errant drones, and could never relish Divinity.'[32] Seduction by the ancients, however, was arguably not the most pressing worry. Assessing the Bible's attitudes to learning and knowledge was a serious enterprise, and one that university-trained ministers could not help but to have been aware of and, sometimes, party to. On the one hand, those in favour of some sort of theological training knew that they could not wholly overturn the arguments put forward in favour of unlearnedness, because the New Testament makes clear the advantages of innocent simplicity if what one is seeking is a relationship with God that would ultimately lead to salvation and true insight. On the other hand, pro-education ministers could argue that the Bible shows through its multivalency that it is underpinned by deep knowledge not only of matters of faith, but also of areas comprising the law, medicine and the natural sciences, via the account of creation. The Bible contains insights into all these fields, so cannot be in principle anti-learning.[33] But even if the arguments in favour of education were germane, there was an arguably even more persistent dilemma or a tension with regard to the state church's expectation that ministers be educated and, therefore, professionalised. As John Morgan's *Godly Learning* shows, some state ministers, especially those we would now class as varieties of puritans, would have been acutely conscious of the contradictions they had internalised. Combing the scripture as exegetes, while understanding that 'a core of revealed knowledge was of a higher order than anything man could discern', puritans were not of one mind on education's utility.[34]

Quaker responses seem remarkably clear in comparison as they deem theological training at university for ministers unnecessary and ungodly. Whereas it might seem that in doing this Quakers were unlikely to win the argument, the training of ministers being inherently justifiable for a range of pragmatic reasons that seem common sense, it was not what was principally at stake. The most pressing issue was one that has already been mooted in the conversion narratives. Just as the individual believer was 'convinced' once they renounced humane learning by allowing God to teach them, the university-educated minister was in a pre-conversion state of alienation. While the Quaker convert had been able to reverse the deleterious effects of learning, the minister might not be able to if now so empirically minded that there was no going back. Quakers therefore employed as one of their most effective arguments the Pauline passage that is ambiguous about the value of literacy itself: 'the letter killeth, but the spirit giveth life' (2 Corinthians 3:6), a quotation also evoked by the Ranters.[35] George Fox, for instance, is suspicious that in the 'beast's power' are those who 'hath the Scriptures in three or four languages' because such thinkers are deluded if they think they can get to the meaning of the Bible through studying it.[36] Fox is here demonstrating the Quaker method of 'violating norms of deference and politeness' through his anticlerical account of the invalidity of education.[37] The use of the word 'wisdom' is different in these texts to the conversion narratives too. Hester Biddle's address to the University of Oxford, for instance, comments on how people can now escape the clutches of the Egyptian taskmaster, the Pharoah, and the 'Oxford' pedant, all of whom are oppressive, rather like the Pharisees in the Bible, since they are 'setting up thy own righteousness and wisdom, which shall grow as ragged as an old garment that moths hath eat'.[38] This is an unusual and striking image that reminds us that what the Quakers wanted to do with their own texts is write in a language their readers could relate to; Biddle is showing that she wants to challenge those working in their 'own ... wisdom'. One other text of this kind, by George Fox, complains that what trained ministers issue forth is not insight, because it originates from 'the wisdom below'.[39] In both instances, Fox and Biddle are not conveying empty jibes: they demonstrate the Quaker usage of plain language that Bauman notes, its intention being 'to redeem others'.[40]

The framing of these issues in a passage short enough to be quoted in its entirety brings together the matters that have been considered so far, as well as introducing new lines of enquiry. The short poem by Susanna Bateman at the end of her 1656 text 'I matter not how I appear to man' shows the will's instinct to transgress, as seen through its desire to take more for itself. The poem shows this pervasiveness of the will through its depiction of wisdom and its other adjuncts, such as language which is building, babel-like, on the wrong foundation:

> Thinks human wisdom I can eas'ly see
> The Scripture can this thing declare to me;
> But it's not known by pleasure, ease or sleep,

Who finds this Pearl must dig both low and deep
And whoso finds before it be his own,
He must sell all to purchase that alone.
And cast up all his stock, and look within,
Before to build this house he doth begin.
Remember Babel, do not build too high,
Nor make a Tower to reach unto the sky,
Nor look without, but turn thy eye within,
See Christ be laid, then build thy House on Him,
Who builds not on this Rock, shall surely fall,
For hee's the Corner-stone uniteth all.
Cease then a while, you humane learned men,
And know your wisdom cannot find out him.
Thou willing and obedient, know it's thee
Whose wall is rent to see this mystery:
It's not the prudent, learned, wise, that shall
Him comprehend, who is the light of all.
Follow the light, for surely 'twill thee bring
Where he is born, then bow and worship him.
No sooner is he born, but thou shalt see,
That Herods nature by its cruelty.
Seeks to destroy that New-born babe in thee.[41]

This poem makes use of a genre found elsewhere in seventeenth-century poetry in works where the flesh and the spirit's differing approaches to learning are considered. As well as Bateman's poem, others in this mode by Andrew Marvell and Anne Bradstreet show the soul and body in what Marvell referred to as 'a dialogue'.[42] In this work, 'A Dialogue between the Resolved Soul and Created Pleasure', we are reminded, in Stanley Fish's words, that what Marvell is in search of is 'self-sufficient' simplicity.[43] Marvell shows that there is an insightfulness to be found when embracing a world view rejecting humane learning, since the reward is an innate experience that had the property of being organic and, more than that, potentially complete. What Marvell's work establishes is that one cannot merely focus on conflict between Quakers and the established church, nor even the learned and the unlearned, though manifestly important to this topic. Non-Quakers and the highly educated, like Andrew Marvell, were also trying to explain the spirit's pre-eminence. Likewise, from the start of Bateman's Quaker poem, readers must reject the intellect that strives for meaning but is incipiently less righteous. From the very first line, Bateman's representation of human wisdom alerts us to the fact that such knowledge does not come from God.

The crux of what is at issue is in fact ontological. As Bateman's poem makes clear in repeated references to the Bible and to language, Scripture does not in fact 'declare' its meanings (line 2). God, the author, is the active agent through 'the light' (line 20). When Quakers use the phrase 'the light' they are often pointing to the spiritual illumination that John's gospel proposes is God's way of delivering supernatural or extraordinary insights. The consequences of this approach are manifest in both theory and in practice. As George Fox established, written texts are not foundational, in the sense of the metaphor of a house's foundations, whereas, in prioritising them, 'is not this to lay another foundation then the holy men of God built upon; which was these things before scripture was written?'[44] His approach in his autobiography is concordant with the polemical pamphlet. In the *Journal*, Fox very often describes how the Bible was an 'opening', or how he 'opened out' Scripture to others. This phrasing reveals that the Bible is a secondary level of revelation, merely, and is also normatively Quaker in that it seeks, in Hilary Hinds's view, to be the 'the rhetorical equivalent of bodying forth in language'.[45] What these 'openings' access is the spirit that is both behind the work, and exists prior to it, eternally.

Another matter that is embedded in Bateman's poem about how 'wisdom cannot find out [God]' is one that is alluded to rather than directly named (line 16). In setting up the Light as the purveyor of knowledge and, even, knowledge itself, Bateman is commenting indirectly on the problem of uncertainty. This is alluded to in the image of Babel and its 'tower' that seeks 'to reach unto the sky' (line 10). Bateman is using a commonplace image of confusion in order to show the limits of those aspiring to build on a foundation that is not Christ the 'corner stone' (line 14). Her figures should be expected to be inexact, since images by their definition are not the same as the concepts to which they apparently allude. In the 'corner stone' she must be referring to faith, but the image of Babel is a little more compressed. It might stand for fallen language, or might, with its images of building, represent the aspiration of human reason, or she might possibly be invoking both concepts simultaneously. The key message, however, is clear, since the framework assumes that the insights of faith are incomparable to those confusedly acquired in other ways. In instructing her readers to 'cease' their search for human wisdom, she is implicitly proposing that faith will bring greater insights than reason (line 15).

Quakers hence did not ascribe to reason positive qualities because they perceived that it was from natural man rather than from God. The ontology that has been traced here speaks of an exterior, supernatural force that becomes internal to each Friend while, in so doing, retaining its extraordinary link to the divine. The objection to rationality is based on the perception that it is tainted with the earthly and humane, so unable to bring about the believer's union with their God. Alternative perspectives, such as that voiced by Nathaniel Culverwell, whose ideas parallel those of the Cambridge Platonists, put a more positive spin on rationality. The possibility to see in reason something of benefit will be important with reference to the discussion, at the end of this chapter, of Isaac Penington, who echoes pro-rationalist ideas.

Writing contemporaneously to the rise of Quakerism, Culverwell makes clear another ontology, one that suggests that reason binds the believer to God. Cambridge educated, Culverwell was part of the group of thinkers at that university who have been seen throughout their work to '[refuse] to oppose the spiritual to the rational'.[46] A posthumously published work, Culverwell's *An Elegant and Learned Discourse of the Light of Nature*, shows that he is thinking about how humane understanding can be given some authority without supplanting the inwardness of spiritual learning. A key statement to this effect is optimistically focused on the unification of God and the believer: 'Whatsoever the secret counsel of [God] issues out and bubbles forth, it is in most rational manifestations. His commands are all rational, his words is the very pith and marrow of reason. His law is the quickening and wakening of man's reason.'[47] Culverwell completes his argument with the observation that right reason is 'in the centre' of each being, thus drawing on natural law theory.[48] Culverwell depicts reason's limitations, but positions himself as an optimist rather than a sceptic. In the intellectual sphere, the best case that religious writers usually made for reason was that it could be sharp enough to give a degree of assurance, and where it was used properly, significant insights could result. 'Though it be but a limited and restrained light, yet it will discover such objects as are within its own sphere with a sufficient certainty', Culverwell observed.[49] A more pessimistic perspective argued that some heavenly matters would always be above or beyond reason's powers of discernment. The analogy most conventionally used by such writers, known as nominalists, was that reason was the candle in man. Its weak light could be compared to the beams of the sun, symbolising God's illumination.[50] Yet Culverwell shows his support for reason through his argument that in 'its own sphere' reason can triumph. He argues that much in the world can be understood, and through that, God's ways intuited.

Unusually, given the framing of the knowledge question by Quakers, examples may be found that support the pro-knowledge arguments to a higher degree. Edward Burrough, who in his conversion narrative focused on turning to the inner light after rejecting vain ways of learning, nevertheless knew 'good education and learning, which in its place is a virtue'.[51] He referred particularly to the teaching of languages to travellers as a case of knowledge used well. The idea that 'worldly' subjects were a species of knowledge that could be augmented and developed through education was not in fact a controversial issue. Arguably, it was more unusual for Quakers to break learning into different categories, discussing the relevance of them.

Isaac Penington was one of the foremost Quakers of the early period, and his works go even further than Burrough's in discussing the origins of religious understanding. For the purposes of this chapter, which is as concerned with immanent Quaker writing as it is with clear-cut Quaker ideas, the text of most significance is one written before he converted. In 1654, when he published *Divine Essays*, Penington was probably a Seeker who had turned away from the established church and the Independency he pursued during the Civil War period. *Divine Essays* is another example of a text that fuses the two ideas: that one can learn from the reason and from the spirit. Penington argues that humans have certain natural capacities for taking them towards God, and reason has a role to play in this process; a higher sort of knowledge is spiritual, and even higher than that is divine knowledge.[52] Throughout this process, reason can play a role in the reformation of individuals and the development of their insight.

This fusion of the spiritual and the natural is what Isaac Pennington proposes though a discussion of 'speculative knowledge' in the section of *Divine Essays* titled 'of knowledge in general'. Pennington notes:

Speculative knowledg [sic] is not to be wholly condemned, it having a necessary use in our present state, (for we have need of more knowledg in every kind then we can possibly experiment) ... yet speculative knowledg alone without practise, without trial, without experience, is not altogether so safe in this state of man: His eye being weak needeth this further help, or he may easily be deceived. His head and his heart must go together, yea, and both must be rightly guided, or he will be apt to mistake and miscarry in every thing.[53]

When Penington refers to 'speculative knowledge' he is describing 'a knowledge by understanding' and he has previously defined it.[54] He contends that the spirit 'most naturally' knows God; Penington is taking on board the hierarchy of knowledge that places revealed knowledge above reason.[55] However, he is not wholly dismissive of the latter, as is evident in the language of integration referring to the insights of eye and heart, which proposes a link between the material and the immaterial. The treatment of experience as a bridge fits this pattern as well, since it brings the speculative to trial.[56] His observation stops short of saying that since different ways of understanding the world and God are available, they are there to be used. Even so, the utility of 'speculative knowledge' is emphasised by it being 'necessary'.

Whereas the Quaker Margaret Abbott observes that if one turns from the Light of Christ, being unable to learn from it, then what one is accessing is 'but the light of nature, or something of a little value', Penington seems to be changing the terms of the debate by degrees.[57] Though having the same sorts of anxieties about wrongly privileging book learning as Abbott, Penington tries to work in the middle ground between the extremes that have been set out in this chapter.[58] Unlike the Quakers at this point, he does not give all over to spiritual insight that looks like self-exultation by another name.[59] He saw a role for reason, proposing that at its highest it could take humans towards an understanding of the nature of God.[60] But, like the Quakers who he would soon join, he also spoke in terms of the inwardness of learning from God, and of that he spoke zealously.

Acknowledging a use for speculation may seem a limited concession, especially given the claims for reason that were being made elsewhere during the century and that have recently been put forward by scholars such as Nicholas McDowell. However, there are several reasons why this is an appropriate response to religious rationalism. Firstly, the question of agency is of key significance, as can be seen when a sceptical perspective is brought to bear on Quaker religiosity. According to Henry Stubbe's account, non-Quakers could demolish Friends' ontology by the contention that they 'mistake *nature* for *grace*'.[61] In other words, their enemies believed that the Light shining in Quakers was part of their own nature and not divine illumination. By contrast, Quakers, in Hilary Hinds's view, instead proposed they were subject to 'referred agency' with the light forming an effectual link between the individual and their God.[62] The assumption that the believer could be overcome by God is much more developed in Quaker writing than in the perspective that reason brings the intellect or the soul to an understanding of God's true nature and laws. Secondly, and contrastingly, Quakers may have been like those puritans that Watkins identified as clinging to 'analytical habits of mind', as they continued to make deductions that have a scholarly method and language.[63] As apparent as this is when one thinks about writers such as Isaac Penington, there is nevertheless a tension at play. Earthly knowledge was by all accounts seen as less potentially insightful and, more than that, more immediately corruptible, because rational perspectives of the divine were generally regarded as limited. Quakers repeatedly referred to their act of turning to the teacher within in order to identify their Christological focus on the inwardly understood spirit of God. Their theories of knowledge, hence, envisaged something more organic and potentially complete than was attainable through reason, thus differing from most of the writers studied in this chapter. Such theories are radical because the Quaker orthodoxy of learning from the spirit led to the empowering of all who could comprehend this power, and this took effect regardless of background or education.

Notes

1 The author wishes to thank Ben Pink Dandelion and Claire Bowditch for reading and commenting on this chapter.
2 G. Campbell and T. N. Corns, *John Milton: Life, Work, and Thought* (Oxford: Oxford University Press, 2012), p. 62. For another example of the demotic nature of radicalism, see Chapter 6.
3 R. Bauman, *Let Your Words Be Few: Symbolism of Speaking and Silence Among Seventeenth-Century Quakers* (London: Quaker Home Service, 1998), p. 37.
4 See T. L. Underwood, *Primitivism, Radicalism, and the Lamb's War:*

Baptist-Quaker Conflict in Seventeenth-Century England (New York and Oxford: Oxford University Press, 1997).

5   S. Eaton, *The Quakers Confuted Being An Answer Vnto Nineteen Queries; Propounded by them, and sent to the Elders of the Church of Duckenfield in Cheshire; wherein is held forth much of the Doctrine and practise Concerning Revelations, and immediate Voices, and against the holy Scriptures, Christs Ministry, Churches and Ordinances &c.* (London, 1653), pp. 12–13. Eaton elaborates on what Quakers consider 'external' matters and so reject: scriptures, ordinances and the ministry.

6   1 Corinthians was particularly important.

7   Eaton describes himself as a 'teacher' on the title page of his pamphlet. He was a Cheshire Independent and found himself the subject of anti-sectarian literature.

8   H. Barbour, *The Quakers in Puritan England* (New Haven, C.T.; London: Yale University Press, 1964), p. 141.

9   See G. Nuttall, *The Holy Spirit in Puritan Faith and Experience* (Chicago, I.L. ; London: University of Chicago Press, 2nd edn, 1992); R. Moore, *The Light in their Consciences: Early Quakers in Britain 1646–1666* (University Park, P.A.: Pennsylvania State University Press, 2000).

10 T. Hobbes, *Leviathan*, ed. John C. A. Gaskin (Oxford: Oxford University Press, 1998), p. 248.

11 N. McDowell, *The English Radical Imagination: Culture, Religion, and Revolution, 1630–1660* (Oxford: Clarendon Press, 2004), p. 178. McDowell provides an overview of Stubbe's career. See also R. L. Greaves, 'The early Quakers as advocates of educational reform', *Quaker History*, 58:1 (1969), 20–30. The author is grateful to Rosemary Moore for sharing her biographical note on Stubbe with her.

12 H. Stubbe, *A Light Shining out of Darkness: or Occasional Queries Submitted To the Judgment of such as would enquire in our Times* (London, rev. edn, 1659), p. 91.

13 G. Fox, *An Epistle to all the People on the Earth; And The Ignorance of all the World, both Professors and Teachers, of the Birth that must be silent, and of the Birth that is to speak, which declares God; and the difference betwixt silence and speaking* (London, 1657), title page.

14 See M. Paxson Grundy, 'Learning to be Quaker: spiritual formation and religious education among early Friends', *Quaker Studies*, 11:2 (2007), 150–79.

15 This contention will be developed later in the chapter. Another account with a focus on rationalism is C. G. Martin, *Milton among the Puritans: The Case for Historical Revisionism* (Farnham: Ashgate, 2010).

16 O. C. Watkins, *The Puritan Experience: Studies in Spiritual Autobiography* (London: Routledge and Kegan Paul, 1972), p. 126.

17 L. M. Wright, *The Literary Life of the Early Friends, 1650–1725* (New York, N.Y.: Columbia University Press, 1935), p. 156.

18 E. Burrough, *A Just and Lawful Trial of the Teachers & professed Ministers of England, By a perfect proceeding against them* (London, 1657), p. 17.

19 M. Ezell, *Writing Women's Literary History* (Baltimore, M.D.; London: The Johns Hopkins University Press, 1993), p. 139.

20 E. Burrough, *A Warning from the Lord to the Inhabitants of Underbarrow, and so to all the Inhabitants in England, Where it shall meet with them, who holds up the false Teachers, and false worship, and who beats, stone, stock, and persecute, and hail out of their Assemblies, those who are sent by the Lord, to speak his word freely* (London, 1654), p. 33.

21 Burrough, *A Warning*, pp. 32, 31, 34.

22 William Dewsbury, *The Discovery of the great enmity of the Serpent against the seed of the Woman, which witnesseth against him where he rules, both in Rulers, Priests, and People* (London, 1655), p. 16.

23 On this aspect of mid-century religio-political writings, see N. Smith, *Perfection Proclaimed: Language and Literature in English Radical Religion* (Oxford: Clarendon, 1989).

24 R. M. Jones, *Spiritual Reformers in the Sixteenth and Seventeenth Centuries* (London: Macmillan, 1914), p. 221. See G. Fox, *Journal*, ed. Nigel Smith (London: Penguin, 1998), p. 27. The entry is from 1648. For a recent contribution to the debate on the influence of Jacob Boehme's writings on early Quakers, see A. Hessayon, 'Jacob Boehme's writings during the English Revolution', in A. Hessayon and S. Apetrei (eds), *An Introduction to Jacob Boehme: Four Centuries of Thought and Reception* (New York, N.Y.; Abingdon: Routledge, 2014), pp. 89–90. On the influence of Jacob Boehme on English seventeenth-century radicals, also see the Introduction in this volume.

25 G. Fox, *A Declaration of the Ground of Error & Errors, Blasphemy, Blasphemers and Blasphemies* (London, 1657), p. 37. He is explaining 1 John 2:3.

26 Wright, *Literary Life of the Early Friends*, p. 71.

27 S. Blackborow, *A Visit to the Spirit in Prison; and an Invitation to all people to come to Christ the light of the World, in whom is life, and doth enlighten every one that cometh into the World* (London, 1658), p. 5.

28 Greaves, 'The early Quakers as advocates', p. 24; Nuttall, *The Holy Spirit*, p. 84, defines the Quakers as anti-formalists and notes the contrasting position of Richard Baxter who believes that learnedness and godliness must be combined in a preacher.

29 J. Harwood, *A Warning from the Lord, to the Town of Cambridge*, [1655], p. 6; *A Warning from the Lord, to the City of Oxford*, [1655], p. 6. Both tracts are identical, only the title changes.

30 For references to Apollo, see Samuel How, *The Svfficiencie of the Spirits Teaching, Without Humane-Learning: Or A Treatise, Tending to Proue Hvmane-Learning To Be No Help to the Spirituall understanding of the Word of God*, 1640, unpaginated. On the learning of Christ, the Disciples, and Apostles, see Thomas Hall, *Vindiciæ Literarum: The Schools Guarded: Or, The Excellency and Vsefulnesse of Humane Learning in Subordination to Divinity, and preparation to the Ministry as also, Rules for the expounding of the Holy Scriptures* (London, 1654), pp. 14–17, p. 56. This text is in part generated in response to the cobbler Samuel How's work.

31 Thomas Aldam *et al.*, *False Prophets and false Teachers described*, 1652, p. 3.

32 Hall, *Vindiciæ Literarum*, p. 57.

33 See K. Killeen, *Biblical Scholarship, Science and Politics in Early Modern England: Thomas Browne and the Thorny Place of Knowledge* (Farnham: Ashgate, 2009).

34 J. Morgan, *Godly Learning: Puritan Attitudes Towards Reason, Learning, and Education, 1560–1640* (Cambridge: Cambridge University Press, 1986), p. 72.

35 See Abiezer Coppe, *A Fiery Flying Roll* and *A Second Fiery Flying Roule*, in *A Collection of Ranter Writings from the Seventeenth Century*, ed. Nigel Smith (London: Junction Books, 1983), p. 111. Quakers were assimilated to Ranters by their antagonistic contemporaries.

36 G. Fox, *The Lambs Officer Is gone forth with the Lambs Message Which is the Witness of God in all Consciences, to call them up to the Bar, the Judgement of the Lamb, in this his day which is come* (London, 1659), p. 2.

37 Bauman, *Let your words be few*, p. 43.

38 E. Hobby, '"Oh Oxford thou art full of filth": the prophetical writings of Hester Biddle, 1629?–1696', in S. Sellers *et al.* (eds), *Feminist Criticism: Theory and Practice* (Toronto: University of Toronto Press, 1991), p. 164.

39 G. Fox, *Here are several Queries Put forth in Print for all, or any of you whose names are here under written, (And likewise for them at Cambridge and Oxford, who are there teaching and training of such up to practice such things as you yourselves are now acting in, or any other of your Societies that will Answer the same) and return your Answer in Print, to the view and satisfaction of many people; who are now questioning whether any of all your practises do proceed from the true Foundation* (London, 1657), p. 11.

40 Bauman, *Let your words be few*, p. 61.

41 S. Bateman, 'I matter not how I appear to man', undated. Thomason gives May 1657 for a date. Even reading can be problematic. In the seven and a half pages that precede the text Susanna Bateman herself offers context for the more compressed ideas in her poem, when saying that sensory evidence cannot be trusted (p. 1). She argues that one gets to knowledge only when one reads the word 'near the heart' (p. 3).

42 A. Marvell, 'A Dialogue, Between the Resolved Soul, and Created Pleasure', in *The Poems of Andrew Marvell*, ed. Nigel Smith (Edinburgh: Pearson, 2007), pp. 33–9. A. Bradstreet, 'The Flesh and the Spirit', in *The Poems of Mrs Anne Bradstreet, 1612–1672. Together with her Prose Remains*, ed. Charles Eliot Norton (S. l.: The Duodecimos, 1989), pp. 259–62.

43 S. Fish, 'Marvell and the art of disappearance', in S. Fish, *Versions of Anti-humanism: Milton and Others* (Cambridge: Cambridge University Press, 2012), p. 213. Fish says that the Spirit and the Flesh are seeking to decouple, not triumph over each other, hence why he describes this process in terms of self-sufficiency.

44 George Fox *et al.*, *A Declaration Against all Poperie, and popish points: and is renounced from them and by them whom the Scorners in scorn call Quakers: and Likewise some Queries to the Pope and his Priests that are guarded with his law*, 1655?, A4v. See Wright, *Literary Life of the Early Friends*, p. 71.

45 H. Hinds, *George Fox and Early Quaker Culture* (Manchester: Manchester University Press, 2001), p. 46.

46 C. A. Patrides, 'Introduction', in *The Cambridge Platonists*, ed. C. A. Patrides (London: Edward Arnold, 1969), p. 10. See, for example, Culvervell's comment on 'the concord that is betwixt Faith and Reason'. Nathaniel Culverwel[l], *An Elegant and Learned Discourse of the Light of Nature, With several other Treatises* (London, 1652), p. 174.

47 Culvervell, *Light of Nature*, p. 120.

48 Culvervell, *Light of Nature*, p. 45.

49 Culvervell, *Light of Nature*, p. 141.

50 This paragraph draws in particular on F. C. Beiser, *The Sovereignty of Reason: The Defence of Rationality in the Early English Enlightenment* (Princeton, N.J.: Princeton University Press, 1996); H. G. Van Leeuwen, *The Problem of Certainty in English Thought: 1630–1690* (The Hague: Martinus Nijhoff, 1963); G. R. Cragg, *Freedom and Authority: A Study in English Thought in the Early Seventeenth Century* (Philadelphia: The Westminster Press, 1975); G. Remer, *Humanism and the Rhetoric of Toleration* (University Park, P.A.: The Penn State University Press, 1996).

51 Greaves, 'The early Quakers as advocates', p. 24.
52 I. Penington, *Divine essays, Or, Considerations About Several Things in Religion Of very deep and weighty Concernment both in reference to the state of the present Times, as also of the Truth itself: With a Lamenting and Pleading Postscript* (London, 1654), p. 93.
53 Penington, *Divine essays*, p. 3.
54 Penington, *Divine essays*, p. 2. He uses reason and understanding interchangeably. See *ibid.*, p. 51.
55 Penington, *Divine essays*, p. 18.
56 He also discusses experience as a life skill: Penington, *Divine essays*, p. 34.
57 M. Abbot, *A Testimony Against the False Teachers of this Generation By one who is come from under them, unto the true Teacher and shepherd of the soul* (1659?), p. 4.
58 Penington, *Divine Essays*, p. 52.
59 See Penington, *Divine Essays*, pp. 18–20, where he writes against the Ranters. On the issue of seventeenth-century radical sects casting aspersions on contemporary sects, see Chapter 1.
60 Penington, *Divine essays*, p. 73.
61 Stubbe, *A Light Shining out of Darkness*, p. 84.
62 Hinds, *George Fox and Early Quaker Culture*, p. 30.
63 Watkins, *The Puritan Experience*, p. 126.

PART II

Radical exchanges and networks

4

~

Secular millenarianism as a radical utopian project in Shaftesbury

Patrick Müller

Shaftesbury and the concept of 'radicalism'

In Philip Kerr's mystery thriller, *Dark Matter*, a crime story set in late seventeenth-century England, Lord Ashley, MP for Poole, features as the ringleader in a dark plot 'to massacre London's Roman Catholics' eventually uncovered by Isaac Newton. According to Kerr's hero Newton, Lord Ashley is a member of the Kit-Kat Club and – consequently, the suggestion is – 'a dreadful snob' following in his grandfather's footsteps, the first Earl having been, as a member of the Green Ribbon Club, responsible for 'a number of plots to kill King Charles', among them the Popish Plot.[1] Although this fictional story about the Shaftesburys and their radical anti-Catholicism cannot be reconciled with fact even by the most daring stretch of any historian's imagination, it nevertheless provides a convenient angle from which to explore the question as to whether and in what way a new interpretation of the third Earl as a 'radical' political theorist is justifiable.

One thing is certain: this Shaftesbury was never the radical political 'activist' or plotter that Kerr makes of him. Yet as a thinker, he clearly developed a marked aversion to Roman Catholicism; for him, French Catholic absolutism embodied the very cultural evils the English nation needed at all costs to avoid. Jean Le Clerc neatly summarised the different concepts associated by Shaftesbury with the two systems of belief then at war in Western Europe, as well as the Earl's understanding of the political systems these stood for; his 'general Aim ... was to establish *Liberty* and *Virtue*, the two most valuable, most useful things, that Men can possess; his Design deserves at least, upon this account, to be applauded by all that equally hate *Slavery* and *Vice*, two things which deserve the most to be abhor'd by Mankind'.[2] What must first be considered, then, is whether the term 'radical' can be applied with any degree of precision to a man who has traditionally been regarded as an aesthete and moralist rather than as a political writer intent on promoting '*Liberty*' and averting the danger he interpreted as '*Slavery*'.

Almost twenty years ago, the seminal work of Lawrence Klein triggered a process of reinterpreting Shaftesbury's thought. Investigating the Earl's agenda as a 'political writer', Klein took his cue from Joseph Rykwert's assertion that the Earl's philosophical concerns were fundamentally 'socio-political'.[3] While Klein conceded that other aspects of the Earl's thought 'were all harnessed to a political project', he hastened to add that this project was 'far from being an exercise in Whig radicalism' but rather a 'legitimation of the post-1688 Whig regime'.[4] In Jonathan Israel's terms, however, Shaftesbury became 'a radical ideologue of the "Glorious Revolution"'.[5] What this chapter offers is a somewhat broader perspective in condensed form, a chronological survey of Shaftesbury's development as an actor on the political scene and as a political theorist. This development will show that, while the Earl was a most pragmatic politician, his mature theoretical views, as expressed in *Characteristicks*, reach beyond the confines of a mere 'legitimation of the post-1688 Whig regime'.

The term 'utopian' as used in the title of this chapter evokes those aspects of Shaftesbury's thought which do not quite fit into Klein's thesis. *Characteristicks* and its unfinished successor, *Second Characters*, are not necessarily understood here as the formulation of – to cite a widely accepted definition of radicalism — a 'political or religious vision different from that required by the state'.[6] One should keep in mind that, in its late seventeenth- and early eighteenth-century context(s), the term 'politics' was always implicitly linked to the role of the Church in the structure of government, and it is here that the Earl's peculiar form of 'radicalism' will come to the fore. What may be found in his writings is a political *and* religious 'vision' that revisits and refines central paradigms of the existing *status quo*, the intention being to turn that vision into a concrete and stable reality. Shaftesbury's idealised vision of Britain's future entailed the implementation of an enlightened cultural utopia which, he believed, was, as a Protestant strong-hold, a viable possibility for the country. At the same time, the Earl painted, in the shadiest of colours, an antithetical, dystopian version of a re-Catholicised England as a kingdom of uncultured darkness. As Manuel de Miranda has argued: 'Shaftesbury was not a democrat, yet he seemed to hold views which indicated his willingness to bring about greater reforms in government than some of his like-minded political allies.'[7] This is a view the author of this chapter would like to endorse, one which means that, although Klein's conclusions are in themselves incontrovertible, his specific focus needs to be widened.

The theoretical assumptions which inform this approach are taken from Richard Ashcraft's introduction to his book on John Locke's *Two Treatises*, the conclusions of which can, to an aston-ishing degree, also be applied to Shaftesbury's work. Like Rykwert and Klein, Ashcraft emphasises the necessary connection between political thought and the underlying social agenda as he argues, for example, that the writing of a political treatise is in itself a 'social action', that one must consider 'the nature of the intended audi-ence' of the text under examination, or that the authors' strategies of 'secrecy and deception' have to be taken into account. Above all, Ashcraft's assertion concerning 'the need to break down the rather firm dichotomy between interests and ideas' is important for the contexts considered here, as is his claim that ideology is 'not by definition a low level of philosophy; on the contrary, a philosophi-cal argument is merely one form of ideological response to those obstacles within the social life-world which inhibit the realization of [an author's] objectives'.[8] This chapter will advance, in outline, a view of Shaftesbury as a thinker whose political views alternated between an emotional zeal for a thoroughly renovated constitution and a most profound pragmatism.

A lesson in avoiding radical opposition: early political career

Although Shaftesbury is generally and correctly regarded as a Whig, his political socialisation was a complex affair. His grandfather was – as the principal wheel in the machine that ground a new, distinctively Whig ideology – one of the leading politicians of the post-Restoration era. The third Earl's biographer has suggested that Shaftesbury experienced the extent of his grandfather's influence even as a boy, and that as a pupil at Winchester College between 1683 and 1685, 'a school where strong Royalist and High Church sentiments reigned',[9] he was daily reminded of his grandfather's role as a staunch, and eventually defeated, champion of the Protestant succession. The following retrospective from a letter to his steward John Wheelock clarifies the enduring and sometimes overburdening vitality of his grandfather's political legacy: 'There is nothing on Earth wanting to me: & I have fullfilld in all respects the Injunctions of my Grandfather & have taken Care of his honour & Name & Posterity: after that ye ill usage & Ingratitude of others had made me despair, & apprehend nothing remaining but Ignominy.'[10] Without jumping to any naive psychological conclusions, if one accepts that Shaftesbury was subject to such enmity in his early youth, the stubborn persistence with which he defended some of his mature views can be more plausibly explained, especially because these Whiggish convictions were, as will be shown later, subjected to severe personal scrutiny at the beginning of his political career. Moreover, his grandfather's example could well have taught him caution when it came to expressing any views publicly and without reserve.

Klein wisely accorded the Glorious Revolution great importance for the development of Shaftesbury's views. As early as 1690, writing to his grandfather's loyal friend Thomas Stringer in the aftermath of the Battle of Beachy Head, Shaftesbury marvelled 'whether immediate death or a future state of health is to succeed this desperate operation on our Body Politick'.[11] There cannot be the shadow of a doubt that Shaftesbury inherited from his grandfather an unforgiving aversion to all things Catholic or Jacobite. He was always suspicious of the ecclesiastical establishment, and especially of High Church politics; in 1691, he gleefully commented on the arrest of Viscount Preston, one of the first Earl's old Catholic enemies, for his involvement in a plot to reinstate King James: 'wee have hetherto ye divertion to see Mother Church so Jaded & y^t whilst The Plott is not turn'd to a Whigg Plott but remains what itt is, a true Church Plott: wee may whilst that lasts sitt merry Spectatours'.[12] This clear position notwithstanding, Shaftesbury, who started his political career at the age of 24 when he entered the House of Commons as MP for Poole, was not a man necessarily influenced by the party line.

The draft Τα Πολιτικα[13] (*Of Politics*), written in Naples between January and April 1712 and probably designed as an initial draft outline for an account of his political career, shows the Earl looking in the mid-1690s for the orientation provided by political role models from both sides of the political spectrum, men who were reputed to be either 'honest' or 'Patriot-like'.[14] This means that the Whigs could not always count on strict allegiance from Shaftesbury; with regard to the Protestant succession, however, he never wavered. His loyalty to this key party policy aside, he had several bones to pick with his fellow Whigs. Even throughout the first decade of the following century, he was to refer to himself and his political friends as 'us Gentlemen of yesterday, who till the Revolution never enjoy'd any thing like Liberty'.[15] Such statements reflect his unflagging loyalty to 'the Old or Country Whigs, more particularly those who had an admiration for the Commonwealth and for its theorists'.[16] In the introduction to an edition of letters from Shaftesbury to Robert Molesworth, John Toland praises Shaftesbury's rigorous attitude towards 'Apostate-Whigs' and records how, by way of recompense, they 'gave out that he was splenetick and melancholy; whimsical and eaten up with vapors'; the Earl's 'bookish' disposition was another easy target for his enemies.[17] To make things worse, 'no government which included men such as Sir Edward Seymour (1633–1708) and, worst of all, the Earl of Danby (1631–1712), was likely to be very sympathetic to the family of the first Earl of Shaftesbury'.[18] The third Earl's own son recorded how the 'fatigues of attending regularly upon the service of the House' affected Lord Ashley's health so 'that he was obliged to decline coming again into Parliament on the Dissolution in 1698'.[19] His grandfather's shadow constantly hanging over him may have been another reason why Shaftesbury increasingly felt that he did not have the stamina necessary to survive in the political scene in London: hated by both Whigs for his constant refusal to follow the party line and Tories for his ancestry, he was in an awkward position from the day he entered parliament.[20]

On the fringes of republicanism: first political writings

This important period, lasting from May 1695 until July 1698, is unfortunately poorly documented. There are, however, two undeniable facts about these early years in Parliament: first, Shaftesbury, as has been seen, was clearly committed to the tenets of the Old Whiggism that had been developed over the last years of his grandfather's career. Second, he met and conversed with a number of men to whom the epithet 'radical' can be applied with considerably less caution, above all the ubiquitous Toland, the Whig theorist Robert Molesworth, and Walter Moyle.[21] There is ample evidence for Shaftesbury's involvement with these men.[22] The first fruit of that was his collaboration with Toland for the pamphlet *The Danger of Mercenary Parliaments*, which was published shortly before the general election in 1698. This frequently overlooked text, informed by the dichotomy not so much between Whig and Tory, but between Court and Country, with its authors endorsing the latter cause, shows numerous affinities with a host of other pamphlets published in the same year, all of which can in fact be regarded as a concerted propagandistic effort of the Country faction. These writings – they include Moyle's and John Trenchard's *Short History of Standing Armies in England* – share a Whig conception of English constitutional and monarchic history following Elizabeth's reign, and especially the years under the two latter Stuarts who were regarded as corrupters of traditional English liberties on account of the increasing influence of Roman Catholicism they were supposed to have allowed. *The Danger of Mercenary Parliaments* in fact contains a detailed reckoning with Charles II, the monarch whose dealings with the first Earl earned him the epithet 'encroaching Tyrant'.[23]

Interestingly enough, *Danger of Mercenary Parliaments* was part of an extended effort on the part of the Country Whigs to remind, in strong terms, the moderate Whig Junto, including Shaftesbury's friend Lord Somers, of its duty towards country and people. This is the first hard evidence showing that he would by no means be satisfied with *any* Whig government – rather, his assent to such a government was predicated on certain conditions the present one did not meet.[24] Another project launched by the circle to which Shaftesbury belonged was a series of new editions of classical, and classically minded, English republicanism, and by implication anti-absolutism,[25] including the writings of James Harrington, John Milton and the republican martyr Algernon Sidney, all of them edited by Toland between 1698 and 1700. Shaftesbury's correspondence offers ample evidence that he had a hand in these and that he regarded, above all, the Harrington edition as a particularly seasonable publication: 'Never could a Book have been publishd in so lucky a Time ... when you consider the late Contest of the

People of England with Nobility & Crown ... you will understand what I mean by the lucky season. For who sees not that Harrington is a Prophet & one inspir'd? if so, he is doubly divine, for his good Sence & his prophetick Spirit.'[26]

It has been argued that it was Shaftesbury, together with 'Trenchard, Molesworth, and Moyle', who 'put the Parliamentary country party on its neo-Harringtonian footing'.[27] Although the edition was, as has been pointed out, a landmark in the process of '[r]ethinking the nature of monarchy', it also 'showed readers that it was possible in 1700 to be both a republican and loyal to a virtuous monarchy', a position which, by and large, characterises Shaftesbury's own views at the time.[28]

With the imminent involvement of the English nation in the War of the Spanish Succession, the negative aspects of Shaftesbury's views became obvious. It is quite clear that he did not want, as he put it – quoting King William – in his second collaborative effort with Toland, *Paradoxes of State*, 'a Popish Prince and a French Government'.[29] This is why he broke, once and for all, with the Tories, some of whose principles he had so far endorsed when he thought them in the nation's best interest. From now on, they stood for all things Jacobite. Toland was, his volatile character notwithstanding, the obvious choice as co-author, having just published *Anglia Libera*, in which he 'reinvented republican traditions by becoming the advocate of a limited monarchy'.[30] On being informed about the publication of that text, Shaftesbury told Toland 'to preserve a Character such as becomes a Man who supports ye Cause of Religion Liberty & Vertue'.[31] The connection that is made here between religion, politics and ethics shows the three pillars Shaftesbury considered indispensable for any proper government. Note, however, that he says 'religion' rather than 'the Church'.

Paradoxes of State was written to reinforce the key speech in which King William asked Parliament for its support of the military alliance he now wished to enter against France. The speech was held on 31 December 1701; the text was published a few weeks later.[32] The general election had not brought the desired Whig majority, and support for the war was waning. From the very beginning of their joint piece, Toland and Shaftesbury made it clear that there was now 'no other real Distinction among us, but of those who are for the Protestant Religion and the present Establishment, and of those who mean a Popish Prince and a French Government', that is, the options were either a constitutional monarchy or absolutism. *Paradoxes of State* is an eminently pragmatic text, attempting to create national unity in order to promote the common cause, that is to say support for the Protestant succession. In the process, not even the Commonwealthmen are spared: 'From what we have said ... it is self-evident that all the *republican* Pretences are quite out of Doors, our *Liberty* being so fully settled, as to be *above all Danger of falling at any Time hereafter under arbitrary Power.*' The authors look back to a time when 'all the *Court*, and a great Part of the *Church*, were in direct Opposition to our civil and spiritual *Liberty*'. Now, in view of the national crisis, it was necessary to overcome those oppositions which had arisen over the past decades, namely those of '*Royalists* and *Republicans*, of the *Court* and *Country party*, of *high* and *low Churchmen*'. The attempt to unite these factions is, of course, biased; the united national front he envisions is Whiggish, favouring a Protestant succession and a Low Church establishment: 'No person in his right Wits can now continue an Enemy to the *Church* or *State* on the Principle of *Liberty*.'[33] It goes without saying that the attempt failed miserably, as these were the principal bones of contention between Whigs and Tories over the coming decades.

Between pragmatic conservatism and a radical critique of instituted religion: *Characteristicks* as a utopian text

Following the sudden death of William in 1702, Shaftesbury was forced to abandon the public political stage. He continued, however, to campaign behind the scenes. When he was not in London, several 'spies' kept him informed of all the latest developments. Moreover, he continued to finance treatises by partisan writers such as Toland or William Stephens[34] and kept in touch with the men he had met during two retreats to Holland between 1698–99 and 1703–04. In an important letter to Jan Van t'Wedde, he repeats his aversion to the notion of a commonwealth with renewed vigour, calling 'this Insinuation that the Whiggs in England think of a Common Wealth other than w^t they enjoy, or that any other is or can ever be practicable in Brittain' a 'base insinuation ... made use of by our Arbitrary Party [i.e., the High Church Tories] to poyson our princes Ear and hinder him from confiding in his People'.[35] Believing as he did in cyclical theories of history,[36] Shaftesbury was convinced both of the destructive and the self-healing powers inherent in historical processes. The Act of Union being imminent, he compared the 'fatal Growth' of the 'Roman Common-Wealth' with the situation of a united Britain which, should it decide to become a commonwealth:

> [It] wou'd immediately tread ye same fatall Path of Greatness. The Over Generouse Spiritts infus'd by Popular Government into so vast a Body so fram'd and Scituated wou'd soon, I fear, employ themselves, and give disturbance to Europe. But as we are happily contrould by the Nature of our mix'd Government, there is little danger from England or even from Brittain as formidable as we may fancy our Selves in such a *Union*. Nothing can be happyer for Europe and Mankind than that this Island shou'd in respect of Government remain as it is Constituted. Shou'd It degenerate into absolute Monarchy, Europe cou'd have no relief from it: but remaining as it is, it will retain the same Power as well as Interest to preserve ye Balance[37] ... To which of these Effects therefore will this Union probably Operate? Not to a Common Wealth surely. this is ye least Fear.[38]

In effect, this seeming inconsistency in Shaftesbury's thought, namely that he could praise Harrington's 'prophetick Spirit' and at the same time be critical of the idea of a commonwealth, cannot be attributed to any general enmity towards the notion but, more than anything else, to the practical difficulties he believed would be involved in instituting it.[39] Moreover, as Toland points out in the preface to his Harrington edition, men are frequently 'cheated by mere Names'; for the circle around Shaftesbury and Toland, the present 'mixt Form of Government' was 'already a Commonwealth' in the proper meaning of the term, it being 'a Government of Laws enacted for the common Good of all the People'.[40]

These convictions explain why, at first sight paradoxically, the avowed champion of the Glorious Revolution was critical of resistance theories:

> But such respect ought ever to be born by all Good People towards every Government that stands upon ye Foundation of Laws & has any thing that may be calld a Constitution that however unjustly things may for a while or on some particular occasion be administerd they will bear with patience those Infirmitys & occasional Corruptions & Mismanagements wch are incident to all Governments ... rather than by a sudden Zeal & Animosity ... attempt to unhinge

the Government itself & stirr up the Minds of the People against their Magistracy & settled Form wch fails not to end in Cruelty & Tyranny. For so the best Commonwealths have been converted into ye most absolute Tyrannys.[41]

This may sound like a patently conservative position, one that is identified as such in many scholarly investigations of the Whigs' attitude towards the revolution.[42]

By the time he wrote that letter, Shaftesbury had already published individually those treatises he was to collect in *Characteristicks* in the following year. *Characteristicks* required subtle rhetorical strategies, especially given the enemy Shaftesbury had now chosen for himself. The 'utopian' elements of the writings gathered there would in reality entail a change of mental attitude in his readers, one which, by way of implication, would dispense not only with all political influence of the Church, but also arguably with all instituted religion. His account of the origins and progress of religion and priesthood in *Miscellaneous Reflections*, the last text in *Characteristicks* and the only one which had not previously been published, is at the same time a propagandistic account of the clergy's perennial lust for and successive rise to power. The examples he chooses are almost invariably taken from ancient historiography, above all from Herodotus and Diodorus Siculus, in whose writings the superstitious practices of ancient Egypt and Ethiopia are juxtaposed with that of Greece.

Unsurprisingly, the former are rejected. Talking about the ecclesiastical constitution of these countries, Shaftesbury reflects on:

> the exorbitant Power of their landed Hierarchy. So true it is, 'That *Dominion* must naturally follow *Property*'. Nor is it possible, as I conceive, for any State or Monarchy to withstand the Encroachments of a growing Hierarchy, founded on the *Model* of these *Egyptian* and *Asiatick* Priesthoods. No SUPERSTITION will ever be wanting among the Ignorant and Vulgar, whilst the Able and Crafty have a power to gain Inheritances and Possessions by working on this *human Weakness*.[43]

The reference to Harrington[44] in this passage is of course not coincidental. Like Shaftesbury, Harrington regarded the ancient commonwealths with their constitutions based on the superiority of 'public interest (embodied in the pattern of ancient virtue)' as vastly superior to constitutions that encouraged the prevalence of 'private interest epitomized in the priestcraft of modern prudence'.[45] The lineage of such prudence, as sketched in *Miscellaneous Reflections*, serves the propagandistic aim of identifying any constitution which grants the Church too much power as dangerous and, consequently, illegitimate. By analogy, the Earl transfers this vision of ecclesiastical dominion and terror to his own age, portraying the High Church divines as contemporary representatives of priestcraft who attempt to secure for themselves political power, not least by means of persecuting 'enemies of faith'. In the year after the Sacheverell trials, which saw Shaftesbury implicated,[46] his patience with the Church was, then, evidently spent.

Shaftesbury's alternative is thus an enlightened project designed to counter any governmental design which includes the clergy in the political power game, a strategy which will, in his view, inevitably lead to both religious and civil strife. His remarks about 'the unnatural Union of *Religion* and *Philosophy*'[47] are reminiscent of the '*Unprosperous Alliance*'[48] between religion and government that had already been diagnosed in the preface to *Select Sermons* of the Low Church divine Benjamin Whichcote, published in 1698, probably as a companion volume to the editions of republican tracts, its purpose being to define the role of religion in government. There, Shaftesbury the pragmatist for the first time delineated the proper sphere of church dignitaries: as harbingers of an enlightened natural religion, illuminating its principles for the 'vulgar', they were meant to become interpreters of the moral order inherent in nature and, as such, stalwarts of virtue.[49] The political sphere ought, by implication, to be left to the secular powers. Absolutism with its religious justification for the monarch's unlimited power was at the other end of the scale.

A famous letter written to Lord Somers on 20 October 1705 attributes to philosopher-statesmen authority in 'discourse of ye Nature of ye Universe, ye Ends of Man, & ye Distinctions of Good and Ill'.[50] There is no real need for instituted religion in this idealistic vision. The three pillars of the state – its political leaders, an eminently rational religion and public virtue – converge in this vision of a state of 'antient Hierarchy'. However, Shaftesbury offers two possible routes which could be taken by champions of the new order: 'No wonder if the amaz'd Surveyors are for the future so apt either to conceive the horridest Aversion to all Priestly Government; or, on the contrary, to admire it, so far as even to wish a Coalescence or

Re-union with this antient *Mother*-Church.'[51] Unlike the more provocative Deist writers of his time, Shaftesbury seemed to prefer the
latter option in his published work, but it is clear that, at the very
least, he flirted with the disaster inherent in the first: it is Theocles
who, in *The Moralists*, embodies, as a philosopher-statesman and
exponent of religious enthusiasm proper, the complete secularism
to which the Earl aspired. The carefully composed private prayer
in one of Shaftesbury's notebooks underlines his unorthodoxy and
independence from devotional forms prescribed by the clergy.[52]

This observation ties in with the following conclusions about
early eighteenth-century religious radicalism: 'The power of the
Enlightenment ... lay in understanding the force of organized religion, and then searching for a set of beliefs which deists, and perhaps
even atheists of the age, could live with and accept. As I have now
come to see, the pantheism I identified in 1981 would lead in many
directions, among them the search to understand all human religiosity and to articulate a universal natural religion.'[53] We have here
the perfect antithesis to Shaftesbury's views about the High Church
clergy as he caricatured it: handmaids of absolutist tyranny, and, as
such, 'Corrupters ... of Morals & publick Principles' and 'the very
Reverse or *Antipodes* to Good Breeding Scholarship, Behaviour,
Sense & Manners'.[54] The Earl's own idealised state was a hotbed of
toleration that defied all excess:

> If modern *Visions, Prophecys,* and *Dreams, Charms, Miracles,*
> *Exorcisms,* and the rest of this kind, be comprehended in that which
> we call FANATICISM or SUPERSTITION; to this Spirit they allow a full
> Career; whilst to ingenuous Writers they afford the Liberty, on the
> other side, in a civil manner, to call in question these spiritual Feats
> perform'd in Monasterys, or up and down by their *mendicant* or
> *itinerant* Priests, and ghostly Missionarys.[55]

The references to the concept of an 'ancient constitution' implied in
Shaftesbury's remarks about 'such a spiritual Sovereignty, so extensive, antient, and of such a long Succession'[56] are much more than
a concession to the radical Whiggism he had imbibed throughout
the late 1690s.

The pragmatism with which Shaftesbury tempers the millenarian zeal[57] that informs his image of 'a Noble Man of Venice'
who 'had receiv'd a settled Government of the most perfect Laws
and Administration, of at least a thousand years past, from my

Ancestours, to be deliverd down again by me to my posterity of a thousand Years to come, or perhaps as long as the world lasts'[58] is indicative of the enthusiasm with which he wanted to embrace a secular utopia of political stability.[59] At the same time, like Neville before him, he acknowledged the far-reaching differences between Venice and England; not only had the latter seen momentous domestic changes, but it was now once more forced to participate in an international conflict with the potential to change the face of its constitution for a long time. This is why Shaftesbury had to act 'a little according to [his] Hott-spur Inclination'.[60] Most of all, he did so in *Miscellaneous Reflections* where the absolutist theorists' justifications of the universal monarchs' '*successive Right*'[61] appear as only a poor copy of that lofty concept of an ancient constitution.

This concept, which is part and parcel of Shaftesbury's under-standing of a classically minded republicanism, as mentioned above, eventually resolves the paradox of Shaftesbury's attitude towards resistance theories. The argument for the alleged conserva-tism of 'Whig justifications of the Revolution' does not take into account that 'ancient constitutionalists did argue that the politi-cal nation, through its representatives, might resist and depose a despotic ruler and settle the crown on a successor'.[62] In fact, his emphasis on this aspect explains Shaftesbury's reluctance to apply the term 'commonwealthman' to himself in public as well as the 'significant interplay of Whig and oppositional elements' in his political career;[63] as Toland wrote in his dedication to the 1700 Harrington edition, '*Those who in the late Reigns were invidi-ously nicknam'd* Commonwealthmen, *are by this time sufficiently clear'd of that Imputation by their Actions, a much better Apology than any Words: for they valiantly rescu'd our antient Government from the devouring Jaws of Arbitrary Power, and ... settl'd the Monarchy for the future ... under such wise Regulations as are most likely to continue it for ever.*'[64]

While Shaftesbury believed in cyclical theories of history, he also believed that this cycle could be broken. His true utopian vision was not so much that of a modern-day version of the Greek city states and the Roman republic, but one of secular millenarianism, that is, a government based on the principles of natural religion, '*likely to continue ... for ever*', without any need for an instituted state reli-gion. Here, Shaftesbury stands in an identifiable tradition, namely that of employing apocalyptic references to expose the ostensibly

115

destructive impact of Catholicism on the English nation, a strategy Whig propagandists had devised during the Restoration crisis.[65] This tradition is suffused throughout both the prose and iconography of *Characteristicks*, the emblematic engraving for the *Inquiry concerning Virtue, or Merit*, designed by Shaftesbury himself and eventually executed by Simon Gribelin for the second edition of *Characteristicks* (1714–15), being the most potent example. Interestingly, the *Inquiry* was the earliest of Shaftesbury's publications, the *editio princeps* appearing in November 1698, and according to a persistent myth it was Toland who had the manuscript published without the Earl's permission.[66] It is, then, certainly not a very bold hypothesis if we assume the text to be just another part of the republican project of Shaftesbury's own circle. The engraving juxtaposes a (Theist) vision of enlightened Whig rule, based on the iconography of the Roman republic, with that of an apocalyptic image of absolutist Tory rule, the 'Savage- God' standing on a pedestal and wielding his weapons to subdue the populace, the 'Mouth of *Hell*' in the form of a Hobbesian, and by implication absolutist, leviathan opening at his back.[67]

In *Characteristicks*, however, such visions were again held in check by Shaftesbury's *realpolitik*. In cases of instability and civil unrest he left the backdoor open for the very practices he detested so much. When Shaftesbury says that the representatives of a polite culture 'may even persecute with a tolerable Grace',[68] this reveals the doubts he had about the practicability of his vision.

The utopian element in *Characteristicks* sees Shaftesbury envisioning an enlightened constitution to be implemented after the end of the War of the Spanish Succession, but at the same time it is constrained by the realities Shaftesbury experienced in that decisive period of British history. As a utopia proper, his is a statement of possibilities, not of fact. Writing in a Harringtonian 'propethick Spirit',[69] a fitting religious image which captures his ideal of the philosopher as the true 'priest', Shaftesbury offered a radical political vision, one which his *Second Characters* were meant to complement with the account of a Whig cultural revolution that 'will make *united* BRITAIN the principal Seat of Arts' based on the '*Virtuoso*-Science'to be spelled out in the treatises the project was to contain.[70] Whenever he allowed his imagination, like that of Theocles, to soar beyond the close confines of his own pragmatism, the utopian elements of his thought opened the possibility

of a more thoroughgoing change to the post-revolutionary constitution, especially with regard to the ecclesiastical establishment.
These aspects of Shaftesbury's philosophy add a new dimension
to the conservative civic humanist who 'replaced a king and his
priests with an oligarchy of nobles',[71] the very tension between his
conservatism and progressivism being contained in the expression
'replaced'. In the end, however, it seems that Shaftesbury thought
the time was not yet ripe for the radical implications of his thought,
which is why these are constantly counterbalanced by a contrary
impulse.[72] In ecclesiastical terms, his 'radicalism' was intended, in
the true sense of the word, as 'a thoroughgoing transformation of
a system, a set of ideas or practices, from the "root" upwards';[73]
however, the set of ideas is merely a 'design'[74] for a universal, anti-
dogmatic and eminently aesthetic religion practised and taught by
philosopher-statesmen. The principal hindrance to implementing
this design were those people Shaftesbury called 'the vulgar'. Their
need for spiritual guidance could only be catered for by a pragmatic
approach which acknowledged the usefulness of the (Low Church)
clergy.

In the broader context of the Earl's political theory, the term
'radicalism', used here to mean 'merely one form of ideological
response to those obstacles within the social life-world which inhibit
the realization of [a writer's and his audience's] objectives',[75] allows
one to see that this is exactly the tension which prevented the buds
of his radical ideas from opening. '[F]or my own part', Shaftesbury
wrote to John Molesworth in the year before his death, 'I am ...
contented with the present Ballance of Power in our Nation, and
with the Authority and Prerogative of the Crown.'[76] Yet driven to
their logical conclusion, his ideas clearly imply a secular constitution in which there is no need for a set of church dignitaries. Given
the state of affairs, however, Shaftesbury was not convinced that
his audience, shaped as it was by the ideological warfare of the
preceding decades, was already prepared to implement ideals which
would, he envisaged, eventually 'bring not Europe only but ... in
a Manner the whole World under one Community; or at least to
such a Correspondence, and Intercourse of good Offices and mutual
Succour, as may render it a more *humane World* than it was ever
known, and carry the Interest of human Kind to a greater Hight
than ever'.[77]

The exit of the '*secular* GENTLEMAN' at the end of *Miscellaneous*

Reflections, 'politely' quitting the scene but hoping to hear more from his Tory antagonists, hints simultaneously to the reader that this utopian discourse is by no means over and thus creates the most challenging of the various 'philosophical fictions' contained in *Characteristicks*.[78]

Notes

1 P. Kerr, *Dark Matter: The Private Life of Sir Isaac Newton* (New York, N.Y.: Three Rivers Press, 2002), pp. 289–90, 299.

2 J. Le Clerc, *Monsieur Le Clerc's Extract and Judgment of the Characteristicks of Men, Manners, Opinions, Times, in Three Volumes. Translated from the French of the XIXth, XXIst and XXIIId Tomes of the Bibliotheque choisie* (London: Egbert Sanger, 1712), p. 72.

3 J. Rykwert, *The First Moderns: The Architects of the Eighteenth Century* (Cambridge, M.A.; London: The MIT Press, 1980), p. 156.

4 L. E. Klein, *Shaftesbury and the Culture of Politeness: Moral Discourse and Cultural Politics in Early Eighteenth-Century England* (Cambridge; New York, N.Y.: Cambridge University Press, 1994), p. 1.

5 J. Israel, *Radical Enlightenment: Philosophy and the Making of Modernity 1650–1750* (Oxford: Oxford University Press, 2001), p. 67. The author of this chapter does not wish to elide the differences between the approaches of Klein and Israel; in fact, their readings differ quite fundamentally, Israel, unlike Klein, insisting on the radical potential of Shaftesbury's thought. Unfortunately, he has so far not made it quite clear why he wishes to see this tag attached to *Characteristicks*, a lack which, it is hoped, will be remedied in Professor Israel's forthcoming contribution, carrying the working title 'Shaftesbury as a pre-eminent Enlightenment Thinker,' to the proceedings to emerge from the 2015 Shaftesbury conference at St Giles's House.

6 T. Morton and N. Smith, 'Introduction', in T. Morton and N. Smith (eds), *Radicalism in British Literary Culture, 1650–1830* (Cambridge: Cambridge University Press, 2002), pp. 1–2.

7 M. L. de Miranda, 'The Moral, Social and Political Thought of the Third Earl of Shaftesbury, 1671–1713: Unbelief and Whig Republicanism in the Early Enlightenment' (PhD dissertation, University of Cambridge, 1995), p. 230.

8 R. Ashcraft, *Revolutionary Politics and Locke's Two Treatises on Government* (Princeton, N.J.: Princeton University Press, 1986), pp. 11, 6, 9, 10, 7.

9 R. B. Voitle, *The Third Earl of Shaftesbury, 1671–1713* (Baton Rouge, L.A. and London: Louisiana State University Press, 1984), p. 15.

10 The National Archives, Kew (hereafter TNA), PRO 30/24/21/178, Lord Shaftesbury to Wheelock, Part 1, 25 August 1709, fol. 97v. See also a much earlier letter to Thomas Stringer where Shaftesbury, aged 18, writes explicitly about 'some most inveterate Enemy's'; TNA, PRO 30/24/21/229, Lord Shaftesbury to Thomas Stringer, 10 December 1689, fols 294–5.

11 Hampshire Record Office, Winchester (hereafter HRO), 9M73/G238/4, Malmesbury Papers, Shaftesbury to Thomas Stringer, 3 July 1690.

12 HRO, 9M73/G238/3, Malmesbury Papers, Shaftesbury to Thomas Stringer, 17 February 1691.

13 TNA, PRO 30/24/24/13, Rider's British Merlin Almanac for 1713, pp. 98–103. For an interpretation, see Klein, *Shaftesbury and the Culture of Politeness*, p. 131.

14 See also John Cropley's remark that 'you must know Ld Hallyfax believes ye late Ld Sunderland was ye Cause of ye not going in the mob Whig way when you were in ye house of Commons': TNA, PRO 30/24/20/134, Part 2, May 1707 fol. 339v.

15 TNA, PRO 30/24/22/4, Shaftesbury to Sir John Cropley, 22 February 1708, fol. 312r.

16 Voitle, *Third Earl of Shaftesbury*, p. 70; see also H. Horwitz, *Parliament, Policy and Politics in the Reign of William III* (Manchester: Manchester University Press, 1977), p. 216.

17 *Letters from the Right Honourable the late Earl of Shaftesbury, to Robert Molesworth, Esq., Now the Lord Viscount of that Name. With Two Letters written by the late Sir John Cropley*, ed. John Toland, 1st edn: 1700 (London: W. Wilkins, 1721), p. viii.

18 Voitle, *Third Earl of Shaftesbury*, p. 51.

19 TNA, PRO 30/24/21/225, rough draught of the life of the third Earl of Shaftesbury by his son, fol. 260r.

20 See the account in Voitle, *Third Earl of Shaftesbury*, p. 77. See also Shaftesbury to Robert Molesworth, 4 November 1708: '[E]ach of [the two parties] enflam'd against me, particularly one, because of my birth and principles; the other, because of my pretended Apostacy, which was only adhering to those principles on which their party was founded', *Letters from the Right Honourable the late Earl of Shaftesbury*, ed. Toland, p. 13.

21 For this 'two-tiered body of Whig critics' as a chimera of radical 'Calves-Head Whigs' and 'Aristocratic or Roman Whigs', see Klein, *Shaftesbury and the Culture of Politeness*, pp. 137–8. Klein refers to A. B. Worden's important introduction to his edition of Edmund Ludlow's *A Voyce from the Watch Tower* (London: Royal Historical Society, 1978), pp. 39–42.

22 In the 1700s, Shaftesbury fell out with some of his former associates:

see Shaftesbury, *Askêmata*, p. 358, and Klein, *Shaftesbury and the Culture of Politeness*, p. 138. All references to the Earl's writings will be to the *Standard Edition: Complete Works, Selected Letters and Posthumous Writings*, eds Wolfram Benda *et al.* (Stuttgart-Bad Cannstatt: Frommann-Holzboog, 1981–2015). Numerals in square brackets refer to page numbers in the 1714–15 edition of the *Characteristicks*. The treatises are: *Miscellaneous Reflections* (I 2); *A Letter concerning Design* (I 5); *Inquiry concerning Virtue, or Merit* (II 2); the *Preface* to Whichcote's *Select Sermons* (II 4); *Askêmata* (II 6).

23 *The Danger of Mercenary Parliaments* (London, 1698), p. 2.

24 For the 'unlikely consonance of radical Whig and Tory voices of criticism', see Morton and Smith, 'Introduction', in Morton and Smith (eds), *Radicalism*, p. 9.

25 Shaftesbury was particularly indebted to Sidney's concept of virtue and to Harrington's as well as Robert Molesworth's exposition of ancient republicanism; see P. Müller, 'Rewriting the divine right theory for the Whigs: the political implications of Shaftesbury's attack on the doctrine of futurity in his *Characteristicks*', in M. Hansen and J. Klein (eds), *Great Expectations: Futurity in the Long Eighteenth Century* (Frankfurt: Peter Lang, 2012), pp. 67–88.

26 HRO, 9M73/G238/12, Malmesbury Papers, Shaftesbury to Thomas Stringer, 22 April 1700.

27 See de Miranda, 'The Moral, Social and Political Thought of the Third Earl of Shaftesbury', p. 207. See also C. Robbins, *The Eighteenth-Century Commonwealthman: Studies in the Transmission, Development, and Circumstance of English Liberal Thought from the Restoration of Charles II until the War with the Thirteen Colonies* (Cambridge, M.A.: Harvard University Press, 1959), pp. 6–7. On resurgent manifestations of radicalism, see the contention advanced in the Introduction in this volume.

28 J. Champion, *Republican Learning: John Toland and the Crisis of Christian Culture, 1696–1722* (Manchester; New York, N.Y.: Manchester University Press, 2003), pp. 109–10. See also Voitle, *The Third Earl of Shaftesbury*, p. 76.

29 *Paradoxes of State, Relating to the Present Juncture of Affairs in England, and the Rest of Europe; Chiefly Grounded on His Majesty's Princely, Pious and Most Gracious Speech* (London: Bernard Lintott, 1702), p. 4.

30 Champion, *Republican Learning*, p. 117. See TNA, PRO 30/24/20/28, Part 1, Toland to Shaftesbury, 19 July 1701 NS, fols 63–4.

31 TNA, PRO 30/24/21, Part 2, 21 July 1701, fol. 324r.

32 Shaftesbury distributed the pamphlet among his Dutch friends; see his

letter to Benjamin Furley: TNA, PRO 30/24/20/55, Part 1, 30 January 1702, fol. 136r.

33 *Paradoxes of State*, pp. 3–4.

34 See J. A. Downie, 'William Stephens and the *Letter to the Author of the Memorial of the State of England* reconsidered', *Bulletin of the Institute of Historical Research*, 50:122 (1977), 253–9.

35 TNA, PRO 30/24/22/2, 17 January 1706, fols 171v–172r.

36 See *Askêmata*, p. 159, note 1.

37 For the Harringtonian sources of the notion of a 'balance' of power, see *The Oceana and Other Works of James Harrington*, ed. John Toland (London: A. Millar, 1737), p. 250.

38 TNA, PRO 30/24/22/4, 29 November 1706, fols 357v–358r.

39 See also Toland's remarks about Harrington's conception of a commonwealth in his 'Life of James Harrington': 'HARRINGTON had demonstrated in his Book, that no commonwealth could be so easily or perfectly establish'd as one by a sole Legislator, it being in his power … to set up a Government in the whole piece at once, and in perfection; but an Assembly, being of better Judgment than Invention, generally make patching work in forming a Government, and are whole Ages about that which is seldom or never brought by 'em to any perfection', *Oceana and Other Works of James Harrington*, ed. Toland, p. xx.

40 *Oceana and Other Works of James Harrington*, ed. Toland, p. viii.

41 TNA, PRO 30/24/21/183, Part 1, Shaftesbury to Benjamin Furley, 22 May 1710, fol. 107v. See de Miranda, 'The Moral, Social and Political Thought of the Third Earl of Shaftesbury', p. 258.

42 See J. Greenberg, 'The confessor's laws and the radical face of the Ancient Constitution', *English Historical Review*, 104:412 (1989), 611–37.

43 *Miscellaneous Reflections*, p. 76 [49].

44 See James Harrington: '*Domestick Empire* is founded upon *Dominion*. Dominion is Property reall or personall; that is to say, in Lands, or in money and goods', *Oceana* (London, 1656), p. 4. The edition in Shaftesbury's library may be found at: www.dozenten.anglistik.phil. uni-erlangen.de/shaftesbury/rr_engfrit.html#h (accessed 29 August 2015).

45 J. Champion, *The Pillars of Priestcraft Shaken: The Church of England and Its Enemies, 1660–1730* (Cambridge: Cambridge University Press, 1992), p. 203. See *Oceana and Other Works of James Harrington*, ed. Toland, p. 37.

46 Six passages from the *Letter concerning Enthusiasm* (1708) were, without naming the author, quoted during the trials; see *Collections of Passages Referr'd to by Dr. Henry Sacheverell in his Answer to the Articles of his Impeachment* (London, 1710), pp. 22, 27.

47 *Miscellaneous Reflections*, p. 106 [80].

48 *Preface*, p. 50.

49 See Klein, *Shaftesbury and the Culture of Politeness*, p. 155. However, this stance only captures the 'official' point of view offered by Shaftesbury to the uninitiated reader.

50 TNA, PRO 30/24/22/4, fol. 285v.

51 *Miscellaneous Reflections*, p. 118 [93].

52 See *Standard Edition* II 6, pp. 532–41.

53 M. C. Jacob, 'The nature of early eighteenth-century religious radicalism', *Republics of Letters: A Journal for the Study of Knowledge, Politics, and the Arts*, 1 (2009), http://arcade.stanford.edu/rofl/nature-early-eighteenth-century-religious-radicalism (accessed 29 August 2015).

54 TNA, PRO 30/24/22/4, Shaftesbury to Lord Somers, 30 March 1711, fol. 356r.

55 *Miscellaneous Reflections*, pp. 116–18 [92–3].

56 *Miscellaneous Reflections*, p. 118 [93].

57 For a discussion of Harrington's alleged millenarianism, see Champion, *Pillars of Priestcraft Shaken*, pp. 199–201.

58 TNA, PRO 30/24/22/4, Shaftesbury to Sir John Cropley, 22 February 1708, fol. 312r.

59 Such references to Venice were of course commonplace in Republican literature. Harrington visited Venice in the 1630s and begins his *Oceana* with an appraisal of this republic which, as the only commonwealth after the decline of the Roman Empire that managed to escape 'the hands of the *Barbarians*, by virtue of its impregnable Situation, has had its ey [sic] fix'd upon antient Prudence, and is attain'd to a perfection even beyond the Copy', *Oceana and Other Works of James Harrington*, ed. Toland, p. 37. See also Henry Neville, *Plato redivivus, or, A Dialogue concerning Government, wherein … an Endeavour is Used to Discover the Present Politick Distemper* (London, 1681), p. 24, where the English gentleman praises the Venetian government as 'the only School in the World, that breeds such Physicians [of State]' which accounts for 'the admirable Stability and Duration of your Government, which hath lasted above twelve hundred years entire and perfect'. The edition cited was in Shaftesbury's library: see www.dozenten.anglistik.phil.uni-erlangen.de/shaftesbury/rr_engfrit.html#n (accessed 29 August 2015).

60 TNA, PRO 30/24/22/4, Shaftesbury to Sir John Cropley, 22 February 1708, fol. 312r.

61 *Miscellaneous Reflections*, p. 118 [94].

62 Greenberg, 'The confessor's laws', p. 613.

63 Klein, *Shaftesbury and the Culture of Politeness*, p. 132.

64 *Oceana and Other Works of James Harrington*, ed. Toland, p. vii.

65 W. E. Burns, 'A Whig Apocalypse: astrology, millenarianism, and politics in England during the Restoration crisis, 1678–1683', in J. E. Force and R. H. Popkin (eds), *Millenarianism and Messianism in Early Modern European Culture*, 4 vols (Dordrecht: Kluwer Academic Publications, 2001), vol. 3: *The Millenarian Turn: Millenarian Contexts of Science, Politics, and Everyday Anglo-American Life in the Seventeenth and Eighteenth Centuries*, pp. 29–41. In this context, Burns points out the significance of the first Earl to whom much of the literature in question was dedicated, p. 30. The concept of 'secular millenarianism' can be connected to the term 'civil religion' used by Mark Goldie to describe Harrington's take on religion. 'Civil religion' is based on a 'Christian-classical eclecticism', and in Harrington (as in Shaftesbury) '[t]he ideal of Christian liberty needed the idea of the Godly civil *imperium*'. See 'The civil religion of James Harrington', in Anthony Pagden (ed.), *The Languages of Political Theory in Early Modern Europe* (Cambridge: Cambridge University Press, 1990 [1987]), pp. 197–224.

66 See the fourth Earl's biography of his father: TNA, PRO 30/24/21, fol. 226. A. B. Worden's suggestion that Toland's editorial interference was far more substantial than hitherto supposed can, at least so far, neither be proved nor discarded: *A Voyce from the Watch Tower, Part Five: 1660–1662*, ed. A. B. Worden, pp. 24, 28–9.

67 'Mouth of *Hell*' appears in *Instructions*, p. 218. See P. Müller, 'Rewriting the divine right theory for the Whigs', p. 85.

68 *Miscellaneous Reflections*, p. 118 [94].

69 For interpretations of Shaftesbury's neo-Harringtonianism, see Klein, *Shaftesbury and the Culture of Politeness*, p. 151, and Champion, *Pillars of Priestcraft Shaken*, pp. 213–18.

70 *Letter concerning Design*, pp. 44 [398], 56 [409].

71 R. Paulson, *The Beautiful, Novel, and Strange: Aesthetics and Heterodoxy* (Baltimore, M.D.: The Johns Hopkins University Press, 1996), p. 4. See Klein's remark that 'Shaftesbury was addressing a context in which mixed constitution and oligarchical politics coincided', *Shaftesbury and the Culture of Politeness*, p. 150.

72 For the conflict, see Morton and Smith, 'Introduction', in Morton and Smith (eds), *Radicalism*, p. 15.

73 Morton and Smith, 'Introduction', in Morton and Smith (eds), *Radicalism*, p. 1.

74 Paulson, *The Beautiful, Novel, and Strange*, p. 3.

75 Ashcraft, *Revolutionary Politics*, p. 7.

76 TNA, PRO 30/24/23/929, March 1712, fol. 98r.

77 TNA, PRO 30/24/27/23, Shaftesbury to James Stanhope, 3 November 1709, fols 7v–8r.

78 *Miscellaneous Reflections*, p. 404 [343]. See P. Müller, '"The able Designer, who feigns in behalf of Truth": Shaftesbury's philosophical poetics', in P. Müller and C. Jackson-Holzberg (eds), *'New Ages, New Opinions': Shaftesbury in his World and Today* (Frankfurt: Peter Lang, 2014), pp. 239–60.

5

~

The diffusion and impact of Baron d'Holbach's texts in Great Britain, 1765–1800

Nick Treuherz

The idea of radical thinkers secretly plotting the overthrow of civilisation as we know it is not confined to our present age. In 1797, John Robison's *Proofs of a Conspiracy against All the Religions and Governments of Europe* explicitly named Mirabaud, supposedly the author of the *Système de la Nature* (1770), as one of the principal proofs in this 'Conspiracy'. Three years later, W. H. Reid's exposé of anti-religious groups in London, *The Rise and Dissolution of the Infidel Societies in this Metropolis* (1800), also picked out this author 'Mirabaud' as a dangerous proponent of atheistic materialism, whose texts were circulating in the capital.[1] Mirabaud was one of a number of pseudonyms used by Paul Henri Thiry, Baron d'Holbach (1723–89), France's foremost atheist in the Enlightenment period. His works were published either anonymously or under pseudonyms – Bernier, Boulanger and Mirabaud – which were usually retained when they were translated into other languages, despite the French reception usually having already ascertained that this was an attempt at anonymity, without managing to unmask the true author. In any case, d'Holbach's texts were frequently banned and burned in France.[2]

In 1799, James Thomson published *The Rise, progress, and consequences, of the new opinions and principles lately introduced into France; with observations* in order to shed light on the dangerous ideas circulating in France. Thomson mentioned the texts *Le Bon Sens*, *Le Militaire philosophe* and *L'Imposture sacerdotale*, in which 'the most odious opinions were delivered'.[3] These French titles, all now known to be by d'Holbach, were offered as proof that the 'corruption of the common people was attempted chiefly by the publication of immoral and impious books'.[4] The subtext is clear: these texts should not be permitted to cause similar problems in Great Britain. Yet to believe Robison and Reid, it was too late. They claimed that texts now attributed to d'Holbach were the subject of abundant underground reading. Robison's and Reid's claims that the *Système de la Nature* was being read by clandestine organisations, intent on instituting its atheist and republican maxims, will here be investigated in order to analyse the extent to which his texts were read in Great Britain before 1800. D'Holbach's undoubted influence on Great Britain has largely been neglected by scholars since Robison's and Reid's claims. What can be known of this underground reading will be considered, apart from the rhetoric and the potentially arbitrary naming by Reid and Robison. A diffusionist study will be attempted to account for the circulation of d'Holbach's text, by tracing the evidence in material bibliography, using new methodology drawn from work in the digital humanities. D'Holbach also maintained a diverse network of British acquaintances, and discussed his works with the likes of Wilkes, Hume and Shelburne. This chapter will also consider how this could have influenced the reactions of British literary circles to the scandalous reputation of his works, using evidence from the periodical press, private correspondence and publishers' catalogues. Rationalist dissenters such as John Jebb, Joseph Priestley and William Godwin were instrumental in bringing d'Holbach's ideas to a wider audience, and should be considered as *passeurs*, or actors of cultural transfer.[5] This will provide insight into the differences and similarities of British and French notions of radicalism. There is, after all, no particularly evident assonance between dissenting rationalism and d'Holbach's atheism, aside from their claim to use reason as a basis for belief. So how did these radical French ideas fare on the radical scene within the British religious context?

This study will be divided into three sections: first, a study of bibliographical data in terms of translations, sales, circulation of, and press reactions to, d'Holbach's works; second, an examination of the possible involvement of d'Holbach himself in the circulation of his works in Britain, as suggested by his relationship with a network of British radicals; third, an analysis of how d'Holbach's ideas were talked about in the published works, correspondence, diaries and marginalia of a range of British philosophers, which demonstrate varying levels of engagement, endorsement, refutation and influence. This chapter will end with a discussion of the first English translation of the *Système de la Nature*, by William Hodgson, a member of London Corresponding Society, whose 1795 edition proved so popular that a second edition was printed in 1797.

The diffusion of d'Holbach's texts: bibliographical data

The first phase of d'Holbach's literary career consisted of radicalising manuscripts of the deceased Frenchman Boulanger and translating English works by the likes of John Toland, John Trenchard and Thomas Gordon.[6] D'Holbach had met Wilkes at Leiden in their university days and they were very close.[7] The Baron also received many British visitors at his biweekly philosophical dinners in Paris, such as Adam Smith, David Hume, Laurence Sterne and David Garrick.[8] D'Holbach travelled to England in 1765, departing in a fit of enthusiasm for what he considered was a politically superior nation, only to return unhappy with the reality: 'mécontent de sa contrée'[9] (unhappy with his country). Between 1766 and 1769, d'Holbach was behind fifteen publications, eight of which were translations from English texts.[10] The *Catalogue des livres de la bibliothèque de feu M. le Baron d'Holbach* contains masses of English books.[11] There is, therefore, an uncontested and veritable influence of British radicalism on d'Holbach's philosophical output. The author's concern, however, is the inverse: how did d'Holbach's ideas and production influence his British readers? To what extent were his texts known?

The archives of one of Europe's most important printers and booksellers, the *Société Typographique de Neuchatel* (STN), show that of the 2,973 copies of books by d'Holbach sold by the Swiss wholesaler, none went directly to Great Britain.[12] This does not mean that none of d'Holbach's texts came to Great Britain directly from other printers, however, as we know that the *Système de la Nature* was printed first by Marc-Michel Rey and then pirated all over Europe.[13] Nor does it mean that British booksellers did not purchase the books via intermediaries. This 'negative' result does not prove that the reading of d'Holbach's texts has been exaggerated, as the following evidence shows. Though one should neither dismiss Robison or Reid as sources, nor take them as accurate reflections of the reception of d'Holbach's works, this chapter aims to use a diffusionist methodology to assess just how much impact the original texts by d'Holbach could have had in Great Britain. Jeroom Vercruysse's *Bibliographie descriptive des écrits du Baron d'Holbach* lists five pre-1800 editions of English translations of works attributed to d'Holbach.[14] Of these, two were translated and printed in the United States of America, and the very rare 1799 edition of *Ecce homo! A critical inquiry into the History of Jesus-Christ* does not help to gauge its impact before its reprint in 1813.[15] The two remaining translations are two editions of the translation of d'Holbach's most famous text, the *Système de la Nature*. This English translation was first published in 1795 and then again in 1797.[16] Given this relative lack of translations, it is fair to say that d'Holbach cannot have been very widely read in Britain prior to 1795, for it would have been in the French original. How can one measure the impact of his various texts on radicalism in Great Britain?

To answer this question, one must first decide which texts he wrote, given that his name appeared on no title page in his lifetime. Though he occupied a central place in the social life of eighteenth-century French philosophy, d'Holbach was totally anonymous in his productions. To overcome this difficulty, the findings of Vercruysse's *Bibliographie descriptive des écrits du Baron d'Holbach* have been used, and accepted, to differentiate between original works authored by d'Holbach and collaborative works, translations, or texts edited by d'Holbach.[17] The first two of Vercruysse's list have not been considered due to their incongruence with the rest of d'Holbach's philosophical corpus.[18] This leaves us with a corpus of fourteen texts.

An indicative answer to the question of circulation can be acquired by looking at the diffusion of d'Holbach's various texts using methodology made available by technological advances. The massive sources of data available through 'Google Books', 'Eighteenth Century Collections Online' (ECCO) and the British Library's '17th and 18th Century Burney Collection Newspapers' may be used in order to show when and by whom d'Holbach's texts were mentioned. By inputting into these three databases the titles of the texts and the names of the various pseudonyms d'Holbach's texts were published under, an impression of the discourse which surrounded these texts in Great Britain may be established.

There are, however, some limitations to this methodology which must be acknowledged. First, it relies on a text which gives information on the diffusion having been digitised in the ECCO or Google Books collections and thus on a necessarily incomplete and transitory corpus. Furthermore, it relies on the Optical Character Recognition (OCR) technology being sufficiently developed to find the search terms entered. Such data can, therefore, only be as reliable as the technology. In gathering the data presented here, there were several occasions when results were found by manually browsing in texts which had given different results, but when the term which should have given these 'accidental' results was entered, the data did not appear. The technology is, therefore, limited.[19] However, these limitations do not alter the disclaimer that the results can only ever be indicative. No methodology is capable of providing exhaustive details of circulation of books in this period.

To establish the data used for this study, the titles of 'original' works attributed to d'Holbach were entered as set out above, that is to say the texts he published as translations were disregarded. Filtering the results by language (English), and by date (1765 to 1800), provided results which required checking to determine their relevance, given that a search for 'Système de la Nature' could produce results for a book with the same title written by Maupertuis; searches for Mirabaud and Boulanger give texts actually written by those authors (not to mention bakery-related results); and terms like 'Bon Sens' – also the title of a book by Jean-Baptiste de Boyer, Marquis d'Argens – and 'Morale universelle' are not limited to the titles of books.

These verified results were then divided into five categories: sale catalogues, both for sale by booksellers, or auctioneers selling the libraries of the deceased; reviews in periodicals (review); mentions in reviews of other works (journal secondary mention); mentions in secondary literature; and newspaper mentions (Burney collection advertisements). These advertised sales are obviously to be taken as indicative of the general circulation of d'Holbach's various anonymous books.[20]

D'Holbach as an author did not 'exist' in the eighteenth century because all his works were published under pseudonyms or anonymously, given the danger of publishing atheistic or anti-establishment texts in absolutist France. While it is perhaps anachronistic to consider all d'Holbach's works as a common corpus produced by a single author, in historical terms there is, nevertheless, a validity and coherence in doing so, in that it allows a snapshot of how anonymity functioned in terms of diffusion. Without a 'name' or reputation, there was naturally less interest in the latest book by the author of the infamous *Système de la Nature*, for example. Of course, very few people knew the identity of d'Holbach as the author of these texts prior to his death. However, it will be interesting to know if any of his British acquaintances seemed to be any more aware of it, and what correlation there is between d'Holbach's correspondents and the holdings of their libraries. The results also throw up some caveats in terms of our anachronistic treatment of the works of d'Holbach as a unitary corpus. In Great Britain, there were multiple errors in the passage of French literary news. Boulanger is sometimes misspelt as Boullanger, some journalists confused Mirabaud with his homophone Mirabeau (Honoré Gabriel Riqueti, comte de Mirabeau, 1749–91); the *Système de la Nature* was attributed variously to Denis Diderot and Claude Adrien Helvétius, as it was in France. Therefore, care must be taken when analysing results.

The mere mention of a book can hide the context in which it is talked about. Searching digitally will bring up mention of d'Holbach's corpus when an English journalist is discussing the publication of the English translation of the *Works* of the Prussian King Frederick the Great, who wrote against the *Système de la Nature*. This type of result has been retained because it shows that the work's title circulated in the British press, which could have led to a curious reader tracking down this book. It is of course not qualitatively the same as Priestley writing about the text in depth, or indeed a catalogue offering the work for sale. For this reason, the results have been divided into five types.

Of the fourteen texts in d'Holbach's corpus, twelve have been retained, because there were no results for the *Histoire critique de Jésus-Christ* (1770) or *Le Tableau des Saints* (1770).[21] In total, there are 121 different instances of references to titles we now know to be written by d'Holbach. There are nine reviews in British journals. There were thirty-nine sale catalogues, selling fifty-five titles. There are thirty-two mentions in other literature and nine mentions in journals where the d'Holbach text is not the principal subject of review. Newspapers carried seventeen advertisements for books by d'Holbach, fifteen of which were for translations of the *Système de la Nature*. D'Holbach is named in none of these instances. By arranging this data into graphic form, one can see that the most talked about text was – unsurprisingly given its prominence in the Enlightenment – *Le Système de la Nature*, which has been established by Robert Darnton, who also tells us that d'Holbach was the second highest selling author in the period, including works he published in collaboration.[22] Also, it shows that all of his different texts were reviewed in English-language journals after the *Histoire Critique de Jésus-Christ*. We can see that there is no systematic infiltration by d'Holbach's texts, which is particularly evident from the *Éthocratie*, which garnered very little reaction: one single review.

D'Holbach and his British contacts

To these digital results can be added piecemeal evidence by, for example, checking the library holdings of canonical figures, when these are available. Given d'Holbach's friendship with Hume, the catalogue of the latter's personal library has been consulted, revealing that Hume possessed both the *Système de la Nature* and the *Système Social*.[23] The question arises whether Hume's friendship with d'Holbach from his visits to Paris was such that he knew that d'Holbach lay behind the various pseudonyms and anonymity of his texts. There are intriguing clues that some English friends knew about d'Holbach's publication activities. It is of course at this point that the distinction between the original writings of d'Holbach and his work as an editor and publicist for manuscripts by Boulanger, Fréret and others becomes less important. What sense of a radical network was there between d'Holbach and his British acquaintances?

John Wilkes's library was subject to two sales, one in 1764 and after his death in 1802, with the first sale catalogue revealing that he owned copies of *Recherches sur l'origine du despotisme oriental* and the *Dissertation sur Elie et Enoch*. The 1802 sale catalogue lists the *Théologie Portative, Boulanger sur Elie et Enoch, Examen Critique de St. Paul, le Bon-Sens, le Christianisme Dévoilé*, and the *Éléments de la morale universelle, ou Catéchisme de la nature*.[24] Wilkes, d'Holbach's closest English friend, actually had one edition of *Recherches sur l'origine du despotisme oriental* printed on his private press in Westminster.[25] Kors also states that Wilkes regularly attended the Baron's philosophical dinners, and was thus known to what Rousseau termed 'd'Holbach's Coterie'.[26] Indeed, the thesis that Wilkes knew about d'Holbach's philosophical output is strengthened by a letter from Wilkes's correspondence with his daughter, to whom he wrote in November 1765: 'The baron and I are more intimate than ever.'[27]

In the little correspondence which remains from d'Holbach, there is a letter to Hume from August 1763 in which d'Holbach mentions a book he is sending with the letter:

> These sentiments have emboldened me to send formerly, though unknown to you, the work you are mentioning to me. I thought you were the best judge of such a performance. [...] However, my late friend's book has appeared since, and there is even an edition of it lately done in England; I believe it will be relished by the friends of truth, who like to see vulgar errors struck at the root.[28]

D'Holbach is here hinting at his role in the wave of anticlerical texts which are published under the pseudonym of Boulanger. In another letter, sent to Hume in March 1766, he lets the Scotsman know that a text is on its way to England from the printer Marc-Michel Rey in Amsterdam: 'We have no News in the republick of letters. The Dutch have Sent, very likely, to Engelland Some copies of Boulanger's *Antiquité dévoilée* in 3 vol, which you have read in manuscript.'[29] This slightly coded missive shows that d'Holbach had shown Boulanger's manuscript to Hume and that he was keen to share his literary success. Now that the publication was complete, he told Hume that it was available, and that he was thus responsible for the publication. This letter, from 1766, was written just prior to the publication of the bulk of texts in d'Holbach's campaign, yet other similar clues like this are absent from his correspondence. There is nevertheless evidence that Hume would have been perfectly aware of the extent of d'Holbach's radical materialistic atheism. In Diderot's letters to Sophie Volland, he recounts Hume declaring to d'Holbach, in the company of eighteen visitors to d'Holbach's *salon*, that he has never met an atheist in his life, to which the Baron replied: 'Monsieur, comptez combien nous sommes ici. Il n'est pas malheureux de vous montrer quinze du premier coup. Les trois autres ne savent qu'en penser'[30] (Sir, count how many we are in this room. I can show you fifteen to start with. The other three have not made up their minds). There were, therefore, some privileged routes of access for news of d'Holbach's books to cross the Channel. However, the dangerous nature of the content of these texts seems to have prohibited d'Holbach from sharing his secret with more than an extremely restricted number of privileged associates.[31] Indeed, in a letter to Wilkes in December 1767, d'Holbach suggests that some of his texts may be easier to find in England than in Paris, where the restrictions on publishing and bookselling prevented easy access.[32] He wrote: 'If there is some good new romance I'll be oblig'd to bring it over along with you, as well as a couple of French books call'd *Militaire philosophe* and *Théologie portative* in case you may easily find them in London, for we cannot get them here.'[33] Given Wilkes had only left Paris ten days previously, and would have only recently returned to London, this could be again a coded reference by his correspondent, informing of the successful publication without writing anything incriminating about his authorship.

Another example of this oblique coding comes in 1770, when d'Holbach writes to Wilkes: 'If the hurry of affairs should leave you any moments to read curious books I would advise you to peruse two very strange works lately publish'd viz *Recherches philosophiques sur les américains* and *Le Système de la Nature* par Mirabaud. I suppose you'll find them cheaper and more easily in London than at Paris.'[34] The fact that d'Holbach does not reveal to Wilkes that he is the author here, and that he describes it as strange, means that one cannot maintain that d'Holbach's English network was definitely involved in disseminating his works. It also tells us that d'Holbach thinks that London must have many more copies of his text, due to the restrictions on the circulation of books in Paris. Was radicalism spreading more quickly in Great Britain?

Cushing gives a list of d'Holbach's closest English friends, which included 'David Hume, David Garrick, John Wilkes, Laurence Sterne, Edward Gibbon, Horace Walpole, Adam Smith, Benjamin Franklin, Joseph Priestley, Lord Shelburne, Sir James MacDonald and [Robert] Foley'.[35] Wickwar has claimed that Shelburne also played a central role in allowing d'Holbach's works to cross the Channel: 'Through the medium probably of Wilkes, Shelburne and Shelburne's librarians, his writings must have been known to many of the earliest leaders of the British movement for radical reform in Church and State.'[36] Unfortunately, Wickwar provides no evidence or support for such a claim. Earl Shelburne, William Petty-FitzMaurice, 1st Marquess of Lansdowne (1737–1805), was a regular attendee of d'Holbach's *salon*.[37] It is known from various correspondence that Garrick sent d'Holbach a copy of Sterne's *Tristram Shandy* and that Sterne enjoyed the company of d'Holbach's *salon*, about which he wrote that he would 'enjoy myself a week or ten days at Paris with my friends, particularly the Baron d'Holbach, and the rest of the joyous sett'.[38] There were, therefore, multiple networks and friendships which could have potentially allowed d'Holbach's texts to penetrate British markets. However, what results from this study is that there is no real or persistent sense that d'Holbach, despite these personal links, was in any way involved in the diffusion of his texts in Great Britain, beyond the realm of three or four privileged men of letters.

What all these quantitative bibliographical results and clues about intellectual networks do not reveal, however, is how these books were read. As Jeffrey Freedman states in reference to the French book trade in Germany, 'it would also be a mistake to draw any firm inferences about how French books were read from the mere fact of their dissemination.'[39] Even the fact that Hume possessed the *Système de la Nature* does not mean he even read it, let alone that he understood its content or agreed with any of its premises. This means, therefore, that one must undertake a further stage of research, to consider the discourse surrounding these books, how they were read and how British thinkers wrote about them, both publicly and privately.[40] Four case studies of British radicals will now be used – William Godwin, Dr John Jebb, Joseph Priestley, William Hodgson – to show how their reading of d'Holbach helped to circulate his ideas.

Reactions to d'Holbach's texts and ideas in Britain: case studies of passeurs

Godwin

William Godwin (1756–1836), the husband of Mary Wollstonecraft and founder of philosophical anarchism, was profoundly affected by reading d'Holbach, and served to diffuse his thought. Godwin's diary reveals that he was an avid reader of the *Système Social*, mentioning it forty-four times in two years, and includes mentions of *La Politique naturelle* and the *Système de la Nature*.[41] This latter text was passed to him in 1781 when residing at Stowmarket by one of his parishioners, a tradesman from London called Frederic Norman, 'a man well versed in the French philosophers', who also initiated him into works by Rousseau and Helvétius.[42] To the twenty-five-year-old Godwin, then a Calvinist minister, the *Système de la Nature* was a revelation. It is in part due to reading d'Holbach that Godwin's Christian faith was shattered. Only one year after reading the text, following a dispute with his congregation, he moved to London and took up a career in writing. He later explained this transition: 'I read the celebrated *Système de la Nature* and became a Deist.'[43] Godwin's correspondence also reveals that materialism was not uncommon, and that reading of the *Système de la Nature* was widespread. In a letter to Wollstonecraft of 15 June 1797, Godwin relates a visit to Elford near Tamworth, where he met with the mill owner and novelist Robert Bage, whose intelligence Godwin admires: 'He has thought much, & like most of those persons I have met with who have conquered many prejudices, & read little metaphysics, is a materialist. His favourite book in this point is the *Système de la Nature*. We spent a most delightful day in his company.'[44] The fact that even in rural areas, men of letters were reading d'Holbach's text, described as 'celebrated' by Godwin, implies that the impact was not minimal, above all on those who admit to it having being the prime force in the shattering of their religious beliefs. This also suggests some semblance of a network of readers.

Godwin sees the malicious effects of Church and State as central to vice in society, a central tenet of d'Holbach's writing and enunciated in the *Système de la Nature*.[45] Several commentators have noticed the influence of d'Holbach's texts on Godwin. Seamus Deane, for example, has written a chapter on Godwin's uptake of d'Holbach and Helvétius, suggesting that '[a]ll of the concepts with which Holbach struggled in his attempt to construct a secular ethic [...] are so faithfully reproduced by Godwin that *Caleb Williams* reads at times like a novelistic version of the *Système Social*'.[46] Others have been more nuanced about this uptake, taking into account that Godwin does not abandon his religious beliefs altogether: 'Helvetius' *De l'Esprit* and Baron d'Holbach's militantly atheistic *Système de la Nature* might have rocked his faith in the relevance of the Christian Gospel to a revolutionary world; but they did not uproot the idea of the Kingdom of God – it simply became the Kingdom of Faith in the Perfectibility of Man. Men who could no longer be served by an outmoded religion might still be exalted by the vision of moral happiness.'[47]

Indisputably, d'Holbach proved to be a strong influence through-out Godwin's life, but it would be remiss to interpret this as a simple process of cultural transfer, with Godwin as some kind of acolyte of French radicalism. Instead, Godwin enters into dialogue with d'Holbach, and is not a philosophical disciple. As one critic has said, 'Godwin departs from his authorities. Firstly, although his phrasing is reminiscent of the *Système de la Nature*, he rejects d'Holbach's pure materialism, and admits the human will as part of necessity.'[48] Godwin's post-1800 reading of d'Holbach is beyond the scope of this study.[49] Yet it is interesting to note that W. H. Reid's *The Rise and Dissolution of the Infidel Societies in this Metropolis* names Godwin in the same class as Voltaire in terms of their pernicious influence on ideas circulating in London: 'To enable the members to furnish themselves with the heavy artillery of Voltaire, Godwin, &c. reading clubs were formed'.[50] Godwin's reading of d'Holbach irrevocably changed the course of his career from Calvinist preacher to political radical. His discussions of d'Holbach and representa-tions of his ideas served to spread radical ideas.

Dr John Jebb

John Jebb (1736–86), an Anglican dissident, was another whose reading of d'Holbach was massively influential both on himself and on the diffusion of the Frenchman's anonymously published ideas. Jebb, who with his wife Ann, campaigned for an extension of the franchise, was a fervent supporter of Wilkes, with whom he shared an interest in radical French philosophy.[51] Reading the *Système de la Nature* in June 1773, he fully engaged with the text, writing detailed annotations in the margins. His posthumous editor posi-tioned his thoughts as replies to his reading, using long quotations from the French original to create a dialogue between Jebb and d'Holbach.[52] Reading these thoughts, which are to a large extent attempts at a refutation of d'Holbach's views, it becomes clear that Jebb, although not yet ready to embrace all aspects of d'Holbach's materialism, was stimulated by his reading, and highlights certain quotations as particularly meaningful, for instance: 'Bien des gens ont regardé Jésus comme un vrai Théiste, dont la religion a été peu à peu corrompue'[53] (Many people considered Jesus as a real theist, whose religion was corrupted little by little). Jebb seems to approve, but nevertheless seeks to establish his faith in Christianity. Jebb explicitly agrees with d'Holbach, whom he calls Mirabaud, to the extent that d'Holbach's moral system retains Christian forms, but established on a different basis:

> In the following words of Mirabaud is expressed my idea of the religion of nature, so far as relates to our duty to our neighbour. He conceives this to be the voice of nature. I only differ from him in thinking it the voice of God. He is right in thus founding morality on fact. And the fact of Jesus's resurrection gives to religion its perfection, and confirms piety a moral duty.[54]

This attempt at agreement encapsulates the way in which Jebb read d'Holbach. He wants to agree, yet is nevertheless distancing himself from the radicalism contained within the French text because of his commitment to Christianity. Radicalism in Britain was not like French radicalism, but it did engage in dialogue with the atheism of d'Holbach. One key difference was of course the different religious contexts of the two nations. Much of what was seen in Britain as excessive anticlericalism on the part of French radicals was simply attributed to the absolutist Catholic environment in which French thinkers were writing. As Page has pointed out, 'Jebb could agree with the anti-religious thrust of d'Holbach's work because he thought the *philosophes* were merely reacting to an irrational and despotic Catholicism. He, on the other hand, as an English rational Christian, knew that true religion was "intelligible to every sensible being".'[55] Page argues that Jebb's relationship to d'Holbach's work is not simply one of stimulation or refutation, stating that Jebb 'agreed with his views on the Trinity and determinism'. Whilst Jebb never embraces the atheistic materialism of d'Holbach, Page finds that 'we might say Jebb adopted a materialism of sorts'.[56] Jebb's career in the Church was effectively ended by his heterodox views and his marginal position of trying to find commonalities with d'Holbach, becoming an outcast Cambridge academic and helping Priestley to form the Unitarian wing of English radicalism.

Jebb's materialist interpretation of Christianity thus aimed to strip the religion of any kind of irrationality, which would allow it to combat attacks from the likes of d'Holbach. Jebb did, after all, write that '[r]eligious awe weakens the mind'.[57] Yet this was no desire to do away with all of religion, but to refine Christianity and establish it on rational grounds. That Jebb's activism was in keeping with radical French philosophy shows that heterodox theology was often a source of political radicalism in Britain.

Joseph Priestley

Without any doubt the greatest role in diffusing d'Holbach's thought prior to the translation of the *Système de la Nature* was played by Joseph Priestley (1733–1804). Priestley met d'Holbach in Paris on a visit in 1774, from which he recalled that 'all the philosophical persons to whom I was introduced at Paris [were] unbelievers in Christianity and even profound atheists'. Priestley claims to have been told that he 'was the only person they had ever met with, of whose understanding they had any opinion, who professed to believe Christianity'.[58] One particular Parisian, thought to be d'Holbach, is afforded special attention in a letter to England: 'I am here in the midst of unbelievers, and even Atheists. I had a long conversation with one, an ingenious man, and good writer, who maintained seriously that man might arise, without any Maker, from the earth. They may despise me; I am sure I despise and pity them.'[59]

Priestley, who defined himself as a materialist, attempted to combat such positions as he had come across in Paris and in David Hume's posthumous *Dialogues concerning Natural Religion* (1779) in his *Letters to a Philosophical Unbeliever* (1780). It would be wrong to see Priestley as influenced by reading d'Holbach, because much of his own thought had been crystallised in the *Disquisitions relating to matter and spirit and the Doctrine of Necessity* (1777), which questioned the notion of the soul and even Christianity: 'The state of things is now such that it appears to me to be absolutely necessary to abandon the notion of a soul, if we would retain Christianity at all. And, happily, the principles of it are as repugnant to that notion, as those of any modern philosophy.'[60]

The eleventh letter of the second edition of the *Letters to a Philosophical Unbeliever* deals exclusively with the *Système de la Nature*, which Priestley describes as a 'work much more celebrated abroad than that of Mr. Hume will probably ever be with us' and a 'bible of atheism'. Priestley affirms the book's European celebrity, and contributes to its British reputation, labelling its author 'much more bold and unreserved than Mr. Hume'.[61] As a writer who himself had openly suggested that the soul was corporeal, Priestley makes attempts to understand d'Holbach and offers long quotations of the *Système de la Nature* in his own English translation. He then adds his comments, which fall between understanding and refutation: 'I will acknowledge with this author, that matter cannot exist without *powers* [...]. Consequently, if matter has been from eternity, these powers, and the motions which are the effects of them, must also have been from eternity.' On the page after this tentative agreement, Priestley turns his comments into refutation, transforming the *Système* into proof of deism: 'I therefore conclude with certainty that a Being superior to every thing [...] created matter itself.'[62] Priestley is far from heaping scorn on this materialistic treatise of atheism, instead attempting to reconcile it with his own Deism. As Schofield states, the '*Système* was the most plausible and seducing thing Priestley had yet met in support of atheism';[63] yet he interpreted d'Holbach's *énergie de la nature* as 'God' and thus rescued the system from the Godless vision it was.

In any case, Priestley's *Letters* definitely served to further diffuse d'Holbach's text and provided it with great publicity in Britain. While he did not fully embrace d'Holbach's atheism, we can agree with Thomson when she states that 'Priestley's materialism was an integral part of his political struggle against hierarchy and authority'.[64] So although Priestley's radicalism was derived from different reasoning to d'Holbach's, their political radicalism was shared and Priestley was open to reading and discussing the banned anonymous texts originating from d'Holbach's *salon*, thus affording them crucial publicity in Great Britain.

William Hodgson

This series of case studies of *passeurs* or 'diffusers' of d'Holbach will end with a study of the first translation of *Système de la Nature*, written by William Hodgson (1745–1851) in 1795. Hodgson was a political radical in his own right with extreme political views, said to be 'chiefly derived from the French philosophers'.[65] A member of the London Corresponding Society, Hodgson was imprisoned on 9 December 1793 for having proposed as a toast 'the French republic', and of having 'compared the king to a German hog butcher'. He was sentenced to two years in Newgate prison and a fine of £200.[66] It was during this incarceration that he wrote his best known work, *The Commonwealth of Reason* (1795), and also translated the *Système de la Nature*. That such a radical figure was responsible for the translation speaks volumes for the potential reception of the book. That Hodgson was also well connected in London offers clues as to his intentions with regard to the translation. His belief in the power of print and the public sphere is confirmed by the publication of his self-defence and attack on the laws which imprisoned him, *The case of William Hodgson, now confined in Newgate*, another text published while Hodgson was still in prison. The translation of the *Système de la Nature* proved so popular that a second edition was published in 1797, also illustrating the popularity which Robison and Reid railed against.[67]

Conclusion

Though there is evidence that d'Holbach's texts circulated, and certain British radicals found intellectual stimulation in them, it seems that Robison, Thomson and Reid were slightly misplaced in their clarion call to close down these scandalous reading societies who were feeding the masses on the dangerous atheism of French radicals like 'Mirabaud'. Indeed, they seem to have followed Augustin Barruel's claims that there existed an international conspiracy derived from the circulation of radical ideas contained in books. Barruel's *Mémoires pour servir à l'histoire du Jacobinisme* had been translated into English and widely reviewed in the English press by 1797.[68] Indeed, in a separate book the following year the translator also made clear the link between the French case, outlined by Barruel, and contemporary British reading societies.[69]

Naturally, d'Holbach was not known as the author of the works which we now attribute to him. Moreover, there was often no connection between these various works for contemporary readers. Indeed, despite the links and network of relations he had in Britain, his anonymity was nearly absolute. Yet this did not prevent his *Système de la Nature* becoming a runaway success in Britain. Our survey of bibliographical data provides evidence to support the view that d'Holbach's *Système* was widely read in Britain. Refutations of his work from various sources also served to further diffuse his work and publicise the 'scandalous' text to potential curious readers.

Additionally, it has been shown how cultural transfer can operate 'under the radar' and how, by studying such transfers, one can study the ways in which radicalism changes when transposed into new contexts. That is to say that literature which was banned and widely reviled in France was integrated into dissenting positions in Britain, where theological debate tolerated such marginal voices as

140

Priestley, Jebb and Godwin. Thus 'radicalism', as a property, is in a way assimilated. This illustrates clearly the differences in radicalism between Britain and France.[70] Ultimately, the importation of d'Holbach's works discussed here is suggestive of, and prepared the way for, underground reading. The extent of this underground reading is difficult to judge – hence why we must rely on bibliographical information given here – prior to the proof provided by the radicalism of the 1820s, when d'Holbach's texts circulated in penny editions and in the journal, *The Deist*, under the direction of agitator Richard Carlile (1790–1843).[71]

Notes

1 Reid is described as a 'Jacobin and obscure littérateur' by I. McCalman, *Radical Underworld: Prophets, Revolutionaries, and Pornographers in London, 1795–1840* (Cambridge: Cambridge University Press, 1988), p. 1.

2 See B. de Negroni, *Lectures interdites: le travail des censeurs au XVIIIe siècle: 1723–1774* (Paris: Albin Michel, 1995). *Le Bon Sens* (1772) was condemned on 10 January 1774, *La Contagion Sacrée*, *Le Christianisme Dévoilé* and *Le Système de la Nature* were condemned together on 18 August 1770. Though 'radicalism' is still an ill-defined category, d'Holbach's atheism, anticlerical and anti-authoritarian ideas, and the fate of his books in France mean there is little dissent in applying the label here.

3 J. Thomson, *The Rise, progress, and consequences, of the new opinions and principles lately introduced into France; with observations* (Edinburgh, 1799), p. 45.

4 Thomson, *The Rise, progress, and consequences*, p. 44. Incidentally, this text makes the mistake of attributing the *Système de la Nature* to Diderot, p. 73.

5 On French–British cultural transfer in the eighteenth century, see A. Thomson, S. Burrows and E. Dziembowski (eds), *Cultural Transfers: France and Britain in the Long Eighteenth Century* (Oxford: Voltaire Foundation, 2010).

6 On d'Holbach's relationship to English Republicanism, see R. Hammersley, *The English Republican Tradition and Eighteenth-Century France: Between the Ancients and the Moderns* (Manchester: Manchester University Press, 2010), pp. 123–34.

7 The closeness of this relationship was interpreted by G. S. Rousseau to have been of a homosexual nature. G. S. Rousseau, *Perilous Enlightenment: Pre- and Post-Modern Discourses, Sexual, Historical*

(Manchester: Manchester University Press, 1991), pp. 129–30. This hypothesis has been thoroughly discredited by A. H. Cash, 'Wilkes, Baxter and d'Holbach at Leiden and Utrecht: an answer to G.S. Rousseau', *The Age of Johnson*, 7 (1996), 397–426.

8 See A. C. Kors, *D'Holbach's Coterie: An Enlightenment in Paris* (Princeton, N.J.: Princeton University Press, 1976).

9 As reported by Denis Diderot, letter to Sophie Volland, 15 September 1765, in *Oeuvres de Diderot*, ed. Laurent Versini (Paris: Robert Laffont, 1997), vol. 5: *Correspondance*, p. 532.

10 Hammersley, *English Republican Tradition*, p. 129.

11 *Catalogue des livres de la bibliothèque de feu M. le Baron d'Holbach* (Paris: De Bure, 1789). For example, d'Holbach's library contained books by Hume, Cudwoth and Toland. D'Holbach's engagement with English deists was not particularly innovative. Voltaire, whose Anglomania was renowned, read extensively the works of English deists: see N. L. Torrey, *Voltaire and the English Deists* (London: Yale University Press, 1930).

12 *The French Book Trade in Enlightenment Europe*, STN archives database at http://fbtee.uws.edu.au/main/ (consulted on 29 August 2015). The STN archives are an invaluable historical resource, but they are very much partial and can only ever be indicative.

13 R. Darnton, 'The life cycle of a book: a publishing history of d'Holbach's *Système de la Nature*', in C. Armbruster (ed.), *Publishing and Readership in Revolutionary France and America* (Westport, C.T.: Greenwood Press, 1993), pp. 15–43.

14 J. Vercruysse, *Bibliographie descriptive des écrits du Baron d'Holbach* (Paris: Minard, 1971), p. xii.

15 Could there be a link between these two translations and the library of Joseph Priestley, who had emigrated to Pennsylvania in the United States having been forced to flee Birmingham after his activities as a dissenter had led to a riot by a mob?

16 *The System of nature: or, The laws of the moral and physical world. Translated from the French of M. Mirabaud ... by William Hodgson* (London: 1795); *The System of nature: or, The laws of the moral and physical world. Translated from the French of M. Mirabaud.* (London, 1797).

17 Vercruysse, *Bibliographie*, p. v, 'Œuvres originales'.

18 Given their rarity and lack of connection with d'Holbach's philosophical programme, both the *Arrêt rendu à l'amphithéâtre* (1752) and the *Lettre à une dame d'un certain âge* (1752) have been disregarded. This leaves us with *Le Christianisme dévoilé, ou Examen des principes et des effets de la religion chrétienne* (1766); *La Contagion sacrée, ou Histoire naturelle de la superstition* (1768); *Lettres à Eugénie,*

ou Préservatif contre les préjugés, (1768); *Théologie Portative, ou Dictionnaire abrégé de la religion chrétienne* (1768); *Essai sur les préjugés, ou De l'influence des opinions sur les mœurs & le bonheur des hommes* (1770); *Système de la nature ou des loix du monde physique & du monde moral* (1770); *Histoire critique de Jésus-Christ, ou Analyse raisonnée des évangiles* (1770); *Tableau des Saints, ou Examen de l'esprit, de la conduite, des maximes & du mérite des personnages que le christianisme révère & propose pour modèles* (1770); *Le Bon Sens, ou idées naturelles opposées aux idées surnaturelles* (1772); *Politique Naturelle, ou Discours sur les vrais principes du Gouvernement* (1773); *Système Social, ou Principes naturels de la morale et de la Politique, avec un examen de l'influence du gouvernement sur les mœurs* (1773); *Ethocratie, ou Le gouvernement fondé sur la morale* (1776); *La Morale Universelle, ou Les devoirs de l'homme fondés sur la Nature* (1776); *Eléments de morale universelle, ou Catéchisme de la Nature* (1790). Collaborative works like *Le Militaire philosophe* (1768), *Recueil philosophique* (1770), works translated by d'Holbach like the *Lettres philosophiques* by Toland, *De l'imposture sacerdotale* (1767) or *De la Cruauté religieuse* (1769), or works which d'Holbach edited have not been taken into consideration, even where this radicalised the original texts, as in the case of Boulanger's *Recherches sur l'origine du despotisme oriental* (1761), *Dissertation sur Élie et Énoch* (1764) or *L'Antiquité dévoilée* (1766). Texts he published either in Diderot and d'Alembert's *Encyclopédie* have not been taken into account, either.

19 When the same information is copied in a second journal, this duplicate mention is retained in the statistics, as the information circulated in a different journal.

20 There is undoubtedly more research to be done on the evidence provided by the sales catalogues of d'Holbach's texts in Great Britain, by searching all the sales catalogues between 1765 and 1800 in A. N. L. Munby and L. Coral (eds), *British Book Sale Catalogues, 1676–1800: A Union List* (London: Mansell, 1977). Checking library catalogues for the number of extant copies of pre-1800 editions has not been done as the unknown acquisition dates preclude the usefulness of the listings, that is to say they could have been acquired after 1800.

21 It is interesting to note that there is no trace in the sources used for *Histoire critique de Jésus-Christ* (1770) apart from its English translation by George Houston: *Ecce Homo! Or A Critical Inquiry into the History of Jesus Christ. Being a Rational Analysis of the Gospels* (Edinburgh, 1799). It was only upon admitting being the translator after the second edition of 1813 that Houston, a Scot, was fined £200 and sentenced to two years in prison at Newgate in November 1815,

after which he fled to America: see McCalman, *Radical Underworld*, pp. 76–8.

22 R. Darnton, *The Forbidden Best-Sellers of Pre-Revolutionary France* (London: Norton, 1996), pp. 194, 199. Darnton's methodology has been subjected to serious criticism, and thus one must treat his results with some scepticism.

23 D. Fate Norton and M. J. Norton (eds), *The David Hume Library* (Edinburgh: Edinburgh Bibliographical Society in association with the National Library of Scotland, 1996), items 871 and 1230.

24 Reprinted in S. Deane (ed.), *Sale Catalogues of Libraries of Eminent Persons* (London: Mansell, 1973), vol. 8: *Politicians*, pp. 94, 118, 131, 135, 150.

25 See the bibliography entry 1763 F2 in Vercruysse, *Bibliographie*. The evidence for this is a manuscript note on the title page. Max Pearson Cushing confuses this with *Le Christianisme dévoilé*, a version of which he claims was printed on Wilkes's private press. The British library catalogue sides with Vercruysse. In any case, Wilkes was in exile in France at the time of the printing of the *Christianisme dévoilé*. See M. P. Cushing, 'Baron d'Holbach: A Study of Eighteenth-Century Radicalism in France', PhD dissertation (New York, 1914), p. 90.

26 Kors, *D'Holbach's Coterie*, pp. 58–9.

27 John Wilkes to Mary Wilkes, 1 November 1765, in *The Correspondence of the late John Wilkes: with his friends, printed from the original manuscripts, in which are introduced memoirs of his life*, ed. John Almon (London, R. Phillips, 1805), vol. 2, p. 188.

28 D'Holbach, letter to Hume, 22 August 1763, in H. Sauter and E. Loos (eds), *Paul Thiry, baron d'Holbach: die gesamte erhaltene Korrespondenz* (Stuttgart: Franz Steiner Verlag Wiesbaden, 1986), p. 19. Loos and Sauter suggest the text in question could be *Le Christianisme devoilé*, but Vercruysse dates this as 1766, and not 1756 as stated on the title page. It is more likely to be the *Recherches sur l'origine du despotisme oriental*, given it is known that one edition was printed in England, on Wilkes's press.

29 D'Holbach letter to David Hume: Sunday, 16 March 1766, in *Electronic Enlightenment*, ed. R. McNamee *et al.*, www.e-enlightenment.com (accessed 29 August 2015).

30 Diderot, letter to Sophie Volland, 6 October 1765, in Versini (ed.), *Correspondance*, p. 537.

31 The danger of these books is illustrated by the case of booksellers Josserand, Lecuyer and his wife arrested for having copies of d'Holbach's *Christianisme dévoilé*. See Diderot's letter to Sophie Volland, 8 October 1768, in Versini (ed.), *Correspondance*, p. 895. This news travelled to England and was reported in the *Annual Register* (1768), p. 180.

32 See R. L. Dawson, *Confiscations at Customs: Banned Books and the French Booktrade during the Last Years of the Ancien Régime* (Oxford: Voltaire Foundation, 2006).

33 D'Holbach to Wilkes, 10 December 1767, in Sauter and Loos (eds), *Korrespondenz*, p. 49. Wilkes left Paris in the middle of the night on 30 November 1767. Wilkes never returned to France, and so could never have brought the requested texts to d'Holbach: see A. H. Cash, *John Wilkes: The Scandalous Father of Civil Liberty* (London: Yale University Press, 2006), p. 201.

34 D'Holbach to Wilkes, 19 March 1770, in Sauter and Loos (eds), *Korrespondenz*, p. 60.

35 Cushing, *Baron d'Holbach*, p. 18.

36 W. H. Wickwar, *Baron d'Holbach: A Prelude to the French Revolution* (New York: A.M. Kelley, [1935] repr. 1968), p. 113.

37 J. M. Norris, *Shelburne and Reform* (London: Macmillan, 1963).

38 Laurence Sterne, letter to John Wodehouse, 20[?] September 1765, in *Electronic Enlightenment*, www.e-enlightenment.com (accessed 29 August 2015).

39 J. Freedman, *Books without Borders in Enlightenment Europe: French Cosmopolitanism and German Literary Markets* (Philadelphia, P.A.: University of Pennsylvania Press, 2012), p. 267.

40 R. Darnton has written at length about the conflict between the different approaches of diffusion and discourse analysis: see notably R. Darnton, *The Literary Underground of the Old Regime* (London: Harvard University Press, 1985), pp. 170–92.

41 *Godwin Diary Project*, http://godwindiary.bodleian.ox.ac.uk/diary/ (consulted on 29 August 2015).

42 Godwin, 'Autobiographical Fragments', in *The Collected Novels and Memoirs of William Godwin*, ed. M. Philp (London: Pickering, 1992), vol. 1: *Autobiography*, p. 44.

43 Godwin, 'The Principal Revolutions of Opinion', in *Collected Novels and Memoirs*, vol. 1, p. 53.

44 Godwin, letter to Mary Wollstonecraft, 15 June 1797, in R. M. Wardle (ed.), *Godwin & Mary: Letters of William Godwin and Mary Wollstonecraft* (London: Constable, 1967), p. 101. For a further discussion of Godwin and Bage, see Chapter 9.

45 [D'Holbach], *Système de la Nature*, vol. 1, p. 173.

46 S. Deane, *The French Revolution and Enlightenment in England, 1789–1832* (London: Harvard University Press, 1988), p. 87.

47 E. E. Smith and E. Greenwell Smith, *William Godwin* (New York: Twayne, 1965), p. 20.

48 A. E. Rodway, *Godwin and the Age of Transition* (London: Harrap, 1952), p. 28.

49 Godwin was also considerably influenced by d'Holbach's writings after the period of 1800, outside the remit of this study. And he corresponded with Shelley about *Système de la Nature*, further disseminating the work.

50 W. H. Reid, *The Rise and Dissolution of the Infidel Societies in this Metropolis* (London, 1800), p. 8.

51 A. Page, *John Jebb and the Enlightenment Origins of British Radicalism* (London: Praeger, 2003), p. 45.

52 John Jebb, *The Works, theological, medical, political, and miscellaneous, of John Jebb*, ed. John Disney (London, 1787), vol. 2, 161–72. Disney published these notes from Jebb's manuscript in a section entitled 'Theological propositions and miscellaneous observations', thus further diffusing sections of the *Système de la Nature* to the 500 subscribers: see Page, *John Jebb*, p. 268.

53 [D'Holbach], *Système de la Nature*, vol. 2, p. 216.

54 Jebb, *Works*, p. 168.

55 Page, *John Jebb*, p. 100.

56 Page, *John Jebb*, pp. 88, 90.

57 Jebb, *Theological Propositions*, in *Works*, vol. 2, p. 139.

58 'Memoirs', in *The Theological and Miscellaneous Works of Joseph Priestley*, ed. J. Towill Rutt (London: 1817), vol. 1, p. 199.

59 Priestley, Letter to T. Lindsey, 21 October 1774, in *Works*, vol. 1, p. 254.

60 Priestley, 'Preface' to second edition of *Disquisitions relating to matter and spirit and the Doctrine of Necessity* (Birmingham: J. Johnson, 1782), p. xxx. For more on the origins of Priestley's materialism see A. Tapper, 'The beginnings of Priestley's materialism', *Enlightenment and Dissent*, 1 (1982), 73–81.

61 Priestley, *Letters to a Philosophical Unbeliever* (Birmingham: Johnson, 2nd edn, 1787), pp. 160, 161.

62 Priestley, *Letters to a Philosophical Unbeliever*, pp. 162, 163.

63 R. E. Schofield, *The Enlightened Joseph Priestley* (University Park, P.A..: Pennsylvania State University Press, 2004), p. 39.

64 A. Thomson, *Bodies of Thought: Science, Religion, and the Soul in the Early Enlightenment* (Oxford: Oxford University Press, 2008), p. 233.

65 T. Cooper, 'Hodgson, William (1745–1851)', *Oxford Dictionary of National Biography* (Oxford University Press, 2004).

66 T. Cooper, 'Hodgson, William (1745–1851)', *Oxford Dictionary of National Biography*. On toasts as radical rituals in late eighteenth-century Britain, see Chapter 7.

67 William Hodgson, *The case of William Hodgson, now confined in Newgate, for the payment of two hundred pounds, after having suffered two years' imprisonment on a charge of sedition, considered and*

compared with the existing laws of the country. By himself (London, 1796).

68 Abbé Barruel, *Memoirs, illustrating the history of Jacobinism*, trans. R. Clifford (London: T. Burton, 1797). Moreover, this book reported the role d'Holbach played in hosting the *salon* at which the *philosophes* met.

69 [Robert Clifford], *Application of Barruel's Memoirs of Jacobinism, to the secret societies of Ireland and Great Britain* (London: E. Booker, 1798).

70 On the French positive reactions to d'Holbach see M. Curran, *Atheism, Religion and Enlightenment in Pre-Revolutionary Europe* (Woodbridge: Boydell Press and the Royal Historical Society, 2012). On the issue of cultural transfers between France and England in the seventeenth century see the introduction to this volume. For radical culture operating 'under the radar', see Chapter 1.

71 McCalman shows d'Holbach was read in underground circles but provides no evidence prior to 1800. McCalman, *Radical Underworld*, pp. 75–93.

PART III

Radical media and practices

6

~

The parliamentary context of political radicalism in the English revolution

Jason Peacey

During at least certain moments of extreme political tension during the English revolution, the process of petitioning Parliament could be a risky enterprise. This might seem to be an unexceptional statement, given scholarly familiarity with the fact that the Long Parliament became nervous about radical agitation during the late 1640s, and with the fact that the ideas of army activists and Levellers centred in no small part upon the assertion of the right to petition, and of the requirement that such demands should be taken seriously by representatives in Parliament. However, the experience of characters like William Bray and Christopher Cheesman is revealing. Bray was arrested in March 1649, not just because he was a known troublemaker – who had been involved in the so-called Ware mutiny in 1647, and who was thought to be a Leveller – or because he had produced a petition 'tending to stir up sedition in the people and mutiny in the army', but also because this petition was printed and 'delivered to divers members' outside Parliament.[1] Cheesman, a cornet in the same regiment as Bray, was likewise arrested in Westminster Hall, on 26 May 1649, for delivering copies of Bray's subsequent printed petitions, issued from his cell at Windsor Castle, and then wrote a detailed account of the incident and of the court martial hearing that followed in a pamphlet entitled *The Lamb Contending with the Lion*. Not the least of Cheesman's ambitions in this latter text was to accuse Oliver Cromwell of having encouraged guards to subject him to brutal treatment, 'running very greedily like so many lions to their pray, pulling and punching of me'.[2]

These two incidents are highly revealing in terms of the relationship between Parliament, print and petitioning, and of the political culture of the period. On the one hand, they are suggestive in relation to the openness and accessibility of the Westminster system and to the fact that petitioning was an accepted and routine practice; and it is notable that, before being arrested, Cheesman had arrived at the Parliament door, informed the Sergeant at Arms about his business, and secured a private meeting with the Speaker of the Commons, William Lenthall. Indeed, upon hearing Cheesman's plea on behalf of Bray, Lenthall apparently responded 'very lovingly, and told me that he would do what he could in the business, and that he would propose it to the House'.[3] On the other hand, however, such incidents suggest that petitioners could find the process of interacting with Parliament challenging and frustrating. Indeed, the aim of this chapter is to suggest that by exploring this tension between the potential for, and the problems of, political participation at Westminster it is possible to highlight new dimensions of our understanding of political radicalism in the English revolution. This will involve enhancing our appreciation of the practices of radical activists, expanding our understanding of who needs to be regarded as 'radical' during the period, and enriching our sense of the process by which radical ideas developed. In each case the aim will be to suggest that students of early modern times have much to learn by thinking about the everyday practices and tactics of political participation, and about the parliamentary context of civil war radicalism.

As a topic for historical enquiry, the fortunes of civil war radicalism have waxed and waned dramatically since the early 1970s. For a long time the expression of innovative ideas was analysed in narrowly ideological ways, understood in relation to socio-economic change, not least in terms of what might be called the uncorking of religious radicalism, and explored in terms of acrimonious debates within the 'public sphere'. Attention tended to focus, in other words, on religious and political activists, not least agitators within the army and groups like the Levellers, and on their contribution to public discourse through high-profile pamphleteering. The result, of course, was a dramatic, and at times intemperate, backlash by those who questioned the relevance of the kinds of character that Christopher Hill had made his own, and who dismissed the views of unrepresentative voices from the fringes of political life. In one famous challenge, for example, John Kenyon questioned 'where all this discussion of obscure left-wing fanatics is getting us', and felt sure that 'some of them were mad'. He concluded that 'the ideas and efforts of these left-wing radicals had no discernible effect on the subsequent course of English developments', and that the kinds of pamphlet which had preoccupied Hill were produced by 'failed shopkeepers, lazy artisans and eccentric academics'. Of course, not all of Hill's other critics, including 'revisionists' as well as somewhat more charitable interlocutors like David Underdown, were so dismissive. Nevertheless, it became fairly common to express concerns about Hill's methodology, in terms of his reliance on contemporary pamphlets and his apparent neglect of manuscripts. And concerted efforts were made to shift attention from 'puritan militancy' to 'the great mass of people … who did not want war' and to the 'conforming majority' who had been left 'largely in the shadows' by Marxist historiography. In other words, it was in direct response to, and reaction against, Hill that revisionist scholars, most obviously Conrad Russell, John Morrill and Mark Kishlansky, chose to challenge the importance of print culture and the trajectories traced by historians of radicalism, and to focus more intently upon the political and religious mainstream, upon moderation and consensus and upon high politics. Thus, while it is true that Morrill accepted that Hill had 'written movingly of the victims of the revolution', he nevertheless insisted that, in the process, scholarship had been misled into focusing on people who merely 'constituted its epiphenomena'.[4] The result was that 'radicals' began to disappear from view, as historians concentrated their attention on politics within Westminster and on political attitudes within the provincial gentry, not least in order to rescue the importance of neutralism and to recover what was claimed to be the perspective of the 'silent majority'.

More recently, of course, there is evidence of a mellowing of historiographical tempers. Eventually, even some leading revisionists began to suggest that the severity of the response to Hill had probably been overblown, that there was a risk of historiographical debates becoming unproductively polarised and that there remained good reasons to recognise the importance of civil war radicals, so long as they were properly understood and contextualised.[5] As a result, recent years have witnessed renewed interest in the radicalism that emerged in the revolutionary decades, not least in work by

Keith Lindley, Ann Hughes and David Como that has engaged in archival research in order to reconstruct radical networks, adopted a much more sophisticated approach to print culture and recognised the value of taking contemporary perceptions about radicalism seriously. However, what has been tended to be overlooked in the debates between Christopher Hill and his critics, as well as in debates between 'revisionists' and 'post-revisionists', is the possibility that radicalism emerged in relation to everyday political practice, and in response to the experience of participating in parliamentary politics. The aim of this chapter, therefore, is to draw attention to neglected voices, including Christopher Cheesman, as well as men like William Sykes, James Freize and John Poyntz, who reveal radical ideas, and who certainly used print, but who do not fit very neatly into the kind of analysis developed by Hill. The purpose of this chapter, indeed, is to draw attention to a fairly wide range of individuals and interest groups who reflected on the nature of representation, participation and political authority, as well as on political accountability and parliamentary privilege, and who did so as a result of their experience of quotidian interactions with, and participation in, Westminster affairs, often in the pursuit of what might be thought to be arcane and prosaic interests and agendas. The focus, in other words, will be on people who sought to participate at Westminster as petitioners and lobbyists, in relation to private grievances and interests, and on the ways in which their tactical awareness and use of print mirrored their frustrated expectations regarding the parliamentary process. By recovering a wealth of evidence about experience-led and 'bottom-up' political thinking, this chapter will demonstrate that radicalism was more pervasive than has generally been recognised,[6] that it sometimes emerged from unexpected quarters and that it often reflected a gradual escalation of tactics and rhetoric.

The argument that follows rests on two foundations, and consists of six points or stages, only the last of which will be addressed in a detailed fashion. In terms of foundations, therefore, it is possible to highlight, first, the development of an 'information revolution' relating to Parliament, with the 'democratisation' and commercialisation of once privileged political information, which became affordable, widely dispersed and eagerly consumed across the country and below the level of the elite. Such information explained how Parliament worked, both in theory and practice, and it even extended to reports of parliamentary speeches and information about the times, places and membership of committees, as well as polemical analysis of the Westminster system and the corruption of its members. The availability, often entirely uncontested, of such information, when placed in the context of an accessible physical environment, indicates contemporary acceptance, sometimes pragmatic but often principled, of parliamentary transparency. Second, it is possible to highlight a growing sense, explicitly fostered by MPs and peers, that Parliament was not just increasingly powerful but also immensely useful. After 1640, in other words, citizens were encouraged to bring their grievances and interests before Parliament, and encouraged to participate in its proceedings, not least through petitioning. This is a topic that has been much discussed in recent historiography, and not least in the arguments of David Zaret, who suggested that petitions, and more importantly printed petitions, constituted and reflected 'public opinion' and that they fostered a 'public sphere'. In fact, printed petitions have tended to be misunderstood, in ways that overplay their importance for 'public' debate while at the same time underestimating their political and constitutional significance. The author's aim here is to demonstrate that printed petitions were used primarily as a non-commercial participatory tool, and to examine what this reveals about perceptions of Parliament and awareness of constitutional issues.[7]

The key point in what represents the first stage of a larger argument is that participation through petitioning was frequently frustrating rather than empowering because of the difficulties involved in securing sponsorship, even for those who could engage directly with representatives and exploit networks of kinship, patronage and friendship.[8] For non-gentry petitioners, of course, it often proved to be extremely difficult to secure support, and Sir John Coke concluded in 1641 that 'the common people do mightily mistake Parliaments'.[9] Ephemeral and non-commercial print culture, however, provided a powerful means of overcoming such problems, making it possible and affordable to make multiple copies of petitions for distribution, discrete and restrained circulation among MPs in the hope of securing support. Parliamentary petitioning thus became part of the tactical armoury of those whose political horizons may otherwise have remained localised. Here one might usefully reflect on the experience of Edmund Felton, whose brother participated in politics by assassinating the Duke of Buckingham in 1628, and who frequently sought to resolve his own grievances by scattering libels around London and Westminster 'in the night time', and by distributing printed petitions 'at the door of the House of Commons' and 'to most or many of the members'.[10] Eventually, it became common to address printed petitions to 'every individual member of Parliament', and many rare examples survive in the papers of individual MPs.[11] As the ejected cleric and Peterhouse fellow Charles Hotham explained in 1653, to fight his case without print was 'near impossible, his bodily strength not sufficing to transcribe so many copies himself ... [while] to have done it by others would have been too vast a charge'.[12]

Analysing printed petitions reveals contemporary perceptions of the role of Parliament *vis-à-vis* local political authorities and other official channels. Many demonstrate a willingness to appeal to parliamentary authorities in the hope of ensuring the proper enforcement of statutes, as with the Somerset beer sellers who used print in 1659 to complain that local excise commissioners were failing to enforce legislation.[13] Examples also reveal appeals being made to higher authorities against decisions made at local levels, in the law courts, and by bodies which were answerable to Parliament. The inhabitants of rural Muggleswick took their demand for a preaching minister to Parliament in 1642, following earlier petitions to the authorities at Durham Cathedral, while Philip Chetwind issued a printed petition from Newgate prison in 1650 after an earlier petition to the Mayor and Aldermen of London had failed because 'it was not in their power' to help him.[14] By examining this kind of ephemeral print, in other words, it is possible to demonstrate how Parliament became part of the tactical armoury of those with local and personal grievances, including fairly humble individuals.

What thus emerges – this being the second point – is that printed petitioning involved not just a direct form of political participation, but also tactical escalation, the latter of which is evident in response to frustrations encountered at Westminster. This sprang most obviously from the way in which members responded to the weight of business, not least the growth of petitioning that was facilitated by print culture, and to the need to prioritise public over private affairs. Excessive workload ensured that many petitioners faced lengthy delays and great expense, and the tendency to postpone consideration of private petitions frequently generated frustration and suspicion. For instance, in early 1647 Hereford corporation explained to the Speaker, William Lenthall, that their petitions had been sidelined by 'affairs of a more general concernment', and they expressed frustration at having waited 'a long time and with much patience'.[15] At least some petitioners, indeed, detected favouritism and 'partiality' in the Commons and its committees.[16]

On the occasions when such ephemeral printed petitions provided a means of responding to participatory difficulties – in what represents the third point of this argument – they tended to reveal awareness of, and unhappiness with, the parliamentary process. One Thomas Hampson, for example, used a simple printed sheet to restate his case ahead of the date on which it was 'appointed to be reported to the Honourable House of Commons'.[17] Thomas Brudenell gave a copy of his printed petition to the MP Bulstrode Whitelocke after his case had been raised and then mishandled.[18] In case after case, indeed, print was used to respond to delays, obstacles and blockages, and such practices reveal how even polite suitors lost patience with the speed at which private matters progressed.[19] In general, however, such exploitation of print represented an escalation of tactics which fell short of taking matters into the public domain, and most printed expressions of frustration were produced for a fairly limited and carefully targeted audience. As such, they represented only a restrained intensification of pressure upon MPs.[20] The Duchess of Hamilton, for example, bemoaned having 'divers times attended in person at the door' with a petition, 'and presented printed copies thereof unto all or more of the particular members'. Her point was not to restate her case, but merely to point out that 'her said petition and case being for above these six months not read (remaining now in the clerks hands), her wants are increased to that extremity that she and her four daughters live merely upon charity'.[21]

Indeed, more than this – and this is the fourth point of this argument – print was often used not merely to draw attention to grievances, but also to rebuke the authorities for ignoring submissions; and it could be employed at any subsequent stage in the parliamentary process, not least when petitions became buried in committees.[22] Colonel Charles Doilie explained that his petition had 'lain in the House ... these four years' and was 'twice ordered to be taken into consideration' but never reported. Doilie's response was phlegmatic, and he expressed hope that this 'was but a disappointment into a better opportunity'.[23] Others, however,

showed signs of thinning patience, including the Lancashire petitioners who resorted to print in February 1642 after two former
petitions had become stuck in committee. Although 'not willing
with unseasonable importunity to interrupt the course of greater
affairs', they nevertheless begged 'that these and other grievances
... after so long expectation, may not be perpetually forgotten'.[24]
Very often, such impatience was expressed in terms of grumbling
about 'constant attendance' and the 'great expenses' that people
inevitably incurred.[25] And the growing sense of frustration which
delays brought men like Richard Chambers is perfectly clear. In his
1646 printed petition, Chambers claimed that he had 'with patience
waited upon God, and your favours, for a seasonable opportunity
to revive his former petition', which had been submitted as long
ago as November 1641, and he explained that he had done so 'out
of a deep sense of your great and weighty affairs in these distracted
times'.[26] By 1652, however, ongoing delays ensured a more exas-
perated tone: he had 'from the first sitting of this parliament to
this present year ... omitted no opportunity by all humble petitions
to seek relief', and he was 'now wearied out and consumed by
expenses and fruitless attendings'.[27] Ultimately, of course, frustration could turn to anger, and Thomas Philpot's printed petition,
'presented at the Parliament-door' in 1654, could not hide his anger
that Parliament had 'again and again' ignored resolutions that no
petitioner should wait more than forty days for a response.[28]

Ultimately, however, frustration with the petitioning process
could be expressed in much more dramatic ways. It may therefore
be argued, fifth, that the print medium provided a means of adopting a more aggressive strategy. The Derbyshire lead miners, for
example, highlight how the kinds of frustrations which encouraged
petitioners to circulate printed petitions also generated inflamed
political rhetoric, even if only in terms of fairly traditional and
imprecise populism. They thus exclaimed that 'prerogative hath
many proctors, by whose power and policy justice is either denied
or delayed; the oppressors, because rich and powerful, cherished,
and the oppressed, though many thousands, ready to perish for
bread, because poor, altogether neglected, and not only so, but
more oppressed, and absolutely exposed to the power of an implac-
able enemy who leaves no way unattempted to destroy them.'[29]
In other instances, however, critiques of the Westminster system
were much more sophisticated. In 1657, East Anglian clothiers

responded to delays in the repayment of parliamentary loans by bemoaning their frequent 'importunity' to MPs over a period of thirteen years, 'besides fifteen weeks attending during this present session'. They now regarded promises that had been made in 1653 as 'conceptions' which had not come to 'a birth of performance', and they wrote of having found 'honour abroad and self-denial not at home, and love to the public thereby, for want of lodging, so cold and feeble'.[30] Some petitioners even detected malign reasons for delays and felt that the system was open to abuse. The Weavers' Company, for instance, thought that rivals had surreptitiously procured an order 'on an unusual day for motions, and contrary to the known rules' of the relevant committee.[31]

On other occasions, the escalation of both tactics and rhetoric which such blockages provoked were sufficiently detailed to involve criticism of individual named MPs. The lawyer, Robert Cole, claimed that a report into his case remained 'in Master [Augustine] Garland's hands', and he was not only willing to name the MP at fault, but also to conclude that 'as yet ... there is not held forth to the free people of this nation any relief'.[32] More dramatic still was the exchange of printed petitions between Thomas Shadforth and George Lilburne, which revolved around the reputation of the MP John Blakiston. Shadforth claimed that Blakiston held damning evidence about Lilburne's activity during the Civil Wars, but Lilburne dismissed Blakiston as 'a supposed member', and accused him of abusing his 'power and interest' by manipulating committees.[33] Colonel George Gill's printed petition, meanwhile, contained detailed allegations about the ways in which Sir William Allenson MP, 'so sharp and so eager an enemy', had abused the parliamentary system and obstructed justice. Gill's persistence resulted in his petition being read and referred to a committee, but he claimed that a report remained undelivered in the hands of another MP, John Downes, for nine months, 'every day almost whereof, I have attended at the door ... at great expenses'. Gill blamed this delay on MPs such as Sir John Bourchier, who 'brought on a particular business of his own' on a day which was 'purposely appointed for mine', such that 'though it hath often been called for, and several times ordered to be heard, yet it could never be heard'.[34]

Ultimately, in what represents the sixth and final stage of this argument, it can sometimes be shown that frustrated expectations and tactical escalations prove to be revealing about the links between low-level quotidian political practice and radical groups like the Levellers. A case in point involves a London leatherseller called Josiah Primatt, which centred upon what has understandably been described as an immensely complicated and 'tortuous' saga relating to the sequestration of collieries in County Durham, and to the local MP, Sir Arthur Hesilrige.[35] These collieries were part-owned by Primatt, and part-owned by Catholic royalists like Thomas Wray. Hesilrige allegedly used his political power to sequester the entire colliery in September 1649, and apparently then leased it back to himself at a low rate, and indeed sought to protect his financial interest in the property by resorting to illegal tactics to prevent Primatt's complaints, and witnesses, from being heard.[36] Such claims were repeated in broadside after broadside, in which Primatt begged for relief from 'the oppression and tyranny' of Hesilrige, and through which he demonstrated his radical credentials rhetorically and tactically.[37] Needless to say, Primatt's language offended MPs, who almost certainly regarded the allegations against Hesilrige as a breach of privilege. However, it is also clear that Primatt's aggressive tactics were deemed to be problematic, and MPs paid particular attention to the fact that he had arranged for the printing of 500 copies of at least one of his texts, the *Humble Petition and Appeal*, and to the fact that he not only delivered 'divers of them to divers members of the House' in December 1651, but also ensured that they became more publicly available. However, what was probably their main concern was that Primatt's frustration had driven him into the arms of John Lilburne and John Wildman. When questioned by the Commons alongside Primatt in December 1651, Lilburne admitted being present when the text was written, although he denied writing it, and admitted that he had been given copies 'to deliver them to several persons', including Speaker Lenthall, Hesilrige and George Fenwick, as well as to anyone else 'who desired to read it'. Wildman, meanwhile, was identified as the petition's penman, and as a key part of Primatt's team of advisors, which also included one Master Levet, as well as lawyers such as Mr Parsons and Mr Lane. The result was that, in January 1652, Primatt's petition was dismissed not just as untrue but also as 'malicious and scandalous'. Copies were ordered to be burnt by the hangman, and Primatt was despatched to the Fleet prison and ordered to pay substantial damages, while the affair was also central to the decision that Lilburne should be banished to the Continent.[38]

Beyond this, when frustration and anger prompted petitioners to consort with radicals it was also possible that they would progress from criticising particular MPs to thinking more generally about the Westminster system. A case in point might be Cornet Christopher Cheesman, with whom this analysis began. Some time after his run-in with the authorities in 1649, Cheesman petitioned Parliament in 1651, in response to his experiences as an agent for sequestrations in Berkshire, in order to expose the 'inhumane cruelties and unparalleled oppressions' of his fellow officials, as well as their financial corruption, at which he was not prepared to 'wink or connive'. Cheesman took his complaints to the authorities in London, only to find himself accused of accepting bribes and suspended from office, and 'put upon an expensive way of prosecution' in order to seek redress, re-employment and his unpaid salary. This he described as 'a mere trick to tire out or discourage him, that thereby the cause of the commonwealth might fall to the ground'. He claimed, indeed, that his enemies 'spun out time from fortnight to fortnight, and three weeks after three weeks, for about three months together'. He noted, therefore, that he was forced to make many 'expensive, long and vexatious journeys to fetch witnesses out of the country', and he complained that at hearings 'the lawyers for their fees, and the commissioners for affection, did weigh so heavy on the side of the offenders, that there could not be one dram of justice allowed the commonwealth and your petitioner'. Cheesman's response involved 'industrious petitioning, writing and printing', but upon discovering that such petitions remained undelivered in the hands of the Speaker he eventually felt compelled to produce a bitter account of the affair, and it is significant that this text, which was addressed 'to every individual member of Parliament', was given the title *The Oppressed Man's Out-cry for Justice*. In it, moreover, Cheesman indicated how experience of interacting with Parliament had taught him that 'though impartial justice and righteousness are the pretended principles of all men in the world, yet ... very few there be which really intend the same, otherwise than only as engines by which they may climb to the top of their ambitious affections and desires.' He had observed how men 'insinuate themselves into the very bowels of the good patriots of this honourable council and commonwealth, under fair and specious pretences of godliness and religion, truth and justice ... by means whereof they possess themselves of great places of honour and profit, which most visibly appears to be their only end.' And he concluded that 'all such men carry on their designs for advancement of themselves, and those of their brotherhood', by 'Machiavellian devices and satanical stratagems'.[39] In other words, Cheesman's mounting frustration led not just to the deployment of print, but also to a radicalisation of his rhetoric. He thus shifted from discrete approaches to officials and MPs in London to printed lobbying, explaining that he 'could not find any better way than to address myself to your honours in print', and then eventually to more public statements, most notably in his *Berk-shires Agent's Humble Address* and then his *Oppressed mans second Outcry for Justice*, both of which were published commercially, or at least made available for sale, by the radical stationer Giles Calvert, respectively in 1651 and 1652.[40] And beyond this, Cheesman's rhetoric also became notably fiery. He thus advised readers 'to avoid being rid upon by subtle politicians, whose aim and ends only is their honour and profits', warned that the nation was likely to be beset by 'bribery, extortion, partiality, perjury and all manner of oppression and cruelty', and railed against 'a grand confederacy' between national and local officials, which 'must needs render the Parliament ... as a mere cipher'.[41]

It is possible, of course, that some petitioners approached the parliamentary process as known troublemakers, and that their radical tactics and rhetoric sprang from their association with men like Lilburne.[42] In the case of Primatt this is certainly possible, given that Lilburne had his own reasons to be involved in the case, in terms of his longstanding feud with Hesilrige and that another of the plaintiffs, George Lilburne, was his uncle. Indeed, Primatt had been consorting with Lilburne for some considerable time and his petitions and complaints were extensively discussed in Lilburne's own pamphlets.[43] And through his association with Bray, of course, Cheesman had been operating on what might be called the fringes of the Leveller movement since 1649. However, while he was clearly a political and religious radical, who stated that 'I do hate persecution for religion', and whose favourite text appears to have been the 'glorious' army declaration of 14 June 1647, and while he was certainly accused of being a mutineer and a Leveller by his enemies, Cheesman strenuously denied that he was a member of any such 'party'. Indeed, it is also worth noting that Cheesman's appointment as an official in Berkshire came after, not before, his arrest in 1649, and that his backers were MPs like William Cawley,

Cornelius Holland and Henry Marten, suggesting that he was much more at home with the new republic than were the Levellers.[44] More importantly, it is possible to show that many other contemporaries developed radical ideas independently of the Levellers, in response to participatory experience, and found themselves drawn towards men like Lilburne, in ways that shed important light on the size and fluidity of the Leveller movement, and on the processes by which it came into being. In 1646, for example, the merchant William Sykes produced a printed sheet for selective distribution, to express frustration at the reception of an earlier printed petition which had demanded free trade, had been 'presented to most members of both Houses', but was 'not so much as publicly read … far less debated and answered'. Sykes felt compelled to 'follow the said petition with this remonstrance', and he outlined increasingly radical views. He demanded the preparation of an ordinance for free trade, by MPs of his own choosing – Alexander Rigby and Henry Marten – and that Parliament 'may not longer delay the discharge of their trust'. He asked: 'Is it not the duty of every trustee in the House of Commons to prosecute the commonwealth's right, and people's privilege?' He also demanded a purge of MPs who were 'patentees, monopolisers, trade engrossers, sellers of people's right, and destroyers of free trade', and the removal of MPs 'out of all other places of public trust'.[45]

Countless other examples could be cited to similar effect, but one of the most striking involves James Freize, one of the long-suffering 'poor prisoners' for debt, whose frustrations with his gaoler and with parliamentary committees led to fruitless petitioning, complaints that MPs blocked a report into his case, and eventually to the deployment of print. Freize explained that he had approached MPs about whom he had read in print and who had developed a public reputation for honesty and probity, and that he had seen Parliament as the obvious way of resolving his personal grievances. Like Sykes, Freize evidently knew a great deal about Parliament and individual MPs, but he also observed partiality in the resolving of grievances, and like Cheesman he began to sound like a Leveller. One pamphlet was called *Every Mans Right*, while another was called *The Outcry and Just Appeal of the Inslaved People of England*. Yet another was called *The Levellers Vindication*, which offered another account of his long and illegal imprisonment and which included provocative ideas and demands. He railed against the abuse of Magna Carta and against political 'juggling', he demanded that those 'intrusted' with public money should be called to 'strict account', and he argued that the law should be translated into English, that 'mercenary lawyers' should be banned from becoming MPs, and that it was necessary to summon a new representative.

And in yet another case, John Poyntz, accused in 1647 of forging an act of Parliament, challenged the jurisdiction of the Lords over a commoner, and reminded MPs that they were 'entrusted', and that they had a responsibility to 'hear, receive and redress the grievances of the people whom you represent, and punish their oppressors, be they high or low, rich or poor, friend or foe, without respect to anything but pure justice'. He even threatened MPs that 'if you resolve to stop your ears against the cries of the people, let us know, that we might fly to some other refuge for protection against those who employ all their power and might to destroy us', and suggested that 'the people of England' might be forced to 'appeal from a Parliament of England'.[46] As with Primatt and Sykes, such disillusionment and such radicalism developed independently of the Levellers, but then helped to draw him into such circles, and in late 1650 he appealed for Lilburne and John Wildman to be his counsel.[47]

This analysis could be extended in various ways. It would be possible to explore similar themes in relation to other forms of participation, from lobbying to public campaigning and even mass protests, and indeed to demonstrate that these were often connected in order to form a participatory spectrum which stretched from the formal, polite and supplicatory to the increasingly demonstrative and even aggressive. However, enough has hopefully been done to make the central point that, by exploring low-level daily parliamentary practices, and the ways in which print came to be deployed tactically and in a variety of ways, it is possible to piece together a picture of important changes to political culture. A variety of more or less ephemeral, and non-public, print genres were appropriated and deployed as tools for participating in parliamentary affairs, not least in order to engage in tactical escalation in the face of frustrated expectations. Printed petitions were thus both an expression of heightened expectations and a manifestation of frustrated hopes. More importantly, such escalations involved ordinary citizens developing an enhanced understanding of how Parliament was supposed to work, did work, and might be made to work better, and finessing their attitudes towards participation and political institutions. They frequently proved willing to criticise the institution and the performance of its members, and to develop a more general critique of the parliamentary system. They were engaged, in other words, in experience-led bottom-up political thinking. And at least occasionally such critiques suggest that our understanding of constitutional conflict in the mid-seventeenth century ought to recognise that intellectual developments originated in political practice. Sometimes this thinking and radicalism is evident in people not normally conceived of as radicals. But it is also evident that groups like the Levellers came into being in no small part through centrifugal forces which brought together disparate and sometimes humble individuals, whose ideas had been forged in the crucible of participatory politics.

Notes

1 *Commons Journal* (hereafter *CJ*), vol. 6, pp. 167–8; *Perfect Occurrences of Every Daies iournall in Parliament*, 116 (16–23 March 1649), p. 911. For Bray, see H. Brailsford, *The Levellers and the English Revolution* (Nottingham: Spokesman, 2nd edn, 1983), pp. 290, 296–8, 300, 306–7; I. Gentles, *The New Model Army in England, Ireland and Scotland, 1645–1653* (Oxford: Blackwell, 1992), pp. 218, 221–4, 229–30, 320.

2 *Perfect Occurrences*, 126 (25 May–1 June 1649), p. 1053; *A Perfect Diurnall of some Passages in Parliament*, 295 (19–26 March 1649), p. 2373; *The Moderate: Impartially communicating Martial Affaires to the Kingdom of England*, 36 (13–20 March 1649), pp. 371–2; C. Cheesman, *The Lamb Contending with the Lion* (London, 1649), sigs A3v–A4v. Cheesman, who claimed not to have been paid for his army service, was accused of being involved in the recent army mutiny, although the evidence against him proved to be limited and he was eventually discharged: Cheesman, *Lamb*, sigs A4v–B4.

3 Cheesman, *Lamb*, sig. A4.

4 J. Morrill, 'John Philipps Kenyon', *Proceedings of the British Academy*, 101 (1999), 452; J. Morrill, *The Nature of the English Revolution* (London: Longman, 1993), pp. 277, 279; D. Underdown, 'Puritanism, revolution and Christopher Hill', in G. Eley and W. Hunt (eds), *Reviving the English Revolution* (London: Verso, 1988), p. 338.

5 Morrill, *Nature*, pp. 281–2; B. Reay, 'The World Turned Upside Down: a retrospect', in Eley and Hunt (eds), *Reviving*, pp. 53–71; J. C. Davis, 'Puritanism and revolution: themes, categories, methods and conclusions', *Historical Journal*, 33 (1990), 693–4; J. C. Davis, *Fear, Myth and History* (Cambridge: Cambridge University Press, 1986), pp. ix–xi,

7–9, 129–37; G. Burgess, 'Radicalism and the English revolution', in G. Burgess and M. Festenstein (eds), *English Radicalism, 1550–1850* (Cambridge: Cambridge University Press, 2007), pp. 63–4.

6 For another example of radicalism as practical and experience led, see Chapter 3.

7 J. Peacey, *Print and Public Politics in the English Revolution* (Cambridge: Cambridge University Press, 2013); D. Zaret, *Origins of Democratic Culture* (Princeton, N.J.: Princeton University Press, 2000).

8 Sir R. Twysden, 'An historical narrative', *Archaeologia Cantiana*, 3 (1860), 155, 170, 171–2, 175–6; *Archaeologia Cantiana*, 4 (1861), 131–2, 134, 146–8, 160–2, 165–70, 172–4, 178, 180–4. For the issues discussed in the following paragraphs, see Peacey, *Print and Public Politics*, ch. 8.

9 British Library (hereafter BL), Additional MS 69871, fol. 98.

10 Lambeth Palace Library, MS 3391, fols 79, 82; *The Humble Petition of Edmond Felton, Gent.* (London, 1642); *Calendar of State Papers Domestic: Interregnum 1652–3*, vol. 36, p. 305. Needless to say, this also seems to have been one of the tactics employed by the Quakers in the later 1650s: see *Diary of Thomas Burton, Esq. member in the Parliaments of Oliver and Richard Cromwell, from 1656 to 1659*, ed. John T. Rutt (London: H. Colburn, 1828), vol. iv, pp. 440–1; G. Fox, *To the High and Lofty Ones* (London, 1655).

11 J. Peacey, 'To every individual member: the Palace of Westminster and participatory politics in the seventeenth century', *The Court Historian*, 13 (2008), 127–47.

12 C. Hotham, *To Every Member of Parliament* (London, 1653).

13 The National Archives, Kew (hereafter TNA), SP 16/479, fol. 84; *The Humble Petition of the Master, Wardens, and Assistants of the Company of Clothworkers of the City of London* (London, 1642); *The Humble Petition of the Parishioners of the Parishes of St. Clement Danes, S. Dunstanes in the West, S. Andrews Holborne, and S. Giles, in the County of Middlesex, in or neere unto Lincolns-Inne-fields* (London, 1645); *The Humble Petition of Divers Persons that Sell Beer in the County of Sommerset* (London, 1659).

14 *A Most Lamentable Information of Part of the Grievances of Mugleswick* (London, 1642); *The humble Petition of Phillip Chetwind, Prisoner in Newgate* (London, 1650).

15 BL, Additional MS 70005, fol. 209.

16 Twysden, 'Narrative', 3, pp. 159–61, 167–70, 173; 'Narrative', 4, pp. 137–42, 144–5, 172; Sir R. Twysden, *Certaine Considerations upon the Government of England*, ed. John M. Kemble (Camden Society, 1849), vol. 45, p. 171.

17 *Sir Thomas Hampson his Carriage upon his case lately questioned for Delinquency* (London, 1647).
18 Longleat, Whitelocke Papers (hereafter WP), Parcel 7, no. 87.
19 Longleat, WP, Parcel 7, no.91; TNA, SP 23/247, 'The Humble Petition of the Reduced Officers', London, 1648, fol. 219.
20 D. Hirst, 'Making contact', *Journal of British Studies*, 45 (2006), 40; Longleat, WP, Parcel 7, no. 85, 'The Case of the Eastland Merchants', undated; WP, Parcel 7, no. 110, 'The Humble Petition of the ... Vintners', undated.
21 Longleat, WP, Parcel 7, no. 102, 'Elizabeth, Duchess of Hamilton Humbly Sheweth' (London, 1653). For the earlier printed petition see *The humble Petition of Elizabeth, Dutchesse (dowager) of Hamilton, and her Foure Orphan Daughters* (London, 1652).
22 Longleat, WP, Parcel 7, no.84, 'The Humble Petition of John Musgrave and Richard Crackenthorpe', undated; *The Humble Petition of Richard Pechell* (London, 1648); *The Humble Address of Sir John Scot, of Scottishtarvet* (London, 1655), sigs A, A2.
23 Longleat, WP, Parcel 7, no. 114, 'The Humble Petition of Colonel Charles Doilie', undated.
24 Parliamentary Archive (hereafter PA), MP 26 February 1642, 'A Declaration of Certaine Particulars', undated.
25 PA, MP 5 May 1648; *The Humble Petition of the Company of Worsted-Weavers of the City of Norwich, and County of Norfolk* (London, 1655); Longleat, WP, Parcel 7, no. 114, 'Colonel Charles Doilie'.
26 *The Humble Petition of Richard Chambers Merchant and Alderman of the City of London* (London, 1646).
27 Longleat, WP, Parcel 7, no. 107, 'The humble Petition of Richard Chambers', London, 1652; BL, 190.g.12/183, 'The Brief Remonstrance and Humble Petition of Richard Chambers', London, 1654.
28 T. Philpot, *To his Highnesse the Lord Protector, And to the right Honourable the Representatives of the People assembled in Parliament: A Preparative to the Humiliation-Day, on the eleventh of Octob. 1654* (London, 1654).
29 BL, Additional MS 6677, fol. 49, 'The Serious Representation of Captain Thomas Robinson', London, 1649; Additional MS 6682, fol. 43.
30 *The Humble Petition of the Real Lenders, upon the Publick Faith, the Clothiers, and all others in the Counties of Essex, and Suffolk, in the behalf of themselves, and all others the like, that are unpaid* (London, 1657).
31 PA, MP 5 May 1648, 'The Humble Petition of Robert Vivers and Henry Benson', London, 1648, pp. 3–5, 6–15; Longleat, WP, Parcel 7, no. 101, 'The Humble Petition of the ... Company of Weavers', undated.

32 Longleat, WP, Parcel 7, no. 83, 'The Case of Robert Cole', undated.
33 *The Humble Petition of Thomas Shadforth* (London, 1649); G. Lilburne, *The humble Remonstrance of George Lilburn, Esquire* (London, 1649), pp. 1, 4–5; T. Shadforth, *Innocency modestly vindicated and truth impartially, though (but partly discovered), by Thomas Shadforth, Esquire, against George Lilburne, Esquire* (London, 1649), p. 4.
34 G. Gill, *Innocency Cleared: or the Case and Vindication of Col. George Gill* (London, 1651), sig. A2, pp. 2, 8, 10–12, 12–14.
35 P. Gregg, *Free-Born John* (London: George Harrap, 1961), pp. 310–11.
36 *The humble Petition of Josiah Primatt, Citizen and Leather-seller of London* (London, 1651).
37 Longleat, WP, Parcel 7, no. 95, 'The Humble Petition of Josiah Primat', London, 1651; *The humble Petition and Appeal of Josiah Prymat of London, Leatherseller* (London, 1651); *The True State of the Case of Josiah Primatt, concerning the Collieries of Harraton in the County of Durham* (London, 1651).
38 *CJ*, vol. 7, pp. 55, 65, 71–3; *The Proceedings of the Parliament upon the Petition and Appeal of Josiah Primat of London, Leatherseller* (London, 1651); *Mercurius Politicus*, 85 (15–22 January 1652), pp. 1353–8, 1364.
39 C. Cheesman, *The Oppressed man's Out-Cry for Justice* (London, 1651), pp. 1, 3–6. For the accusations of bribery and the fight with his rivals, see: *Calendar of the Proceedings of the Committee for Compounding*, ed. M. Green (London: HMSO, 1889–92), vol. i, pp. 177, 351, 390–1, 402, 405, 409–10, 412, 417, 426, 430, 432, 436–7, 443, 447, 473, 477–8, 482, 503, 517; TNA, SP 23/15, p. 107; TNA, SP 23/74, pp. 269, 277, 283.
40 C. Cheesman, *Berk-shires Agent's Humble Address To The honourable Commissioners for Compounding* (London, 1651), pp. 2–3, 5, 11, 16; C. Cheesman, *The Oppressed mans second Outcry for Justice* (London, 1652), pp. 6–7.
41 Cheesman, *Berk-shires*, p. 45; Cheesman, *The Oppressed mans second Outcry*, pp. 6–7.
42 *The Humble Petition of Samuel Chidley* (London, 1652); *The humble Representation of divers afflicted Women-Petitioners to the Parliament, on the behalf of Mr John Lilburn* (London, 1653).
43 J. Lilburne, *A Just Reproof to Haberdashers-Hall* (London, 1651), *passim*. See also *Lieut. Colonel John Lilb. Tryed and Cast: or His Case and Craft discovered* (London, 1653), pp. 3–17.
44 Cheesman, *Lamb*, sigs A2v, A4, B, B2; Cheesman, *Berk-shires*, pp. 8, 11, 41, 45; TNA, SP 28/258, part 4, fol. 448. For his spirited but perhaps ill-advised 'counsel' to Charles II, see *An Epistle to Charles*

the Second King of England, and to every individual Member of His Council (Reading, 1661).

45 *The Humble Remonstrance of William Sykes* (London, 1646). For the earlier petition, see *The Humble Petition of William Sykes and Thomas Johnson* (London, 1645).

46 PA, MP 28 Aug. 1648: 'The Humble Petition of John Poyntz', undated; J. Poyntz, *The Humble Petition and Appeal* (London, 1648); PA, MP 25 Nov. 1648, 'To Every Individual Member', undated; *An Appeal to each individual Member of the present Parliament and Army, in the case of John Poyntz aliàs Morris, Mary his wife, Isabella Smith, Leonard Darby and John Harris* (London, 1648); *The Case and Vindication of John Poyntz, alias Morrice, and his Friends* (London, 1648), p. 7; CJ, vol. 6, p. 86.

47 *The humble Petition of John Poyntz, alias Morris* (London, 1650).

7

∼

Toasting and the diffusion of radical ideas, 1780–1832

Rémy Duthille

In modern England, health-giving, or toasting – a term used with increasing frequency after its coining c. 1700 – was a political and contentious act marking the drinker's allegiance to a patron and, later, to a cause. Each of the political crises that affected Britain in the seventeenth and eighteenth centuries had its spate of quarrels, riots and prosecutions involving people drinking, or refusing to drink the health, or the damnation, of the Duke of York, James III, William of Orange, Dr Sacheverell or John Wilkes, to name but a few.[1] While toasting helped cement communities in hardship or exile, such as the Jacobites, more generally toasting became a partisan weapon, ambiguously signalling allegiance to persons and groupings, but also to values. By the early nineteenth century, indeed, it was integral to the rich repertoire of practices deployed by the radicals during ritualised dinners, as James Epstein has thoroughly demonstrated.[2] Frank O'Gorman argued that, as election rituals, toasts crucially articulated the parties' convictions and sense of history and identity, so much so that 'piecing together the innumerable toasts at election dinners it is sometimes almost possible to reconstruct the entire belief system of those present'.[3] This chapter supports this claim. Most dinners displayed the harmony and conviviality wished for by organisers and guests alike. However, there is evidence that toasts could fail in their ritual function and provoke strife instead of unifying reformers around shared ideals and goals. Toasting thus provides a particularly promising entryway into political discourse, as it shows both how solidarity is being built around shared values and goals, and how those common objectives might be challenged and negotiated.

The foundation of the Society for Constitutional Information (SCI) in 1780 heralded new developments. While political toasting and counter-toasting was part of the 'politics of pleasure' flourishing during the Wilkite agitation,[4] the 1780s saw the institutionalisation of radical dinners and the increasingly frequent and regular publication of toast lists in the press. The SCI minute books provide systematic account of toasts over a long range of years, from 1780 to 1793.[5] Toast lists were carefully drafted and the order of precedence was negotiated and agreed to in advance. During the dinner toasts were preceded by 'sentiments', which could be very long speeches if the speaker was a famous orator or a guest of honour. The concluding toast was a brilliant envoy which might have little thematic relevance to the preceding speech. Each guest rose and gave a toast in turn, answering what was said before.

Investigations into material culture might shed some light on symbolic aspects of toasting. The nature of beverages probably depended above all on the social standing of the drinkers. The late Stuart beer v. wine political divide had long faded away and by the end of the eighteenth century punch united the middling orders across party differences.[6] Plebeian radicals drank porter while reformers from the middling ranks favoured Madeira, port or punch but there is no evidence that this choice was in any way politicised. Pottery was specifically crafted for radical circles in the 1790s – a toby jug with black printing designs of Paine and Burke, a mug printed with 'La Guillotine' – but we have yet to learn how those objects functioned.[7]

Epstein's analysis is based on exceptionally exhaustive accounts. But toasts must all too often be interpreted without reference to the symbolic paraphernalia because lists of toasts published in the press were usually incomplete. Before the 1800s the press provided detailed coverage only on special occasions, such as celebrations of the 4 November or 14 July, by major societies, not local societies in the provinces. When the toast list formed the bulk of the press article, it inevitably acquired a metonymic value, becoming shorthand for the ideological principles defended by a particular set of people, and this process involves problems of interpretation both for the eighteenth-century reader and for the historian, who might be compared to a literary critic trying to reconstruct a *commedia dell'arte* show on the basis of a prompt book or a sketchy account.

Toasting was also a widespread social practice that was not by any means restricted to banquets but included informal gatherings in alehouses, taverns, private homes or Newgate prison, the site of a flourishing radical culture in the 1790s. For Newton E. Key, 'commensality can best be viewed as a continuum: from solitary dining; to private dining with family and friends; to clubs reserved for members; to feasts that were publicized and were restricted only by tickets bought or freely distributed; to outdoor, inclusive feasts'.[8] What Key wrote about the reign of Charles II is also valid for late eighteenth-century Britain. Toasting cultures in the two periods, however, differed, if only because places of sociability changed and the blurred boundaries between the public and the private were being redefined. By the 1790s, gentlemen's clubs had become much more socially exclusive; radical societies wished to retain their independence from parties, and 'outdoor, inclusive feasts' were avoided as they could turn into occasions for riots. Most importantly, radical sociability, including drinking and toasting practices, was shaped by government surveillance, judicial repression and loyalist harassment.

Toasting can be analysed as a ritual providing one bears in mind that there were degrees of ritualisation, from low-key, informal tavern encounters to highly codified forms.[9] Though a full theorisation is impossible in the scope of a chapter, toasts will be analysed here as speech acts and as a rituals of interaction from the perspective of pragmatics and Erwing Goffman's sociology.[10] Toasting normally performs an integrative function in radical societies and its highly codified formal properties shape the message, encouraging irony, parody and subversion. But in politically volatile contexts this ritualisation also encouraged breaches of decorum and outrageous performances, involving violence and strife.

The practice of toasting in radical societies, such as the SCI or the London Corresponding Society (hereafter LCS), served an integrative function, fostering solidarity and mobilisation. Convivial drinking helped to hold the group together, while the regularity of rituals structured the society's time around a specific, symbolic festive calendar. Well managed toasting rounds achieved a balance between the group and the individual: each member of the society accepted common rules while enjoying his own moment of glory when giving his toast. Values were seemingly transmitted in a very literal sense as the glass and speaking turn went round from one member to the next.

Throughout its period of existence, the SCI held anniversary dinners which were an annual occasion for the members to socialise and commune around shared values and historical references. Toast lists from 1780 to 1793 show both stability and change, signalling ideological mutations. The first toast was 'The Majesty of the People', followed by others to the president, treasurer and stewards of the society.

Toasts to the traditional liberties of England, such as 'The Navy of England – Volunteer Crews – and no Press Gangs', coexisted with others supporting international causes and struggling patriots, especially the Insurgents during the American War and the United States after independence. In 1785 the SCI drank to 'The United States of America; and may the Cause of Freedom flourish in every Region of the Globe'.[11] Toast lists thus displayed the characteristic coexistence of English constitutionalism and universal aspirations which persisted in modified forms well into the nineteenth century.[12]

But they also charted change, as increasingly frequent references to the Irish Volunteers and the Scottish reformers in the 1780s testified to the progressive British scope of the SCI's ideology and networks.[13] Draft lists also gave some insight into the debates about wording, reflecting discussions on the society's values and priorities. In the late 1780s, in the context of the dissenters' renewed campaign against the Test and Corporation Acts, the SCI was moving away from toleration towards a more pressing demand for liberty, as can be seen in the crossed-out manuscript: '25. May universal Toleration prevail through all the World; and May no Person suffer in his Civil or religious Capacity for his peculiar religious Opinions by any Penal or exclusive Laws.'[14]

The leading members of the society were given a special homage, especially Richard Price, 'the Friend of the Universe', and Cartwright, dubbed, interestingly, both 'the Father of Reform' and 'the Father of the Society'. Deceased members were also honoured, alongside their forebears in the struggle against tyranny.[15] Those rituals of remembrance reinforced the society's self-identification as heir to the heroic Commonwealthmen of the previous century. This heritage is even more central to the identity of the Revolution Society, whose object was the celebration of the Glorious Revolution, hence toasts to:

25. The immortal Memory of Alfred the great, and may all the Kings of the earth imitate his example.
26. The immortal Memory of Hampden, Pym, Russell, and Sidney.
27. The memory of Andrew Marvell, Milton, Locke, the late Mr Thomas Hollis and the late Dr John Jebb.[16]

Such rituals of remembrance helped to build a sense of historical continuity legitimising the reformers' indefatigable endeavours. The radicals identified with the opponents to Charles I and the Commonwealthmen, as they too considered themselves as defenders of liberty pitted against arbitrary rulers. As for the 1688 Revolution, it was celebrated as a 'glorious' yet incomplete achievement calling for further reform.[17]

The generation active in the revival of radical activism after 1815 was keenly aware of that necessity. While new celebrations were created, such as the annual 'Purity of Election dinner' celebrating Sir Francis Burdett's election in Westminster in 1807, the radicals also drew on and enriched their repertoire of toasts. Some healths were drunk throughout and beyond the period considered in this chapter; those perennial classics pointed to the continuity of grievances and demands, and to the changing nature of the many-headed hydra of despotism. Thus 'the liberty of the press, the bulwark of English liberty' had as much urgency, but a different resonance, in the time of Wilkes and general warrants, and that of the taxes on knowledge and the unstamped press.

Examples abound of toasts keeping alive a radical tradition by reinvigorating hallowed phrases. In 1818 a banquet was held in the honour of the then seventy-eight-year-old Major Cartwright. Though the Major was too ill to attend he wrote a valedictory speech that was read out in response. The title of his 1776 pamphlet was revived as a toast showing the continuity of the radical movement with a new generation carrying on with the fight: 'Take your choice – a civil government, or a military despotism; – in other words, Burdett's bill, or Castlereagh's bayonet.'[18] Another veteran was Coke of Norfolk, who had voted against the American War in Parliament.[19] But perhaps the most spectacular instance of an appeal to a radical tradition was Cobbett's return from the United States with the remains of Thomas Paine in October 1819. A series of dinners was given in the North of England, with Cobbett explaining he wanted to 'erect a colossal statue to his memory', and toasts being drunk to 'the memory of our famous countryman, Thomas

Paine, the "Noble of Nature", "the Child of the Lower Orders", illustrious from his unrivalled talents, and still more illustrious from the employment of those talents in the cause of the "oppressed of all nations"'. Those dinners also paid homage to Cartwright and to the Peterloo 'martyrs'.[20]

The publication of toast lists and dinner accounts in the press was crucial in establishing the pan-British scope of the reform movement, at least ideally, showing the popularity of the cause in Britain and the international solidarity with patriots abroad. Such favourable press coverage was essential to keep up the reformers' spirits in periods of repression and to diffuse toasts from one place to another, since reformers took up and adapted toasts drunk elsewhere. The process was certainly not just one of imitation of metropolitan toasts in the provinces. Newspapers in Manchester, Sheffield and Edinburgh were very active in diffusing toast lists across Britain. For instance, the *Manchester Herald*, a paper that ran from April 1792 to March 1793, regularly reported dinners given by many societies in England and Scotland, covering a broad section of opposition and radical circles, from the newly created artisan societies to the moderate Foxite Friends of the People.[21] The toast lists of so many societies across Britain tended to show a unity of purpose and contained cross references expressing solidarity among reformers. In the *Manchester Herald*'s account of the Sheffield 'patriotic fête' celebrating French military victories in October 1792, the first toast was to 'the French Republic'; others were given to '[t]he London, Manchester, Norwich, Stockport, Edinburgh, and Glasgow societies for Parliamentary Reform, and all other similar societies in the Nation'.[22] Similarly the *Edinburgh Gazetteer*, from November 1792 to January 1794, published reports from England and did its utmost to cover the activities of new reform societies forming across Scotland, thus bolstering the morale of reformers living in isolated or very loyalist areas.

The publication of toasts drunk in France and the United States highlighted the international nature of republicanism. Thus, the *Edinburgh Gazetteer* published a letter from Philadelphia about the 'sumptuous feast' given to the French ambassador Edmond-Charles Genet on his arrival in Philadelphia in May 1793. The toasts celebrated the friendship of the two republics and sent dire warnings to monarchies: 'The arm of Hercules to those who combat the hydra of despotism. May the last Freeman rather perish than bend under the yoke of Despotism. The years 1776 and 1792, which declared America and France Republics. May the heads soon be under one Cap, the BONNET ROUGE, the Cap of Liberty.'[23] In the 1820s toasts served to display both patriotic feeling and sympathy for foreign freedom fighters and liberal politicians in South America and Greece, while toasts such as 'the Glorious Revolution of Spain'[24] linked liberal aspirations abroad to a British tradition.

The increasing number of toast lists published in the press testified to the radicals' perceived potency of the genre. Such perlocutionary agency comes from both the formal properties of the toast, and from the performance in a context of interaction.

There were two basic structures, which could occasionally be combined: a noun phrase – sometimes preceded by 'to' and followed by a relative clause or other modifiers – and optative clauses starting with 'may'. These two structures were simple and flexible enough to allow a rich generative process. The first enabled the unfurling of rolls of honour, or to list grievances or items of a reform programme. As for optative clauses, they allowed for an immense variety of matter and tone, serious or jocular, as the many jestbooks and toastmaster's guides published in the period testify. The optative toast had a pithy style that tallied well with the experimental nature of much of radical writing: by opening fresh imaginary perspectives it allowed for idiosyncrasy and provocation and could serve to test the boundaries of the socially and politically acceptable.[25] Rather than defining closed, coherent ideologies, toasts reflected inchoate, evolving structures of feelings.[26] Whereas the lists of toasts given in conservative circles were rather short, always beginning with 'the King' or 'Church and King', and then moving down an unproblematic hierarchy to praise local worthies, with no or few optative clauses,[27] the radicals exploited the generative formulaic pattern of the toast to voice new ideas. The convivial context of drinking facilitated this process; Spencean circles in particular organised singing and drinking competitions giving rise to toasts such as 'May the barren land of our country be manured with the blood of our Tyrantry'.[28]

Another key feature shaping the message was its binary form, which reduced issues to clear-cut alternatives. Toasts were powerful weapons in the battles for the redefinition of political vocabulary, as they played on key oppositions such as liberty/slavery or aristocracy/people. Thus many toasts were moulded in set structures, which

176

can be formalised as: A rather than non-A, may B replace non-B, as in 'Dr Priestley, and may reason and philosophy ever prevail over fanaticism and ignorance'.[29] Pledging a toast, then, essentially meant taking sides. It could not accommodate complex argument or qualified endorsements of values and people, which explains why the publication of toast lists without the associated speeches could be misleading and was often wilfully misinterpreted. Perhaps the best example is the toast given by Richard Price at the 4 November 1790 dinner of the Revolution Society: 'The Parliament of Great Britain, and may it become a National Assembly.'[30] This caused offence as it was widely interpreted as a sweeping defence of the French Revolution and a call for another in Britain. In fact it did not completely reflect the tenor of the foregoing speech and Price felt compelled to reply to his numerous critics that he only advocated a thoroughgoing parliamentary reform, which was totally different.[31] In a rapidly moving context, pronouncements took on new, unexpected meanings, and recantations only fuelled the suspicion of ulterior motives.

On the other hand, toasts, with their easily recognisable and imitable structure, lent themselves admirably to parody. By toasting Burke, 'The SWINISH MULTITUDE. Mr Burke, and may he long serve the cause of the people, by *writing against them*',[32] radicals and dissenters seized on an unfortunate expression in *Reflections on the Revolution in France* to praise the people as the source of sovereignty and express their belief that truth would ultimately prevail. In the 1800s reformers in Lancashire strove to reclaim loyalty from their Tory opponents by appropriating and subverting their own symbols, calendar and toasts. Counter-celebrations of the King's birthday were staged with reformist toasts couched in constitutionalist rhetoric, while a group in Liverpool chose Pitt's birthday to drink parodic toasts such as 'Middling Classes of Society annihilated'.[33]

Irony, of course, worked both ways, and loyalists published satirical accounts of radical dinners. On 14 July 1791 *The Times* gave a list of toasts allegedly drafted by the Revolution Society before its Bastille Day celebration, praising Voltaire and Mirabeau, Nero and Caligula, Wat Tyler, Jack Cade, Oliver Cromwell, and the Gordon Riots of 1780. The journalist displayed such a mastery of the radicals' classical and French revolutionary tropes, such as 'May the dagger of *Brutus* be tempered on the anvil of French

Republicanism', that parody is at times virtually undistinguish-able from the original. Thus, some of the most outrageous regicide rhetoric, like 'May the purple stream of Royalty be soon visible at Paris', was voiced in the impeccably loyalist *Times*. [34]

Such accounts implicitly acknowledged the rhetorical potency of the radical toast list, a type of writing that was taken seriously enough to be countered by parody. Conservative anxieties about mob violence, levelling and a resurgence of the violence of the 1640s, already central in Burke's *Reflections*, could hardly be exagger-ated.[35] The authorities knew that toasting, like communal drinking and singing, cemented radical communities, and in their paranoid way they interpreted it as evidence of a 'system' or a plot to ensnare gullible artisans and lead them to treasonable thoughts and, later, actions.[36] The authorities considered popular toasts as an index of public opinion and were forced to acknowledge that inns and taverns had become politicised spaces. The loyalist associations that spread through many regions of Britain in the winter of 1792–93 made every effort to ban seditious speech, bring the offenders to justice and intimidate publicans who tolerated radicals on their premises.[37]

From 1792 on, the performance of toasting was enacted in a context of spying and intimidation, though the intensity and nature of repression varied in time and across social divisions. A related obstacle was that of respectability. The radicals had two options to counter their loyalist opponents, who tried to disqualify them by denying them any form of respectability. The LCS and most other societies strove to redefine and appropriate it to back their claims to political seriousness and legitimacy. On the other hand, a few others, essentially the Spenceans, flouted middle-class con-ventions. Toasting straddled the blurred, contested line dividing the 'respectable' from the 'unrespectable':[38] whereas it signalled a sense of order and decency in imitation of formal elite dinners, it also entailed the danger of excessive drinking and violence. The LCS held its meetings in taverns but forbade its members to drink and smoke, and its magazine criticised intemperance and profane toasting.[39] Francis Place, the arch-exponent of respectability, tried to reform the tavern-centred artisan culture, once declaring: 'I hate taverns and tavern company. I cannot drink.'[40] Others were actu-ated by class feelings. A gentleman reformer rather than a staunch radical, John Cam Hobhouse expressed a marked dislike for the bibulous culture of electioneering and political dinners.[41]

Besides loyalist pressure and the dictates of respectability, the third crucial parameter governing the situation of interaction lay in the gendered notions of masculine honour. For Alexandra Shepard, early modern male drinking rituals could threaten any social norm, except the exclusion of women from political power, which was unambiguously upheld.[42] This argument can be extended to the period considered here. Though by the late eighteenth century a polite, Addisonian model of gentlemanliness competed with rougher types,[43] in all-male parties, toasting and inebriation encouraged aggressive masculinity. It is most likely that John Horne Tooke, once John Wilkes's favourite drinking companion, gave bawdy after-dinner toasts, especially after sterner members like Dr Price left the room, but press articles kept to euphemisms such as 'mirth' or 'utmost conviviality'. Male radicals never toasted Catharine Macaulay or Mary Wollstonecraft, possibly for fear of casting aspersions on their female modesty. Perhaps more importantly, their pretentions to respectability precluded any association with earlier aristocratic, libertine practices of drinking to the 'toasts of the town'. As for the bawdy bumpers drunk by the 'unrespectable' ultraradicals, they can hardly be said to advance women's lib.[44] This state of affairs seems to have changed little over the period. Several female reform societies were founded around 1818;[45] at least one of them drank toasts, and elsewhere in Lancashire, reformers of both sexes appear to have held dinners together.[46] Male reformers occasionally toasted 'the heroines of our age and country, the Female Reformers',[47] but honoured them as mere auxiliaries to their cause. When ladies participated in radical dinners, they sat in the gallery and 'waved their handkerchiefs in sympathy' during the toasts and speeches.[48]

Drinking places became 'arenas for testing the courage of men's political convictions'.[49] Toasting indeed wielded violence, channelling aggression into wit and politeness, or mounting challenges to other men's masculinity. Reactions ranged from imitation, cheers and signs of approval to taunts, physical violence, aggression or judicial proceedings. In the situation of interaction each participant had to deploy face-saving strategies. A tract distributed by the APLP tells the story of an 'ill-looking stranger', a favourite trope of loyalist writing, who gives a toast to Paine in an inn, is repulsed, and ousted from the company, while the other guests – people from the local community – drink bumpers to Church and King.[50] The loyal toast symbolises the reunion of the community around shared values, endowing the moralistic tale with a comforting sense of closure.

Far from being merely symbolic, punishment could take practical, damaging forms. In December 1792, the *World* reported the story of a commercial traveller who invited his customers to dinner:

> After Supper the Party began to drink toasts; and the Traveller took upon him to propose Mr. THOMAS PAINE as a toast, which so enraged the company, that they seized him with almost an unanimous consent, and would have proceeded to *thrust him up the chimney*, had not a person in company interfered. The next morning all those Persons who had the preceding day favoured him with orders, sent him notice to strike them out of his books; for *they would have nothing to do with any Person who was a Friend to* M. PAINE *or his* DOCTRINES.[51]

Physical violence was replaced by economic retaliation, a potentially more effective weapon. All kinds of horrible things happened to those who drank radical toasts: when a Cornish miner drank Tom Paine's health and 'perdition to all Kings of the earth', 'his jaw became locked, and he died on the spot, in the most excruciating torments. He left a pregnant wife, and four helpless infants behind him.'[52] Deterring and vindictive rather than factual, this kind of loyalist writing turns the perlocutionary violence of the toast against the blaspheming drinker.

Prosecution was another, more extreme, response to controversial toasting. John Thelwall allegedly toasted 'the lamp-iron in Parliament street' and cut the froth off a glass of porter, saying 'So should all tyrants be served'. Thelwall's guillotining of his glass of porter was presented by the prosecution as an act of 'compass[ing] and imagin[ing] the King's death' but the perlocutionary effect remains ambivalent as Thelwall may have been advocating the regicide and also trying to make his friends laugh.[53] Such an uneasy mixture of high seriousness and fun contributed to destabilise accepted hierarchies.

Punishments could be harsh. While the English radical leaders were acquitted in London, in Scotland three men – a flax-dresser, a mason and a tailor – were condemned to four months' imprisonment and a heavy fine for 'riotous behaviour' after celebrating French victories and drinking seditious toasts such as 'George the Third and last King'.[54] Nor did the high and mighty go unpunished.

In 1798 the Duke of Norfolk was dismissed from two offices he held, and Fox was expelled from the Privy Council for drinking 'the Majesty of the People!' at Whig dinner parties.[55]

Loyalist pressure was very strong in polite circles, making it increasingly dangerous to give even Whiggish toasts in public: 'So apprehensive are the Chartered Companies of being infected with the spirit of freedom, that they have more than once turned out of the room a solitary individual who has dared to propose a toast or attempted to sing a song in opposition to their own sentiments, and thus at once given a proof of politeness and courage.'[56] In rare instances, a courageous individual could shatter the consensus. Samuel Parr did so shortly after the Priestley riots of July 1791, using the rule obliging him to toast Church and King in his turn to affirm Whig principles in defiance of the Tory assembly:

> At first, he resolutely declined. But the obligation of compliance being urgently pressed upon him – rising, at length, with firmness and dignity – with a manner of impressive solemnity, and with a voice of powerful energy, he spoke thus – 'I am compelled to drink the toast given from the chair; but I shall do so, with my own comment. Well, then, gentlemen – Church and King. – Once it was the toast of the Jacobites; now it is the toast of incendiaries. It means a Church without the gospel – and a king above the law'.[57]

The body language displaying manliness and respectability was as integral to the performance as the brilliance of the speech. This episode was used for hagiographic purposes by Parr's biographer William Field, and later found its way into the *Oxford Dictionary of National Biography*, a sure sign that toasting could be a memorable test of steadfastness.

The loyal toast at the centre of the Parr anecdote was used to silence opponents and unmask traitors: it became a test of loyalty, and merely omitting to drink it was seen as tantamount to treason.[58] Parr's flamboyant gesture was available only to gentlemen radicals, not to plebeians who would never be invited to a Tory gathering in the first place. Giving a radical toast in public places frequented by the upper- and middling orders, such as coffee houses and reputed taverns, meant holding one's ground, both figuratively and literally. A case in point already discussed by critics is that of Charles Pigott and William Hodgson. While engaged in conversation at a London coffee house in September 1792, Hodgson called George III

'German Hog Butcher' loud enough for a member of the APLP to hear it. Several customers came up and tried to force the two men to drink to 'the King and the Royal Family'; as they refused to comply they were arrested and brought to trial for 'uttering seditious and inflammatory words'. Later witnesses swore that Pigott and Hodgson had drunk toasts to France and the 'overthrow of all monarchies'.[59]

The defence insisted on Pigott's and Hodgson's manly fortitude, and relied on a man's right to drink and give toasts without being spied on. John Thelwall chimed in:

> Where is the man whose conversation and sentiments never lay open to misrepresentation? Where is the man who never, in the gaiety of youthful passion, gave utterance to an idle expression, or drank a ridiculous toast, which if gravely repeated, with the colourings of a malignant commentator, might not be tortured into evidence of intentions from which his soul would have revolted?[60]

On another occasion an LCS member told the court that he was 'very much intoxicated': 'I do not know what the man who gave them meant by the toasts. I drank them.'[61] This line of defence was self-defeating as it contradicted the radicals' professed steadfastness and honesty of purpose, damaged their pretensions to respectability and echoed the loyalist trope of the violent, drunken rabble that served to dismiss popular political expression and agency.

The dangers entailed by toasting were exploited by *agents provocateurs*. In 1816, John Castle, a government informer, gave: 'May the last of Kings be strangled with the guts of the last priest.' Henry Hunt refused to drink what he called in his autobiography 'a vulgar and sanguinary toast ... a piece of brutality which had not even the miserable merit of being original, he having copied it from one of the French anarchists ... I remonstrated against such blackguardism, and declared that I would not remain in the room if there was any repetition of it.'[62] Hunt's narrative of the incident is but one of several competing versions that were published in the context of a trial revolving on Castle's testimony.[63] It enabled him to state the toast was *not* a standard radical toast and to style himself as an upright reformer.

Toasting indeed forced a man to show how far he was ready to go. This is why it was used by the radicals to test one another's loyalties and limits. Toasting-related quarrels multiplied after Francis

Burdett's election as MP for Westminster in 1807, both reflecting and fuelling personal rivalries and differences over strategy. The alliance with the Whigs was a thorny problem which the drafting of toast lists could bring to the fore. In 1821, when Hobhouse warned that to 'drink a toast to *"radical reform w[ould] be to offend the Whigs"'*, Burdett retorted that those who refused such a toast were not entitled to give a speech on radical reform. He also objected to toasts like 'the *House* of *Russell'* as too aristocratic.[64] Finally the quarrel was patched up; 'radical reform' was expunged and Hobhouse boasted he 'contrived to name almost all the MPs present'.[65]

A further point of contention was the ordering of toasts. The orators at the top of the list were given an opportunity to hold forth, while those speaking at the end of the dinner would address an almost empty room or befuddled guests. Negotiations over the toast list could be magnified in press reports so as to attack rivals. In 1818 the Westminster Committee chose Hobhouse to run for the parliamentary election rather than Cartwright, Cobbett's candidate. Cobbett published a diatribe against Hobhouse and his Benthamite allies because they had managed to place one of them third on the list and had relegated Cartwright far below. On seeing their list of toasts, 'the rage which I flew into … rendered it impossible for me to hold my tongue'. Cobbett demanded that the list should be altered. According to him, the Benthamites gave in for fear he might challenge the orders of toasts and humiliate them during the dinner. 'The history of this base intrigue', as Cobbett styled it, gave him a golden opportunity for self-promotion and settling of scores.[66]

The increasing frequency of such quarrels from the 1810s should not be seen merely as signs of the ineffectual character of radicalism but as the downside of two positive developments. First, the expansion of the radical press provided more outlets for such polemics. More significantly, the competition for leadership sharpened because the post-1807 radicals played for higher stakes as election to the Commons had become a credible prospect, at least in a few constituencies.

Toasts were thus a potent but dangerous vehicle of radical values and aspirations. They provoked discussion, and potential dissension, from pre-dinner arrangements to the actual performance and beyond, whether they were imitated, challenged or subverted. Reporting and misreporting embroiled their authors in controversies and retaliation. They were therefore part of a developing nexus comprising oral and written discourse, pamphlets, press reports and rumours, under the less than benevolent gaze of the law and the courts of justice. Crucially, toasts contributed to make radical voices heard in public places, catching the public mood and spreading political slogans well beyond the pamphlet-reading public.

But the very public nature of the business of toasting meant it was torn by contradictions. Ironically toasts worried both loyalists and the leaders of the reform movement, who attempted to tone them down and channel them into acceptable forms. Nevertheless, toasting was never kept under total control. The irruption of outrageous, divisive, indictable toasts risked at any moment to undermine neat pre-dinner arrangements and derail whatever movement there was. Toasts thus bear testimony to the formidable – the radical? – potency of the individual voice.

Notes

1 On the Restoration, see: N. E. Key, '"High feeding and smart drinking": associating Hedge-Lane Lords in Exclusion Crisis London', in J. McElligott (ed.), *Fear, Exclusion and Revolution: Roger Morrice and Britain in the 1680s* (Aldershot: Ashgate, 2006), pp. 154–73; T. Harris, *London Crowds in the Reign of Charles II: Propaganda and Politics from the Restoration until the Exclusion Crisis* (Cambridge: Cambridge University Press, 1987), ch. 7 especially. On toasting under James II and during the Glorious Revolution: T. Harris, *Revolution: The Great Crisis of the British Monarchy, 1685–1720* (Harmondsworth: Penguin, 2007), pp. 64, 83, 86, 90, 111, 152, 356 and elsewhere. On Jacobite toasting and malicious prosecutions for 'seditious words', see P. K. Monod. *Jacobitism and the English People, 1688–1788* (Cambridge: Cambridge University Press, 1993), ch. 8 especially.

2 J. Epstein, *Radical Expression: Political Language, Ritual, and Symbol in England, 1790–1850* (Oxford: Oxford University Press, 1994), pp. 147–65.

3 F. O'Gorman, 'Campaign rituals and ceremonies: the social meaning of elections in England', *Past and Present*, 135 (1992), 113.

4 J. Brewer, *Party Ideology and Popular Politics at the Accession of George III* (Cambridge: Cambridge University Press, 1976), p. 191.

5 The minute books are held at the National Archives in Kew (hereafter TNA), TS11/1133, TS11/961 and TS11/962.

6 On the politicisation of drink and beverages in the seventeenth century,

see A. Smyth (ed.), *A Pleasing Sinne: Drink and Conviviality in Seventeenth-Century England* (Cambridge: D. S. Brewer, 2004); on punch: K. Harvey, 'Ritual encounters: punch parties and masculinity in the eighteenth century', *Past and Present*, 214:1 (2012), 165–203.

7 D. Duff, 'Burke and Paine: contrasts', in P. Clemit (ed.), *The Cambridge Companion to British Literature of the French Revolution in the 1790s* (Cambridge: Cambridge University Press, 2011), p. 59; D. Bindman, *The Shadow of the Guillotine: Britain and the French Revolution* (London: British Museum Publications, 1989), p. 141.

8 N. E. Key, 'High feeding and smart drinking', p. 163.

9 F. O'Gorman, 'Political ritual in eighteenth-century Britain', in J. Neuheiser and M. Schaich (eds), *Political Rituals in Great Britain 1700–2000* (Augsburg: Wissner, 2006), pp. 17–36.

10 Goffman's concept of 'stigma management' was used to describe the London Corresponding Society's strategies to attain respectability; see M. T. Davis, 'The Mob Club? The London Corresponding Society and the politics of civility in the 1790s', in M. T. Davis and P. A. Pickering (eds), *Unrespectable Radicals?: Popular Politics in the Age of Reform* (Aldershot; Burlington, V.T.: Ashgate, 2008), pp. 21–40.

11 TNA, TS 11/961, General Audit Dinner, 14 December 1785, fol. 119.

12 J. Belchem, 'Republicanism, popular constitutionalism and the radical platform in early nineteenth-century England', *Social History*, 6 (1981), 9.

13 TNA, TS 11/961, General Audit Dinner, 14 December 1785, fol. 119.

14 TNA, TS 11/961, General Audit Dinner, 10 May 1786, fol. 139.

15 For example, John Jebb and Thomas Day in 1786: TNA, TS 11/961, fols 138, 204.

16 British Library, London (hereafter BL), Additional MS 64814, Minute Book of the Revolution Society, 'Anniversary Public Dinner', 4 November 1790, fols 40–1. See also the SCI dinner, 16 December 1789: D. H., 'Letter', *Gentleman's Magazine* 64 (1789), 1183.

17 On celebrations of the Glorious Revolution by radicals and other groups, see: H. T. Dickinson, 'The eighteenth-century debate on the "Glorious Revolution"', *History*, 61 (1976), 28–45; K. Wilson, 'Inventing revolution: 1688 and eighteenth-century popular politics', *Journal of British Studies*, 28 (1989), 354–64; R. Duthille, 'Célébrer 1688 après 1789: le discours de la *Revolution Society* et sa réception en France et en Angleterre', in T. Coignard, P. Davis and A. C. Montoya (eds), *Lumières et histoire/Enlightenment and History* (Paris: Honoré Champion, 2010), pp. 245–62. On resurgent manifestations of radicalism, see the Introduction in this volume.

18 'Meeting of Major Cartwright's Friends', *The Times*, 19 August 1818.

19 See for example *Guardian*, 31 May 1823.

20 Public dinner in Liverpool: *Manchester Observer*, 4 December 1819.

21 *Manchester Herald*, 16 February 1793.

22 *Manchester Herald*, 27 October 1792.

23 'Extract from a Letter from Philadelphia, 22 May', *Edinburgh Gazetteer*, 9 June 1793.

24 *Examiner*, 9 April 1820.

25 On the experimental nature of radical writing in the 1790s, see M. Philp, 'The fragmented ideology of reform', in M. Philp (ed.), *The French Revolution and British Popular Politics* (Cambridge: Cambridge University Press, 1991), pp. 50–77; J. Barrell, *Imagining the King's Death: Figurative Treason, Fantasies of Regicide: 1793–1796* (Oxford: Oxford University Press, 2000); J. Epstein, *In Practice: Studies in the Language and Culture of Popular Politics in Modern Britain* (Stanford, C.A.: Stanford University Press, 2003), p. 97. On radical writing in the eighteenth century, see also chapters 2 and 9.

26 On 'structures of feelings', see R. Williams, *Marxism and Literature* (Oxford; New York, N.Y.: Oxford University Press, 1977), pp. 128–35.

27 This tended to change with more complex toasts given in the Pitt Clubs from the 1800s; see M. McCormack, 'Rethinking "loyalty" in eighteenth-century Britain', *Journal for Eighteenth-Century Studies*, 35 (2012), 418.

28 The Spenceans were followers of utopian thinker Thomas Spence (1750–1814). The 'Society of Spencean Philanthropists' was formed in 1815 to promote Spence's land plan, a scheme involving communal land ownership and democratic management of public affairs at the parish level. While Thomas Evans focused on the dissemination of Spence's ideas, Arthur Thistlewood engaged in direct action, with the so-called Cato Street conspiracy in 1820. They survived into the 1820s despite government surveillance and repression, and their ideas contributed to Chartist land nationalisation schemes in the following two decades. On Spenceans and toasting competitions, see I. McCalman, *Radical Underworld: Prophets, Revolutionaries and Pornographers in London, 1795–1840* (Cambridge: Cambridge University Press, 1988), p. 120.

29 Revolution Society, Anniversary of the Glorious Revolution, 5 November 1791, in *Glasgow Courier*, 10 November 1791.

30 BL, Additional MS 64814, Minute Book of the Revolution Society, 4 November 1790, fol. 40.

31 This toast was convincingly interpreted as an example of the occasional discrepancy between radical aspirations and rhetoric. See D. O. Thomas, *Ymateb i Chwyldro: Response to Revolution* (Cardiff: University of Wales Press, 1989), p. 41; Philp, 'Fragmented ideology of reform', p. 55.

32 Celebration of the Glorious Revolution in Manchester, 4 November

1792, in *Edinburgh Gazetteer*, 16 November 1792; see also *Courier and Evening Gazette*, 9 November 1795; *London Chronicle*, 5 November 1790. In this as in all subsequent quotations the italics occurred in the original.

33 K. Navickas, *Loyalism and Radicalism in Lancashire, 1798–1815* (Oxford: Oxford University Press, 2009), pp. 208, 217–18.

34 'Revolution Society. Monday, July 11, 1791', *The Times*, 14 July 1791. Tyler and Cade were leaders of popular revolts in 1381 and 1450 respectively.

35 P. J. Kitson, '"Not a reforming patriot but an ambitious tyrant": representations of Cromwell and the English Republic in the late eighteenth and early nineteenth centuries', in T. Morton and N. Smith (eds), *Radicalism in British Literary Culture, 1650–1830: From Revolution to Revolution* (Cambridge: Cambridge University Press, 2002), pp. 183–200.

36 J. Epstein and D. Karr, 'Playing at revolution: British "Jacobin" performance', *Journal of Modern History*, 79:3 (2007), 514.

37 The largest one was the Association for Preserving Liberty and Property against Republicans and Levellers (APLP), founded by John Reeves in November 1792. The most recent major account of loyalist writing is K. Gilmartin, *Writing against Revolution: Literary Conservatism in Britain, 1790–1832* (Cambridge: Cambridge University Press, 2007), pp. 19–54.

38 On respectability, see Davis and Pickering (eds), *Unrespectable Radicals?* On the issue of unacceptable practices as manifestations of radicalism, see also Chapter 1.

39 M. T. Davis, 'The Mob Club?', in Davis and Pickering (eds), *Unrespectable Radicals?*, p. 31; *The Autobiography of Francis Place (1771–1854)*, ed. Mary Thale (Cambridge: Cambridge University Press, 1972), pp. 131–2; Paramython, [Letter to the editor], *Moral and Political Magazine of the London Corresponding Society* (London, 1796–7), vol. 1, p. 264.

40 E. P. Thompson, *The Making of the English Working Class* (Harmondsworth: Penguin, 1963), p. 63.

41 'The Diary of John Cam Hobhouse', ed. Peter Cochran (henceforward Hobhouse Diary). 'Introduction', p. vii; http://petercochran. files.wordpress.com/2009/12/00-introduction.pdf (accessed 29 August 2015). For other disparaging comments, see for example the entry for 6 November 1819.

42 A. Shepard, '"Swil-bols and tos-pots": drink culture and male bonding in England, c.1560–1640', in L. Gowing, M. Hunter and M. Rubin (eds), *Love, Friendship and Faith in Europe, 1300–1800* (Basingstoke; New York, N.Y.: Palgrave Macmillan, 2003), pp. 110–30.

43 P. Carter, *Men and the Emergence of Polite Society: 1660–1800* (Harlow: Longman, 2000); M. McCormack, *The Independent Man: Citizenship and Gender Politics in Georgian England* (Manchester: Manchester University Press, 2005).

44 On toasting and eroticism, see J. Skipp, 'Masculinity and social stratification in eighteenth-century erotic literature, 1700–1821', *Journal for Eighteenth-Century Studies*, 29:2 (2006), 253–69. One who toasted Catharine Macaulay was Samuel Johnson, to ridicule her: see James Boswell, *Life of Johnson*, ed. R. W. Chapman (Oxford: Oxford University Press, 1980), p. 344.

45 J. Fulcher, 'Gender, politics and class in the early nineteenth-century English reform movement', *Historical Research*, 67:162 (1994), 66–7; Epstein, *Radical Expression*, p. 158.

46 Further research is needed to determine whether toasting reflected the change provoked by the Queen Caroline affair in 1820, which for an influential critic 'decisively shifted radical men away from a misogynist libertinism toward the chivalrous ideal': A. Clark, *The Struggle for the Breeches: Gender and the Making of the British Working Class* (Berkeley, C.A.: University of California Press, 1995), p. 174.

47 *Manchester Observer*, 4 December 1819.

48 *Cobbett's Evening Post*, 3 March 1820, quoted in Fulcher, 'Gender, politics and class', p. 68.

49 J. Epstein, '"Equality and No King": sociability and sedition: the case of John Frost', in G. Russell and C. Tuite (eds), *Romantic Sociability: Social Networks and Literary Culture in Britain 1770–1840* (Cambridge: Cambridge University Press, 2002), pp. 47–8.

50 *John Bull's Second Answer to His Brother Thomas*, quoted in K. Gilmartin, 'Counter-revolutionary culture', in Clemit (ed.), *Cambridge Companion to British Literature of the French Revolution*, p. 137.

51 'Yorkshire Loyalty', *World*, 17 December 1792.

52 *True Briton*, 2 March 1795, quoted in Barrell, *Imagining the King's Death*, pp. 101–2.

53 *A Complete Collection of State Trials and Proceedings for High Treason and Other Crimes and Misdemeanors from the Earliest Period to the Year 1783, with Notes and Other Illustrations, Compiled by T. B. Howell, Esq. F.R.S. F.S.A. and Continued from the Year 1783 to the Present Time by Thomas Jones Howell, Esq.* (London, 1818), vol. 24, col. 742–3. For the legal framework, see Barrell, *Imagining the King's Death*, pp. 30–46.

54 J. D. Brims, 'The Scottish Democratic Movement in the Age of the French Revolution' (PhD dissertation, University of Edinburgh, 1983), pp. 270–1.

55 L. Reid, *Charles James Fox: a Man for the People* (London: Longman, 1965), p. 365.
56 *Morning Chronicle*, 21 November 1792.
57 W. Field, *Memoirs of the Life, Writings, and Opinions of the Rev. Samuel Parr with Biographical Notices of Many of his Friends, Pupils and Contemporaries* (London: Henry Colburn, 1828), 1:309; L. W. Cowie, 'Parr, Samuel (1747–1825)', *Oxford Dictionary of National Biography* (Oxford: Oxford University Press, 2004).
58 See comments on toasts drunk during Fox's election dinner in *True Briton*, 14 October 1794.
59 J. Epstein, 'Equality and No King', p. 46. Epstein's account, based on Charles Pigott's own defense in *Persecution. The Case of Charles Pigott: Contained in the Defense He Had Prepared and Would Have Delivered* (London, 1793), tallies with the deposition in the Old Bailey *Proceedings Online*, trial of William Hudson, 4 December 1793; http://www.oldbaileyonline.org/browse.jsp?div=t17931204-54 (accessed 29 August 2015).
60 J. Thelwall, *The Natural and Constitutional Right of Britons to Annual Parliaments, Universal Suffrage, and the Freedom of Popular Association* (London, 1795), in G. Claeys (ed.), *The Politics of English Jacobinism: Writings of John Thelwall* (University Park, P.A.: Pennsylvania State University Press, 1995), p. 56.
61 LCS secretary John Ashley, quoted by P. A. Brown, *The French Revolution in English History* (London: Allen and Unwin, 1918), p. 116.
62 H. Hunt, *Memoirs of Henry Hunt, Esq. Written by Himself, in His Majesty's Jail* (London, 1820), vol. 3, p. 344. The toast, however, was fairly common in parts of London: see J. Champion, '"May the last king be strangled in the bowels of the last priest": irreligion and the English Enlightenment, 1649–1789', in Morton and Smith (eds), *Radicalism in British Literary Culture*, p. 29.
63 Thompson, *Making of English Working Class*, pp. 693–4.
64 D. R. Fisher, 'Westminster', in D. R. Fisher (ed.), *The History of Parliament: the House of Commons 1820–1832*, 2009'; www.historyofparliamentonline.org/volume/1820-1832/constituencies/westminster (accessed 29 August 2015).
65 Hobhouse Diary, 4 April 1821, p. 26; http://petercochran.files.wordpress.com/2009/12/29-18211.pdf (accessed 29 August 2015).
66 W. Cobbett, 'To Henry Hunt, Esq. Letter I', *Cobbett's Weekly Political Register*, vol. 33, no. 1, 3 January 1818, pp. 27–9. On the political background of the dinner, see Thompson, *Making of English Working Class*, p. 510.

PART IV
Radical fiction and representation

8

⁓

Contesting the press-oppressors of the age: the captivity narrative of William Okeley (1675)

Catherine Vigier

In the 1670s, religious dissenters were faced with increasing hostility from an Anglican church determined to stamp out what was called 'nonconformity'. A nonconformist was originally a person adhering to the doctrine but not the usages of the Church of England, but the repressive apparatus of the Clarendon Code established a clear line between those who conformed and those who refused. From the Act of Uniformity (1662) onwards, nonconformity was the target of ferocious persecution. At the same time, heavy censorship aimed at depriving nonconformists of any means of defending their positions in print. Yet the repression was not simply aimed at ending religious polemic. It was above all an attempt by those at the helm of the state, the 'men of property', to suppress freedom of organisation and of discussion and to put an end to the political debate of the Civil War years. This meant re-establishing a single state church that was controlled from above, and reducing its critics to silence. The responses of those Protestants who were excluded – Presbyterians, Independents, Quakers and others – differed widely, but in their opposition to the established Church they suffered equally. This chapter focuses on the literary response to this oppression, specifically that which was organised by of a group of personalities working with the publisher Nathaniel Ponder in the 1670s. Not only did Ponder publish Andrew Marvell's highly successful satire *The Rehearsal Transpros'd*, but he also used a more popular genre, the captivity narrative, to continue the polemic under the nose of the censor. This chapter aims to show how the captivity narrative of William Okeley reproduced elements of Marvell's satire while making the case against religious tyranny within the framework of a story of slavery in Barbary.

William Okeley's captivity narrative, *Ebenezer; or, A Small Monument of Great Mercy, Appearing in the Miraculous Deliverance of William Okeley*, was first published in 1675.[1] It has undergone considerable scrutiny by researchers since the 2000s, following the publication of a series of carefully documented articles on the captivity narrative by Nabil Matar[2] and Linda Colley's critically acclaimed *Captives*.[3] While these researchers have highlighted the suffering of captives sold into slavery on the Barbary Coast, their work approaches the captivity narrative as a primary historical source, that is, as an eyewitness account of captivity. Although Colley accepts that Okeley's text involves much 'cut and paste', she suggests that we should not read too much into authors' failure to stick to the historical truth. In Okeley's case the text was rewritten to bring out what he regarded as the deeper moral truth of his experiences, she argues.[4]

Yet there is a strong case to be made for treating captivity narratives as literary texts which were constructed in the light of the political and ideological debates of the age in which they were written. This approach has been strongly advocated by Daniel Vitkus, who argues that scholars need to pay more attention to the political environment in which captivity narratives were produced. We should thus view the narrators as figures in multilayered texts which were often produced for ideological reasons. He points to the way in which writers like Rabelais used the captivity narrative for satirical purposes.[5] From early modern times, the genre was highly codified, containing a number of indispensable elements as well as the inevitable claims regarding the truthfulness of the account. Such claims were made necessary by the scepticism, if not outright derision, with which the voyagers' claims were often greeted. Parodies of the travel and captivity narrative were as popular as the narratives themselves, as can be seen from the immense success of *The Legend of Captain Jones*, which mocked Captain John Smith's account of his voyages.[6]

The standardised format of the narrative and its location in a far-off land allowed for veiled criticism of events nearer home. Anne Duprat suggests that it was precisely the stereotypical nature of the captivity narrative that allowed it to express ideas that might otherwise be censored: 'By basing themselves on the apparently unchanging ideological framework of the antagonism between Islam and Christianity, between Barbary States and European powers, these narratives give new form to the expression of religious, social and political conflicts inside European society, conflicts which could often be freely expressed in writing about the Other and within the stable narrative programme of the captivity scenario.'[7] The seventeenth-century captivity narrative should therefore be considered as a potential bearer of political content, to a much greater extent than some contemporary historians have been willing to acknowledge. In *The Literary Culture of Nonconformity*, N. H. Keeble reminds us of Christopher Hill's invitation to consider seventeenth-century texts as 'cryptograms to be decoded'.[8] This is as true of the captivity narrative as it is of other forms of literature.

The captivity narrative of William Okeley is particularly rich in this regard, when set against other texts published by Nathaniel Ponder in defense of nonconformity in the 1670s. Vitkus has emphasised the militant Protestantism and virulent anti-Catholicism of the narrative, saying 'there are many signs of a Calvinistic, providentialist agenda in Okeley's text, and the revival of antiroyalist Protestantism in England may account for the printing of the text after so many years, in 1675.'[9] Anti-royalist or not, Calvinists were in considerable difficulty in the 1670s. The hopes for freedom of conscience promised in the Declaration of Breda had been dashed. The Anglican Tories in Church and Parliament were determined to suppress religious nonconformity, which was now being called dissent.[10] In the words of Martin Dzelzainis and Annabel Patterson: 'England was now manifestly a persecuting state, seeking to achieve religious uniformity through coercion.'[11] A number of prominent dissenters had placed their faith in the idea that religious toleration would be defended by the King through the Declaration of Indulgence (1672). Such hopes of royal support faded as the King withdrew the Declaration in March 1673 under pressure from Parliament. Meanwhile, members of the Anglican clergy had been busy writing polemics denouncing Calvinism and other forms of religious dissent. The future Bishop of Oxford, Samuel Parker, had published *A Discourse of Ecclesiastical Politie* (1669) (henceforth *Discourse*),[12] followed by *A Defence and Continuation of the Ecclesiastical Politie* (1670)[13] (henceforth *Defence*), and *Bishop Bramhall's Vindication of himself ... together with a preface shewing what grounds there are of Fears and Jealousies of Popery* (1672) (henceforth *Preface*).[14] These attacks on liberty of conscience were answered by John Owen, leader of the Independents, and then by Andrew Marvell in his satire *The Rehearsal Transpros'd*, the first part of which (henceforth *RT*) was published in 1672[15] and the second (henceforth *RT2*) in 1673.[16]

The Rehearsal Transpros'd was immensely successful and its many jokes at the expense of Parker were relayed in the coffee houses and public meeting places. It was said that the King himself had read it and found it very funny. It was the King's appreciation of the satire which saved Marvell and his printer Nathaniel Ponder from the full wrath of the censor, and the work was allowed to circulate in spite of Parker's efforts to have it suppressed. Nonetheless, Marvell and Ponder were confronted with great difficulty in producing the work, which was published anonymously and was not licensed when it first appeared.

Nathaniel Ponder was active in defending the nonconformist cause throughout the 1670s. Although he did publish mathematical and scientific works, his main output was nonconformist polemics and religious tracts. In 1670–71 he published a book by Robert Perrot, minister of Dean, in Bedfordshire, who had been ejected from his living. He was closely involved in the publication of works by John Owen, and his first publication was a folio volume of Owen's writing.[17] He was later to gain fame as the publisher of *The Pilgrim's Progress*. In his study of John Bunyan, Christopher Hill described Ponder as 'a political and religious radical'.[18] The publication of the Okeley captivity narrative comes as a departure from Ponder's typical publishing activity: it was his first, and only, venture into the field of the captivity narrative. This chapter will argue that Okeley's captivity narrative is best understood as part of the corpus of work published by Ponder in response to the attacks on religious dissent. The text contains numerous references to Marvell's satire and ends with an appeal to the English to defend their liberties or risk losing them. Yet on the surface the narrative appears as a simple tale of misfortune at sea.

The story describes how William Okeley was captured by Turkish pirates in August 1639. He was on board the *Mary*, bound for the puritan colony of Providence Island in the West Indies.[19] He narrates his experiences as a slave in Algiers, his escape in a canvas boat after five years' captivity and his return to England. The

story follows the conventions of the captivity narrative, recount-
ing departure, danger, crisis, struggle and capture, arrival at the
slave market, the master, the temptation to convert, escape and
homecoming. It contains various paratexts; over a hundred lines
of verse, an introductory preface and some lines of verse at the end
which appear to be an epitaph for William Okeley. The book was
printed in the cheaper octavo format, which suggests that it was
aimed at a popular audience. It was reprinted in 1676, a second
edition appeared in 1684, and a third edition was printed in 1764.
This publishing history suggests that the narrative met with some
success.

While it has been customary to regard Okeley's narrative as an
eyewitness account of slavery in Algiers, and the *Mary* was indeed
captured by pirates in August 1639, it is worth pointing out that
the narrative could have been written by anyone familiar with the
history of the Providence Island Company. Okeley may well have
existed, but his existence was not necessary for the story to have
been written. Information relating to the ill-starred voyage of the
Mary is contained in the records of the Providence Island Company.
The colony was founded by Puritan grandees grouped around the
Earl of Warwick in 1629–30, but rapidly became a base for privateering missions against the Spanish. The *Mary* was on a mission to
find a silver mine in the Bay of Darien. If no silver was found, the
ship was to be used for privateering.[20] Marvell could have learnt
of Providence Island and the loss of the *Mary* through his link
with the former Oxford scholar John Oxenbridge, who spent time
in Bermuda and became governor of the Somers Island Company
under Cromwell.[21] There were many links between Bermuda and the
Providence Island colony, whose first settlers came from Bermuda.
Governors of Bermuda like Philip Bell and Nathaniel Butler went
on to serve in Providence Island.[22]

Indeed, the central image of the Okeley narrative, of the five
Englishmen rowing across the sea to safety, is prefigured in Marvell's
poem 'Bermudas', which depicts Englishmen rowing across the
water, protected from storms and religious persecution by the hand
of Divine Providence: 'What should we do but sing his praise/That
led us through the wat'ry maze.'[23] While Marvell's poem refers to
the escape from 'prelates' rage', the Okeley narrative includes a reference to Herbert's 'Church Militant', and the idea of escape across
the sea, away from religious persecution.[24] N. Smith has underlined

the idealistic view of the puritan colonies presented in 'Bermudas'. The same can be said of the Okeley narrative, which makes no reference to the more disreputable aspects of the voyage of the *Mary* –hunting for silver, privateering – but presents it as a godly undertaking. Some elements of Okeley's story do not correspond to the historical record. For example, John Randal, who is presented as 'a glover by trade'[25] in the Okeley narrative, was a gunner on the *Expedition*'s voyage to Providence in 1638 and is on record as a planter and slave owner.[26]

Okeley tells us that he did not write the text himself and was convinced to publish his story by others: 'I thought a long while that it was not worth the while to trouble the world with my particular concerns, till the importunity of several ministers and others (both in city and country) overcame my reluctance, in whose reasons I did acquiesce.'[27] Linda Colley suggests that Okeley was helped to publish by Anglican ministers: 'In Okeley's case, we can be reasonably sure who these auxiliaries were. A deeply religious man, he was urged to publish his experiences by some Anglican clergymen, and it was probably they who also helped him shape and style his narrative.'[28] Anglican ministers did help publish captivity narratives, but it is not likely that they would have published with Ponder given his role in the attacks on Samuel Parker. Second, the title, *Ebenezer*, is a clue to the author's political and religious orientation. The Hebrew word, meaning 'stone of help', is a reference to 1 Samuel 7:12; it refers to an account of God saving the Israelites from an attack by the Philistines. Nonconformists often likened their situation to that of the biblical captives in Babylon.[29] *Ebenezer* is also the title of a sermon John Owen preached before General Fairfax and his army in thanksgiving for the lifting of the siege of Colchester in 1648.

Okeley's narrative includes a woodcut depicting scenes of capture, sale and torture of slaves in Algiers; 110 lines of verse entitled 'Upon this book and its Author'; a preface, laid out in the form of a sermon, indicating the moral lessons to be drawn from the account and the narrative itself. Also provided is a list of other publications by Ponder, which includes *RT*. The book, including the lines of verse, was entered in the Stationers' register on 29 March 1675.[30] The lines of verse are striking in that they promise to reveal information about the author and the publication but in fact do no such thing. Instead Okeley launches an attack on those whom he designates as 'press-oppressors': 'This author never was in print before/And (let this please or not) will never more./If all the press-oppressors of the age/would so resolve, t'would happiness presage.'[31] For the reader considering the books and pamphlets on sale at Nathaniel Ponder's bookshop, this reference to the 'press-oppressors' may have been easier to interpret than for a modern readership. In *Defence*, Parker wrote that he had had enough of answering the impertinent authors who assailed him and vowed to give up writing, which of course he did not do. This allowed Marvell to accuse him of lying in the opening pages of *RT*.[32] Okeley's opening lines thus might serve to remind the politically informed reader of the promise which the clergyman made but failed to honour, and also to designate Parker as the target of the narrative.

In *RT* Marvell accuses Parker of being an enemy of the press: Parker is, by his own admission, '*none of the most zealous Patrons of the Press*' (italics in original). Marvell also accuses him of wanting to silence the press. He mocks the Bishop's irritation with the press and his description of it as that '*villainous* engine'. Finally, Marvell links the Bishop's hostility to the press with his desire to suppress religious dissent. Marvell follows Milton in likening the printer's letters to teeth, which resist censorship by springing up just as armies spring from serpents' teeth in the legend of Cadmus: 'Their ugly Printing-Letters, that look but like so many rotten-teeth, How oft have they been pull'd out by (Sir John) B.(irkenhead) and L.(Estrange) the Publick-Tooth-drawers! And yet the rascally Operators of the Press have got a trick to fasten them again in a few minutes that they grow as firm a Set, and as biting and talkative as ever.'[33] The Okeley verse echoes Marvell's imagery, saying: 'Had but some monk this history to dress,/He would have made the iron teeth of th'press/Turn edge and grin, to chew the stuff and style.'[34] Okeley seems to suggest that the iron teeth of the press are only effective in the hands of those who contest the corruption of the Catholic Church. One of the nonconformists' main objections to Bishop Bramhall was that he was considered to have worked towards a rapprochement between the Catholic Church and Protestantism.

Okeley the poet appears reluctant to write when he says 'He should as soon another voyage take,/As be obliged another book to make.'[35] This assertion allows him to denounce the hostile climate facing those writers who defend Scripture. The book is likened to the tiny pinnace which goes off from shore. The embattled author who is alone on hostile seas, dependent on a favourable audience for salvation, is likened to the Protestant sailors who fought the Armada. The verse describes the difficulties encountered in publishing a book: 'For Whoso prints a book goes off from shore/to hazard that which was his own before/As one poor pinnace overmatched that fights/With an armado, so doth he who writes.'[36] The same imagery of the writer in hostile seas is used by Marvell in *RT2*, when, in explaining his decision to enter the fray a second time, and his reluctance to do so, he exclaims: 'I took it to be part of my gratitude to go no more to Sea, having been sufficiently tossed for one man upon the billows of applause and obloquy to put me in mind of a Shipwrack.'[37] Okeley's tone is more pious, but remains accusatory, using the metaphor of the sea battle to identify a number of enemies of Scripture:

> If Books (like goodly merchant ships) set forth,
> Laden with riches of the greatest worth;
> With councils, fathers, text-men, school men manned;
> With sacred cannon mounted at each hand;
> Are hard beset, and forc'd to make defense
> Against armed atheism, pride and impudence,
> How can this little cockboat hope escape
> When scripture suffers piracy and rape.[38]

In *RT2* Marvell uses the image of piracy to justify his attack on Parker by saying 'no man needs Letters of Mart against one that is an open Pirate of other men's Credit'. He then accuses Parker of desecrating Scripture, 'seeming to have forgot not only all Scripture rules, but even all Scripture expressions; unless where he either distorts them to his own interpretation, or attempts to make them ridiculous to others; Insomuch that, of all the books that ever I read, I must needs say I never saw a Divine guilty of so much ribaldry and prophaneness.'[39]

Okeley complains in his poem about the censorship of pious Christian writers and hints at the way that nonconformists face the full force of the law when they venture into print: 'These miracles and all the sacred store/Which faith should grasp and piety adore/Meet with arrests, arraignments and a doom/More harsh than tales of heathen Greece or Rome.'[40] The verse then returns to the issue of truth and its defenders: 'An heaven-born truth (like poor men's infants) may/For lack of godfathers, unchristened stay/And find no priest; when every stander-by/Will be a gossip to a great man's lie.'[41] The reader is compelled to reflect on the identity of the 'great man' who is accused of telling a lie here.

There is an allusion to the wider political context too. In denouncing the times, Okeley claims that Noah's Ark 'by infidelity itself lies drowned'.[42] This image may be designed to recall the disasters which befell the English fleet in the course of the Anglo-Dutch wars, the subject of Marvell's Painter Poems. In the 'Second Advice to a Painter', the navy directed by a drunken Clarendon is likened to the Ark directed by an inebriated Noah when the disaffected sailor cries 'He taught us how to drink, and how to drown'.[43] The image of the drowned ship is used by Marvell to represent the betrayal of the nation in 'The Last Instructions to a Painter', when he writes, 'our merchantmen, lest they be burned, we drown'.[44] He is referring to the burning of the English fleet by the Dutch in 1667 as a result of the self-serving behaviour of the high officers of the Admiralty and the corrupt politicians he held responsible for the Anglo-Dutch wars.

At the end of his verse, Okeley makes a sectarian remark about the price, saying: 'Meanwhile this narrative (all plain and true)/ Is worth a sixpence to a Turk or Jew,/But to a Christian (were the story gone),/The preface is a pennyworth alone.'[45] This is a way of highlighting the importance of the preface, as distinct from the story itself. The writer uses the preface to discuss truth and lies in narrative, and in so doing makes some very direct references to the polemic around *RT*. Rather than talking about captivity, Okeley begins to discuss the practice of story writing, and the way in which some writers invent fictitious events and places in order to attract an audience. The writers of such stories, instead of sticking to the truth, invent places and topographies to suit themselves: 'And lest *Mare del Zur* should still be a desolate wilderness, have courteously stocked it with the Painter's Wife's Island and *terra incognita*'; Okeley suggests that some writers in particular are prone to this type of inaccurate description, saying 'at this rate are we dealt with by this kind of men who love to blow up lank stories into huge bladders and then put something in them to make them rattle to please children, and yet they are but bladders still, though swelled with the tympany and wind colic.'[46] While this passage appears to be a simple assertion that the author is writing a truthful account, it also refers to a key passage in *RT* in which Marvell mocks Parker for mistakenly locating Zurich on the South Shore of Lake Leman. Marvell refers to this as 'the *Terra incognita* of Geneva'.[47] The phrase *terra incognita* became part of a running joke in *RT*. This reference at the beginning of the preface would make the connection with Marvell's satire for politically aware readers. Martin Dzelzainis and Annabel Patterson observe that 'Parker's slip in locating Geneva on the south side of Lake Leman rather than at its western end' became 'the subject of a competitive exchange between coffeehouse wits'.[48] The joke about Parker's faulty geography was subsequently criticised by Henry Stubbes in his response to Marvell, when he said: 'But I might complain of the Geography of this railer.'[49] Yet this would only have kept the joke in the public mind. Okeley may have added the reference to swollen bladders to underscore the object of mirth, for Marvell had also joked that Bishop Parker's head had 'swelled like any Bladder with wind and vapour'.[50]

Okeley returns again and again to the question of truthfulness, saying that 'it were unpardonable to strive to recommend the wonderful providences of God to the genius of this age by a lie or to talk deceitfully for Him.'[51] In this he makes a direct reference to *RT*, where Marvell satirises Parker's *Preface*, saying he (Parker) will make you '*a Preface that shall recommend you ... to the Genius of the Age*'.[52] This echoes Parker's pompous justification for writing the preface to Bramhall, which Marvell exploited to great comic effect in *RT*. Okeley is using Marvell's (and Parker's) phrases to suggest that the Bishop is a liar.[53] The Okeley preface also alludes to another joke: when he writes 'Let others make tragedies to gratify the bookseller and cheat the simple buyer',[54] he is in fact referring to a passage in which Bishop Parker claimed that he had written his preface in order to gratify the bookseller's request, which Marvell had much fun with in *RT*. Thus the opening paragraphs of Okeley's preface refer to a number of jokes – the reference to *terra incognita*, the Bishop swollen with wind like a bladder and his writing for the gratification of the bookseller.

The writer of the Okeley preface also comments on the question of style, and denounces 'lean, barren stories, larded with the additaments of fruitful invention, as if they had been penned by the pattern of Xenophon's *Cyrus*'.[55] He also criticises 'those romances which are the issues of fine wits', saying 'what clumsed things are the Cassandras'.[56] *Cassandra*, by Costes de la Calprenède, was a type of romance popular with royalists during the Interregnum. Similarly, in *RT*, Marvell accuses Mr Bayes (Parker) of imitating the style of popular romances: 'By the language he seems to transcribe out of the *Grand-Cyrus* and *Cassandra*.'[57] Though hostile to *Cassandra*, Okeley does not hesitate to make use of the French language when he wishes to cite a useful proverb, which suggests that he perceives his audience as being among the educated classes. This show of linguistic proficiency may be a way of inciting the reader to question the real identity of 'William Okeley'.

Okeley also invokes science in support of his arguments, affirming that works of art are clumsy things when compared to the perfection of God's work as seen under a microscope. He points to the perfection of the bee's sting when studied under a microscope and compares this perfection to the clumsiness of a manmade object such as a needle. This is reminiscent of Marvell's 'Last Instructions to a Painter': 'With Hooke, then, through the microscope, take aim', where the artist is advised to look at the scene as through a microscope.[58] Marvell's interest in the microscope has been pointed out by Nigel Smith, who adds that the poet represents painting as an inferior art to that of empirical investigation.[59] The same idea is present in Okeley: 'Look upon the subtle point of the finest needle through a microscope, and you will soon be satisfied that art is but a dunce.'[60] This incitation to study the world in depth may have an added meaning in Okeley's preface: the writer warns against the reader taking a childish pleasure in the 'gilded covers and marbled leaves of books', while failing to understand the deeper matters couched within them. The reader is told to search beyond the surface meaning of the narrative: 'Here then will be the reader's danger lest all his spirits should evaporate in a confused admiration that a boat, a little canvas boat, should like the ark convey so many persons so many leagues safe to shore, whilst he misses the true intent and meaning of it.'[61]

The captivity narrative itself contains a number of biblical and mythological references which echo those used by Marvell in *RT*. The most striking of these is a reference to the early modern myth concerning the origins of Islam. The Okeley text is fiercely hostile to Islam and contains a scene in which the narrator insults his captors by denigrating their religion. Okeley tells his masters that Islam was a religion cobbled together by the outlawed monk Sergius and Abdallah the Jew. He refers to Sergius, 'that Nestorian monk who clubbed with Mahomet in the cursed invention of the Alkoran'.[62] Marvell uses the same myth to insult Parker in *RT*, referring to 'those two that clubb'd with Mahomet in making the Alchoran'.[63] According to Martin Dzelzainis and Annabel Patterson, Marvell's source is Samuel Purchas, who refers to Sergius and Abdallah, 'A Nestorian monk of Constantinople and a paynime Jew'.[64] The expression 'clubb'd with Mahomet' is not used by Purchas, so Okeley may have borrowed it from Marvell, although Daniel Vitkus points out that different versions of the legend were in circulation in England.[65] It is nonetheless remarkable that Okeley should have insulted his captors using the same expression that Marvell used to insult Parker. Okeley also refers to the legend of the Albanian national hero, Scanderbeg, who wielded a mighty scimitar, known as Castriot's scimitar. This weapon was only potent in the hand of one who had the support of God and thus, according to the legend, could not be used by the Grand Seignior, but only by its owner, who had 'the arm of God'. Thus Okeley concludes that 'none can work with God's means that has not God's arm'.[66] In *RT*, Marvell uses the image of Castriot's scimitar to deride Parker: 'No worth the man that comes in the way of so dead doing a tool, and when wielded with the arm of such a Scanderbag as our Author.'[67] Like the legend of Sergius the monk, the legend of Scanderbeg is part of the repertoire of anti-Islamic myths circulating in seventeenth-century Europe.

Okeley does not restrict his sources to anti-Islamic mythology, however. He is keen to demonstrate his knowledge of foreign languages and is fond of using Latin and French expressions. He refers to Ovid's legend of Alcyone to explain the calmness of the Mediterranean waters during the captives' escape. In *Metamorphoses*, Alcyone was transformed into a kingfisher, which had the power to calm the seas during the period in which it nested on the ocean.[68] A Christianised version of this legend is used by Okeley: 'The same God that commands a calm for the Halcyon commanded Halcyon days and nights for us, till under the wings of his gracious care he had hatched his purposes of mercy into perfect deliverance.'[69] We find the same image from *Metamorphoses* in *RT2*, when Marvell says sarcastically that if the course of action advocated by Parker were followed, 'the whole year would consist of Halcyon Holy-dayes, and the whole world free from Storms and Tempests would be lull'd and dandled into a Brumall quiet'.[70]

The tone of the Okeley narrative is overwhelmingly religious, with a multitude of references to the Bible and to the Psalms in particular. References to the captivity in Babylon are frequent, but Okeley insists that the slave should rebel against his condition of servitude. After a long period of captivity, the captive risks becoming resigned, he argues. He uses a biblical image to describe this: 'We seemed as if our ears had been bored, and we had vowed to serve our patrons forever.'[71] The source of this imagery is Exodus 21:6, which states that when a Hebrew servant refuses freedom out of love for his master 'his master shall bore his ear through with an awl; and he shall serve him for ever'.[72] In *RT*, Marvell denounces those who uncritically accept Parker's arguments as those 'whose ears are of a just bore for his fable'.[73] Okeley feared becoming like those slaves in Babylon who forgot Canaan and settled down to work, for 'long bondage breaks the spirits' of slaves, he said.[74]

Okeley's narrative raises the issue of slavery and freedom in the context of captivity in Barbary. The Turk was a tyrannical figure that could be readily identified by the reading public, but could be also used as a cover for discourses on tyranny closer to home. In *RT*, Marvell takes issue with Parker's argument that princes had to have the power to bind their subjects to that religion that they considered *'most advantageous to publick peace and tranquillity'*.[75] Parker intended that the magistrates should have the power to enforce religious practices. In this view, contested by Marvell, rulers were right to impose the religion that they saw as most appropriate for the maintenance of public order; Marvell suggests that the Bishop would approve of the fact that the Turk had established Islam among his subjects as the *'Religion that he apprehends most advantageous to publick peace and settlement'*.[76] He insinuates that Parker is behaving like the Turk: 'And 'tis indeed the very thing proposed in your *Ecclesiastical Politie*, that you might be row'd in state over the ocean of Publick Tranquility by the publick Slavery.'[77] Marvell expresses outrage at Parker's declaration that nonconformists should face *'Pillories, Whipping-posts, Galleys, and Axes'*.[78] He ironically suggests that more galleys would have to be built, to contain all the nonconformists. Then he conjures up an image of the King at the head of a Spanish-style Inquisition, 'busied in his Cabinet among those Engines whose very names are so hard that it is some torture to name them ... so a peculiar Rack for every Limb and Member of a Christians body.'[79] Parker's words are an insult to the King, he implies. A captivity narrative describing scenes of torture in Algiers could act as a warning to those who were complacent about the repression of nonconformists in England.

The Okeley text contains a long warning about the dangers of taking freedom for granted. While the text is aimed at the godly community of believers, interspersed as it is with biblical quotations and psalms, it clearly had several purposes for those who produced it. It carried the polemic around *RT* to a wider audience, and suggested that, even if the nonconformists were sent to the galleys, they would come back and state their case. The theme of liberty is clearly underlined in the preface, with the insistence that if the English did not value their freedom and defend it, they risked losing it. In publishing Okeley's narrative, Nathaniel Ponder and his collaborators defended freedom of speech and freedom of conscience at a time when it was not profitable to do so. Their opponents in the polemic with Parker had many resources at their disposal, and Marvell clearly understood this when he complained that Parker was using Bramhall as a 'stalking horse' to come within shot of the nonconformists. It can be argued that those working with Ponder decided to use a similar strategy. They chose a popular literary genre, the captivity narrative, adding a preface and lines of verse in order to restate the case for liberty. Marvell may have written the narrative himself, though this is difficult to prove conclusively. What is clear is that the text was influenced by Marvell's ideas and his literary and political culture. One final point on Okeley's identity is worth making. The anonymous editor of the third edition of his narrative (1764) wrote: 'Mr. Okeley was Steward or Bailiff to the Ancestors of Sir Danvers Osbourn, at Chickson, between Ampthill and Shefford in the said country, and always esteemed a very pious good man.'[80] If this information were true, it would mean that Okeley was steward to the King's Chief Minister, Thomas Osborne, Earl of Danby. Osborne was targeted by Marvell in *An Account of the Growth of Popery and Arbitrary Government* (1677), wherein Marvell alleged that the Earl was in league with the bishops to undermine English liberties.[81] Whatever his real identity, Okeley was a radical voice in the struggle against the repression of nonconformists in the 1670s.

Notes

1 W. Okeley, *Ebenezer; or, a Small Monument of Great Mercy Appearing in the Miraculous Deliverance of William Okeley, John Anthony, William Adams, John Jephs, John ---- Carpenter, from the Miserable Slavery of Algiers with the Wonderful Means of Their Escape in a Boat of Canvas; the Great Distress and Utmost Extremities Which They Endured at Sea for Six Days and Nights; (and) Their Safe Arrival at Mayork, with Several Matters of Remark During Their Long Captivity and the Following Providences of God Which Brought Them Safe to England* (London: Printed for N. Ponder, 1675), in D. Vitkus (ed.), *Piracy, Slavery and Redemption: Barbary Captivity Narratives from Early Modern England* (New York, Chichester: Columbia University Press, 2001) (hereafter Okeley), pp. 127–92.

2 N. Matar, 'English accounts of captivity in North Africa and the Middle East, 1577–1625', *Renaissance Quarterly*, 54:2 (2001), 553–72.

3 L. Colley, *Captives: Britain, Empire and the World, 1600–1850* (London: Jonathan Cape, 2002).

4 Colley, *Captives*, p. 92.

5 D. Vitkus, 'Barbary captivity narratives from early modern England: truth claims and the (re)construction of authority', in *La guerre de course en récits (XVIe-XVIIIes). Terrains, corpus, séries*, online publication of the CORSO project, November 2010, p. 2; www.oroc-crlc.paris-sorbonne.fr/index.php/visiteur/Projet-CORSO/Ressources/La-guerre-de-course-en-récits (accessed 29 August 2015).

6 A. T. Vaughan, 'John Smith satirized: the legend of Captaine Jones'. *The William and Mary Quarterly*, 3rd Series, 45:4 (1988), 712–32.

7 A. Duprat, 'Introduction', in *The Mediterranean Corsairs in Narrative: Territories, Corpus and Series*, online publication of the CORSO project, November 2010, p. 3; www.oroc-crlc.paris-sorbonne.fr/index. php/visiteur/Projet-CORSO/Ressources/La-guerre-de-course-en-recits (accessed 29 August 2015).

8 N. H. Keeble, *The Literary Culture of Nonconformity in Later Seventeenth-Century England* (Athens, G.A.: University of Georgia Press, 1987), p. 119.

9 D. Vitkus, *Piracy, Slavery and Redemption*, p. 125.

10 Keeble, *The Literary Culture of Nonconformity*, p. 41.

11 M. Dzelzainis and A. Patterson (eds), *The Prose Works of Andrew Marvell*, vol. 1: 1672–3. (New Haven, N.J.; London: Yale University Press, 2003) (hereafter *Prose Works 1*), p. 5.

12 S. Parker, *A Discourse of Ecclesiastical Politie, Wherein the Authority of the Civil Magistrate over the Consciences of Subjects in Matters of External Religion is Asserted; The Mischiefs and Inconveniences*

of Toleration are represented, And all Pretenses Pleaded in Behalf of Liberty of Conscience are Fully Answered (London, 1669).

13 S. Parker, *A Defence and Continuation of the Ecclesiastical Politie. By Way of a letter to a friend in London. Together with a letter from the author of the Friendly debate* (London, 1671).

14 S. Parker, *Bishop Bramhall's vindication of himself and the episcopal clergy, from the Presbyterian charge of popery ... together with a preface shewing what grounds there are of Fears and Jealousies of Popery* (London, 1672).

15 A. Marvell, *The Rehearsal Transpros'd: Or, Animadversions Upon a late Book, Intituled, A Preface shewing what grounds there are of Fears and Jealousies of Popery* (London, 1672) (hereafter *RT*), in *Prose Works 1*, pp. 41–203.

16 A. Marvell, *The Rehearsal Transpros'd: The Second Part* (London, 1673) (hereafter *RT2*), in *Prose Works 1* pp. 221–438.

17 F. Mott Harrison, 'Nathaniel Ponder', *The Library*, 15:3 (1934), 257–94.

18 C. Hill, *A Turbulent, Seditious and Factious People: John Bunyan and his Church* (Oxford: Clarendon Press, 1988), p. 289.

19 Okeley, p. 147.

20 The National Archives, CO 124/1 and CO 124/2, Providence Island Company Records, 1630–50.

21 N. Smith, *Andrew Marvell: The Chameleon* (New Haven, N.J. and London: Yale University Press, 2012), p. 113.

22 K. Ordahl Kuppermann, *Providence Island, 1630–1641: The Other Puritan Colony* (Cambridge: Cambridge University Press, 1995), pp. 25–8.

23 A. Marvell, 'Bermudas', in *The Poems of Andrew Marvell*, ed. Nigel Smith (Harlow: Pearson Longman, rev. edn, 2007), p. 56; see also Smith, *Andrew Marvell: the Chameleon*, pp. 113–14.

24 Okeley, p. 141.

25 Okeley, p. 157.

26 P. W. Coldham, *The Complete Book of Emigrants, 1607–1660* (Baltimore, M.D.: Genealogical Publishing, 1987), p. 195.

27 Okeley, p. 144.

28 Colley, *Captives*, p. 92.

29 Keeble, *The Literary Culture of Nonconformity*, p. 278.

30 *A Transcript of the Registers of the Worshipful Company of Stationers, from 1640–1708 A.D.* (London, 1913), vol. 2: 1655–1675, p. 505.

31 Okeley, p. 127, lines 1–4.

32 *RT*, pp. 43–4.

33 *RT*, pp. 44–6.

34 Okeley, p. 129, lines 64–6. According to the *Oxford English Dictionary*, to 'turn edge' means to have the edge turned back, to become blunt.
35 Okeley, p. 127, lines 5–6.
36 Okeley, pp. 127–28, lines 11–14.
37 *RT2*, p. 247.
38 Okeley, p.128, lines 15–22.
39 *RT2*, pp. 245–6.
40 Okeley, pp. 128–9, lines 39–42.
41 Okeley, p. 129, lines 51–4.
42 Okeley, p. 128, line 26.
43 Marvell, 'The Second Advice to a Painter', in *The Poems of Andrew Marvell*, p. 337, line 138.
44 Marvell, 'The Last Instructions to a Painter', in *The Poems of Andrew Marvell*, p. 389, line 712.
45 Okeley, p. 131, lines 104–7.
46 Okeley, p. 132.
47 *RT*, p. 150.
48 *Prose Works 1*, p. 12.
49 H. Stubbes, *Rosemary and Bayes, or Animadversions Upon a Treatise Called The Rehearsal Trans-prosed, In a Letter to a Friend in the Countrey* (London, 1672), p. 7.
50 *RT*, p. 75.
51 Okeley, p. 134.
52 *RT*, p. 53.
53 *RT*, p. 52.
54 Okeley, p. 133.
55 Okeley, p. 132.
56 Okeley, p. 134.
57 *RT*, p. 53.
58 Marvell, 'Last Instructions to a Painter', in *The Poems of Andrew Marvell*, p. 369, line 16.
59 Smith, *Andrew Marvell: The Chameleon*, p. 204.
60 Okeley, p. 134.
61 Okeley, p. 135.
62 Okeley, p. 160.
63 *RT*, p. 65.
64 S. Purchas, *Purchas his Pilgrimages. Or Relations of the World and the Religions Obserued in All Ages and Places discouered, from the Creation vnto this Present In foure partes.* (London, 1613), p. 200: see footnote in *Prose Works 1*, p. 66.
65 Vitkus, Introduction to Okeley, p. 126.
66 Okeley, p. 136.
67 *RT*, p. 151.

68 Ovid, *Metamorphoses*, trans. D. Raeburn (London: Penguin, 2004), Book XI, lines 410–748, pp. 442–58.
69 Okeley, p. 137.
70 *RT2*, p. 321.
71 Okeley, p. 157.
72 Exodus 21:6, in the 1611 *King James Bible*.
73 *RT*, p. 90.
74 Okeley, p. 157.
75 *RT2*, p. 273.
76 *RT*, p. 106.
77 *RT2*, p. 324.
78 *RT*, p. 107.
79 *RT*, p. 108–9.
80 W. Okeley, *Eben-Ezer:, or, a small monument of great mercy* (London, 3rd edn, 1764), British Library copy.
81 See Smith, *Andrew Marvell: The Chameleon*, p. 1.

9

~

Ways of thinking, ways of writing: novelistic expression of radicalism in the works of Godwin, Holcroft and Bage

Marion Leclair

Since the works of Gary Kelly[1] and Marilyn Butler[2] in the 1970s, William Godwin, Thomas Holcroft and Robert Bage are usually considered as part of the same group of politically committed novelists who enthusiastically supported the French Revolution in the last decade of the eighteenth century. The four writers originally considered by Gary Kelly were Godwin, Holcroft, Bage and Elizabeth Inchbald, but the group has expanded since, as more and more studies born of this revived interest in the literature of the revolutionary period claimed other novelists, principally Mary Wollstonecraft, Mary Hays and Charlotte Smith, for the same 'Jacobin' group.

The grouping is justified by the presence in their works of similar political and moral values which, by the standards of eighteenth-century politics, branded those who upheld them as 'radicals': a deep aversion for the injustice of the social and political institutions of their time as well as a belief in the natural equality of men, in the possibility of intellectual and moral progress through education and in the right of private judgement. These values echo the ideals of the French Revolution, but are also indebted to the older tradition of dissent and, especially in late eighteenth-century England, of the kind of rational dissent embodied by Joseph Priestley or Richard Price.

The influence of this intellectual and moral tradition on Jacobin novelists, who either came from dissenting backgrounds themselves, or were close to dissenting circles, has in the last twenty years elicited more and more interest from scholars anxious to reassess the influence of the French *philosophes* on British radicals and to consider the work and thought of the latter from a longstanding and more Anglo-centric perspective.[3] This accounts partly for the change in name, from 'Jacobin novels' to 'radical novels', as the works of Godwin and the others are increasingly referred to.

Yet, both designations – other variations, ancient and modern, on the same theme exist as well: 'speculative novels', 'novels of opinion',[4] 'novels of reform',[5] 'political novels',[6] 'rational novels'[7] – convey the same impression that the significance of such novels lies in their intellectual and political content rather than in their literary form. They are mere 'vehicles', to use a word Godwin employs in the preface to *Things as They Are; or the Adventures of Caleb Williams* (hereafter *Caleb Williams*),[8] for the radical ideas of their authors; or, as J. M. S. Tompkins puts it: '[their] intellectual energy … taking its source from the ethical, social and political views of the authors, streamed through the novel as through a well-worn channel of access to the public. Its torrential passing did not much modify the channel.'[9]

Critics after Tompkins have endeavoured to challenge this view and to gain some recognition for the literary innovations of the radical novel and their consistency with the writers' radical agenda. Thus, some attempts have been made at linking the formal characteristics of radical novels with the radical ideas they express. Pamela Clemit, for example, sees the plot of flight and pursuit in Godwin's *Caleb Williams* as 'a symbolical enactment of relations between government and the governed as set out in *Political Justice*',[10] Godwin's groundbreaking treatise of political philosophy. She also relates the ambiguity of certain passages of the novel, in which the burden of interpretation seems to be thrown onto the reader, to Godwin's emphasis on the importance of private judgement both in *Political Justice* and *The Enquirer*, a collection of essays published in 1797. Gary Kelly and Ronald Paulson see as a formal consequence of the doctrine of necessity developed in *Political Justice* (published in 1793, and revised in 1796 and 1798),[11] the 'unity of design'[12] claimed by Godwin and Holcroft for their novels: the plot must be a tight chain of events linked to one another by causal relations, rather than a loose series of unconnected episodes. However, the *doxa* on radical novels and novelists remains that they 'deployed existing novelistic conventions as a means of advancing a radical critique of society'.[13]

This chapter will show that radical novelists do modify existing novelistic conventions and, to this extent, contest the prevailing novelistic order of the day; and that their commitment to the pursuit and propagation of truth, their defence of men's equality and distrust of established authorities are reflected in the form of their novels. Three components of this prevailing order will be focused upon: style, plot and 'plan of narrative', a phrase used by the Scottish philosopher and poet James Beattie to describe what today we would call the narrator, or type of narration, chosen by a novelist.[14] Examples will mostly come from the works of Bage, Holcroft and Godwin, where subversion of novelistic conventions is most evident.

There is no apparent similarity between the respective styles of Godwin, Holcroft and Bage. The elegance of Godwin's style was often noted by reviewers, Bage was praised for his wit and 'peculiarly sprightly and pointed style',[15] while Holcroft was declared to be better at satire than at expressing lofty sentiments which he could not succeed in making sound very natural. But in the works of all three there is evident criticism of the conventional style of novels. In Bage's *James Wallace*, a gruff country squire makes fun of 'the lingo of novel books';[16] a more obviously authorised character makes a similar point in Bage's first novel, *Mount Henneth*: 'I confess, Henry, that I am incapable of going through the orderly detail of ruby lips, and rosy dimples. [...] I well remember, how sick the novel writers have often made both thee and me, with a profusion of epithets heaped upon their object, without any regard to number, or propriety. I will offend the truth, or thee, with one that is not strictly just.'[17]

The style of novels is criticised for being redundant, formulaic and untrue to things as they are. Similar observations can be found under the pen of Holcroft, in the preface to his first novel, *Alwyn*: Holcroft points out the 'poverty of style' of novels, writing that they have 'but one set of phrases, one languid, inanimate description' and 'a want of knowledge of the human heart, of men and manners'. Like Bage, he finds fault with the formulas and the untruthfulness of the style of novels, and adds a further charge of 'languidness' and lack of energy.[18] These observations are echoed in Godwin's essay 'Of English Style', published as part of a collection of essays in *The Enquirer*, in which he seeks to define 'the perfection of style':

The beauty of style consists in this, to be free from unnecessary parts and excrescencies, and to communicate our ideas with the smallest degree of prolixity and circuitousness. Style should be the transparent envelope of our thoughts. [...] It is an ill mode of composition, where we find an author expressing his thought in ten words, when it might have been expressed with equal discrimination and grammatical propriety in five. The five additional words are so much dead and worthless matter mixed up with the true and genuine substance. [...] The forcible expression of passion demands closeness and compression.[19]

Godwin's essay and the scattered remarks on style we find in the novels of Holcroft and Bage show that all three consciously reflected on style and had, albeit in an embryonic form for Holcroft and Bage, a certain stylistic programme for their novels, which rejected the conventional style in which novels were written. Interestingly, none of them specifies the faulty novels they have in mind. One can suppose that they are thinking of the mass-produced sentimental novels and gothic romances published by the Minerva Press and disseminated through the country to a rapidly growing readership by the circulating libraries. In such conditions, with novels being an eminently marketable ware, it is no wonder that their style declined, as Godwin explains in a manuscript essay on 'History and Romance' which was published only after his death:

Novels, as an object of trade among booksellers, are of a peculiar cast. There are few by which immense sums of money can be expected to be gained. There is scarcely one by which some money is not gained. A class of readers, consisting of women and boys, and which is considerably numerous, requires a continual supply of books of this sort. The circulating libraries therefore must be furnished; while, in consequence of the discredit which has fallen upon romance, such works are rarely found to obtain a place in the collection of the gentleman or the scholar. An ingenious bookseller of the metropolis, speculating upon this circumstance, was accustomed to paste an advertisement in his window, to attract the eye of the curious passenger, and to fire his ambition, by informing him of a 'want of novels for the ensuing season'.[20]

If the style of novels did indeed decline, the three novelists would only be criticising, sensibly enough – as many others did beyond the small group of 'Jacobin' novelists[21] – bad writing in novels written quickly and unthinkingly to meet the demands of the reading public. But beside the reproach of bad writing, all three seem to voice a more fundamental reproach regarding the tendency of novels to beautify things and gloss over truth. Instead, Godwin recommends a 'transparent' style free of all ornaments but 'those metaphors and ornaments of composition, which shall be found to increase the clearness or force with which the author's ideas are communicated to his readers'.[22] If one turns from the theory to the practice and considers Godwin's novels, it is clear that Godwin tried to apply this ideal of transparency and scarcity of ornament. The opening pages of *Caleb Williams*, for example, are remarkable for a certain dryness of expression which, although it cannot be kept up for whole chapters together and is less manifest in Godwin's later works, is arguably characteristic of Godwin's style. The following passage from the first chapter, in which Caleb relates his encounter with Mr Falkland, is especially revealing of Godwin's dryness of style. The opening paragraph of the chapter exhibits the same literary quality, but, since its dryness could be ascribed to soon-to-die Caleb's panting despair, it is perhaps less representative:

> In the summer of the year Mr. Falkland visited his estate in our county after an absence of several months. This was a period of misfortune to me. I was then eighteen years of age. My father lay dead in our cottage. I had lost my mother some years before. In this forlorn situation I was surprised by a message from the squire, ordering me to repair to the mansion-house the morning after my father's funeral.[23]

The shortness of the sentences and systematic lack of conjunctions to link the sentences together, a trope known as asyndeton, are striking; so is the simple, not to say, plain vocabulary: 'a period of misfortune', for instance, to refer to the death of both parents, is so very flat that is seems hardly adequate for the situation described here. Of course, the sentences in the novel are not always as short and some *are* linked by conjunctions. But even when they are longer, they tend to be so by accumulation and mere coordination, with series of clauses linked by 'and', rather than by complexity of structure and subordination. Stylistic ornaments are, on the whole, rare and rather austere, certainly not of the flashy Burkean sort: a few sentences based on ternary rhythm and the double negations, such as 'my curiosity was not entirely ignoble', that Godwin's biographer William St Clair sees as Godwin's stylistic idiosyncracy and which Mary Hays imitates in her own novels. As far as vocabulary is concerned, Godwin's preference for simple, generic, rather abstract words is visible throughout the novel.

If we accept this simple, 'transparent' style as the norm for Godwin novels, deviations from the norm become pregnant with meaning. It is probably no coincidence if many of the sentences in the second chapter, where Collins takes over the narration of the story, begin with an inversion, breaking away from the subject–verb–complement pattern, as the prepositional clause is shifted to the beginning of the sentence: '*Among the favourite authors of his early years* were the heroic poets of Italy. *From them* he imbibed the love of chivalry and romance ... *With these sentiments* he set out upon his travels ... *By inclination* he was led to make his longest stay in Italy, and here he fell into company with several young noblemen whose studies and principles were congenial to his own. *By them* he was assiduously courted.' It is probably no coincidence either if examples are more numerous in this chapter of such stylistic ornaments as ternary rhythm, as in 'He believed that nothing was so well calculated to make men *delicate, gallant and humane* ... His dignity was then heightened by certain additions which were afterwards obliterated, an expression of *frankness, ingenuity and unreserve*', or metaphors – such as the assimilation of values and principles, of education through exposure to the world compared to the drinking of a beverage: 'He *imbibed* the love of chivalry and romance; while his imagination was purged with a certain *infusion* of philosophy; it was not possible for him to have *drunk* so deeply of the *fountain* of philosophy.'[24] Consistently enough, the shift from Caleb's to Collins' narrative, from a narrator who, at least at the beginning of the novel, seems to embody the Godwinian ideals of free enquiry and plain speaking, to a loyal old servant with a liking for the Burkean ideals of 'chivalry' and hierarchy, entails a corresponding shift from a simple to a more ornate style.

Thus, the simple style advocated by Godwin both in the theoretic essay on style and in his novelistic practice is not merely an aesthetic preference, but a philosophical and political choice as well: his equating of beauty with truth, while all ornament is seen as truth-distorting sophistry, harks back to a Puritanism and Platonism characteristic of Godwin's early thought and, before him, to the intellectual tradition of dissent. But, at a time when an elaborate rhetoric had come to be associated, in the debate on the French Revolution, with Burke and the conservative politics which the radicals were fighting, the rejection of ornament was also a political signature: the stylistic badge of radicalism, more or less worn by all radical-minded writers anxious to be seen as rational propagators of truth rather than mind-dazzling sophists.

In the light of this radical stylistic programme, more similarities between the respective styles of Godwin, Holcroft and Bage appear: a striking scarcity of adjectives and descriptions, for example, which often makes it very difficult for the reader to picture characters and places, and is all the more surprising as picturesque descriptions of romantic scenes were becoming a well-established novelistic convention at the time. In this light, we can also see Bage's wit and Godwin's careful prose as two parallel, rather than conflicting, attempts at drawing the style of novels away from its conventional literariness, towards spontaneous oral conversation in the case of Bage, and non-fictional prose-writing in the case of Godwin.

In their treatment of plot, the three novelists depart as well from set novelistic conventions. At the risk of oversimplifying things, one can argue that most eighteenth-century novels follow one of three possible plots: the traditional plot of romance, centring on the trials and tribulations of a pair of lovers who are eventually united at the end of the novel – which may be called the romantic plot;[25] the picaresque plot of a young man's varied adventures as he enters upon the world's stage; and finally, in the second half of the century, the gothic plot of flight and pursuit. This classification raises many objections and certainly fails to account for the richness and diversity of eighteenth-century novels. It will be used here to try and identify the most conventional models on which radical novelists could draw.

Most of Bage's novels and Holcroft's *Anna St Ives* (1792) are built around a romantic plot; the rest of Holcroft's novels and Bage's *Man As He Is* (1792) use the picaresque plot; and the gothic nature of the plot of *Caleb Williams* has often been underlined by critics.[26] However, it may be argued that these conventional plots undergo more substantial modifications at the hands of radical novelists than is usually acknowledged.

The tightening of plot in the novels of Godwin and Holcroft resulting from their commitment to the doctrine of necessity is pointed out in most studies on the radical novel. The explicit social significance given to conventional plots has also been underlined: the gothic plot of flight and pursuit and the romantic plot of abduction become, explicitly so, stories of social, political, economic and domestic oppression in eighteenth-century England. This chapter will not give these ideas further consideration but will discuss another way in which, arguably, conventional plots are modified in the radical novel. They are, as it were, levelled by radical novelists. The levelling[27] is, in the first place, social: the plots are made to put characters of different social statuses on an equal footing. In the levelled gothic plot, the victim and oppressor change places several times over the course of the story, the victim acquiring a power over his oppressor which disrupts the normal social order. Godwin's *Caleb Williams* is perhaps the most obvious example of this role shifting: Caleb discovers that his aristocratic master once killed a man, then is pursued by his master who fears for his reputation if his secret should be revealed, but this master is eventually forced by Caleb to confess his guilt before a court. The situation occurs again in one of Godwin's last and lesser known novels, *Cloudesley*, in which a younger son inherits a peerage by faking the death of the rightful heir. When Cloudesley, to whom the rightful heir has been entrusted, visits the lord twenty years later to threaten him with revealing the imposture, the lord acknowledges the power Cloudesley has gained over him and its socially disruptive potential:

> You possess a fearful power over me. Use it with moderation and temperance. Remember that I am a nobleman. Can you bear to trample me in the dust, to thrust me forth to universal scorn? [...] You were born the son of a cultivator of the earth, belonging to a cast of society essentially inferior to mine. In the order of things you could not approach to anyone of the blood of the Altons and the Danverses, but to offer your services, and to receive our commands. A concurrence of circumstances has put it in your power to destroy me.[28]

In the romantic plot, the social levelling comes from the inversion of the gendered rags-to-riches story of virtue rewarded by social ascension. In the orthodox version of the story – as may be found, for example, in Richardson's *Pamela* – it is a young woman of obscure birth who eventually marries into rank and wealth. The version that consists in having a young man marry a girl of a superior social status is more socially subversive, as underlined in Michael McKeon's study of *Pamela* in *The Origins of the English Novel*;[29] marriage, in this case, instead of conferring rank on virtue, thus confirming the legitimacy of a social hierarchy, degrades rank without elevating virtue. It is this socially subversive version of the romantic plot that we find in many radical novels. And if in Bage's *James Wallace* and *Hermsprong*[30] the hero eventually turns out to be of noble birth, there is no such last-minute saving grace for Frank Henley in *Anna St Ives* or Tom Sutton in *Mount Henneth*; yet both marry into nobility.

Plots are also subjected to a structural levelling, to the extent that the conventional hierarchy of characters and plots, main and secondary, is subverted – a subversion for which Bage may have been indebted to Sterne's playful deconstruction of narrative in *Tristram Shandy*.[31] In Bage's novels, the conventional pair of female friends or sisters with contrasting characters – one serious and sensitive, the other bolder and wittier – is usually turned on its head: the female wit engrosses the reader's interest while her serious friend remains in her shadow, as was noted by eighteenth-century reviewers. His works also include instances of side characters changing category in the course of the novel: in *Man As He Is*, for example, Mr Bardoe only appears towards the end of the novel and is first introduced as the comic type of the English eccentric; yet, he suddenly becomes the hero's intimate friend and mentor, and his marriage to the hero's sister at the end of the novel confirms him as one of the main characters of the novel. Thus, the line between main and secondary characters seems to blur. In fact, the romantic plot in Bage's novels tends to be integrated into a wider plot: reduplicated into up to four intersecting love stories which all end in marriage and the constitution of a little colony, it becomes less a story of love and marriage than of the progressive constitution of the colony; and the characters in this enlarged plot work, so to speak, as an ensemble cast, in which the traditional hierarchy of characters disappears.

The hierarchy between main plot and subplot also seems to blur. The most striking example is perhaps *James Wallace*, in which the main plot and the subplot are even inverted: the Richardsonian plot of virtue – Paulina – seduced by a lovable rake – Sir Everard Moreton – is only the subplot of the novel, while the main plot centres on the amour of the lively daughter of a Liverpool merchant and her domestic servant James Wallace.

To conclude on this point, a third kind of levelling will be considered, this time in the picaresque plot. In this case, the levelling is less social than moral: it does not so much put the characters on an equal footing as it empties the plot of its conventional morals of progress. Disconnected though the episodes of the conventional picaresque plot may be, they are organised along an ascending axis which shows the gradual progress, moral or social or both, of the hero: as the story unfolds, he or she becomes more experienced, more successful and/or more virtuous; his or her progress is thus ascendant. But in Holcroft's *The Adventures of Hugh Trevor* or Godwin's *Fleetwood; or, The New Man of Feeling* (1805)[32] the authors' interest in 'the progress of mind'[33] deprives the picaresque plot of its usual direction. Convinced that 'the characters of men originate in their external circumstances',[34] Holcroft and Godwin see the novel as a means of reconstructing the development of an individual's mind by showing the various impressions he receives and how they shape his character. Progress, in this sense, is morally neutral and more or less synonymous with development, without any implication of amelioration: it applies to Hugh Trevor's growing understanding as well as to Fleetwood's growing egotism and misanthropy; it is a linear, horizontal evolution in time, rather than an ascending move. The picaresque plot thus becomes an amoral narrative of interaction between world and mind, tending more and more towards the *Bildungsroman*. The disappearance of a clearly expressed morality in the novel is also linked to the disappearance of a clearly identifiable moral voice in the novel, which will be discussed next.

Grossly speaking, it may be argued that three main 'plans of narrative', to use Beattie's phrase, were available to a writer at the end of the eighteenth century: the narrative by letters, the retrospective first person narrative in the tradition of the confession and the third person narrative, often with an ironic narrator. All radical novels use one of these three conventional types, with more or less substantial alterations which, however, all follow the same path towards the eviction of a clearly identifiable authoritative voice from the novel.

The epistolary plan of narrative is the one least favourable to the clear expression of a moral authority because its peculiarity lies precisely in its allowing several characters to express themselves in the first person, which puts them apparently on a level with each other. There are indeed means by which the author can make sure that the voice of his authorised characters will be heard over those of over-eloquent rakes. But, interestingly, Bage makes very little use of them in his four epistolary novels. Unlike Richardson, he does not rely on the paratext to make his meaning less ambiguous: all his six novels were published anonymously, some have no preface, and in those which have one, the playful, ironic tone in which the preface is written confuses the author's character and meaning more than it explains them. Within the novels, the impressive number of letter writers prevents the easy identification of a relater-in-chief, and those letter writers who could be considered as Bage's mouthpieces are not even given systematic pride of place. In *James Wallace*, Bage gives the last word to a very eloquent rake – the only case in eighteenth-century literature, notes Peter Faulkner[35] – who concludes the novel with a witty raillery at 'the pleasure of matrimony' and the 'upright commerciants of Liverpool' that the reader has just seen settle in a happy colony. If other novels by Bage are anything to go by, there is little risk of mistaking Sir Everard for the voice of the author. But his witty scepticism and vehemence are so engaging that they force the reader to see the happy few of the little colony through his eyes, and to find their virtue and happiness somewhat petty:

> Sir Everard Moreton to James Lamounded, Esq.: Mr. Preceptor, I have a very great opinion of your *savoir faire*, especially in the articles of sugar and rum; but for your *savoir vivre* – none. You give advice, I allow, with great dignity; the only difficulty is to get anybody to take it. Before *I* do, it must be mixed up in a different way. Whatever you expatiate upon, comes mended from your delightful pen. How the pleasures of matrimony are rendered captivating by it! How smooth they be and tranquil! No storm through the whole of this charming voyage over seas of milk and honey; nor does the water thereof even curdle or turn sour upon the stomach, nor creates it ever crudities and indigestions. Permanent too! Rather a new epithet this; but genius is always creative [...]. Debauchees and sharpers ... In the grace of God, I believe they are not equal to the upright commerciants of Liverpool; nor do they get up matrimony so sweetly: But for the manufacture of wit, mirth, and good humour, I doubt the abilities of your artists must fall short; and curse me if I don't prefer these looms to those for the weaving of saints.[36]

The disappearance of a clearly identifiable moral voice can be observed as well in radical novels adopting a third person narration, such as Bage's last two novels, *Man As He Is* and *Hermsprong: or Man As He Is Not*, in which Bage uses an ironic third person narrator that recalls the works of Fielding. But while critics often underline the normative role of Fielding's ironic narrator, who 'set[s] off the narrative and the characters from immediate contact with the reader and keep[s] the reader aware of the author's controlling presence and his message',[37] Bage's narrator exerts no such mediation between narrative and reader. In *Hermsprong*, the reader is suddenly told in chapter ten that the narrator, who had seemed so far to be exterior to the fictional world he describes, is in fact one of the characters of the story:

> At the conclusion of our sixth chapter, we left Mr. Hermsprong bidding good morrow to the Reverend Dr. Blick. In the course of his morning's walk, he saw a young man taking angles with a Hadley's quadrant. This was my humble self; but I hate egotism; and when I have occasion to mention this self, it shall be by the names of Gregory Glen; the first of which I derive from my godmothers, the latter I inherit from my mother.[38]

The narrator goes on speaking about himself in the third person as 'Mr. Glen' throughout the novel. The brutal shift from one type of narration to the other has an obvious comic effect. But since it does not change the perspective from which the story is told, for Glen still tells his story in the third person and not in the first, it may seem a little gratuitous. But it is, arguably, more than a mere comic device. For in drawing Glen into the fictional world of the story, Bage deprives him of the distance necessary to establish his authority as final and absolute; his word can have at best just as much authority as that of a sympathetic letter writer in an epistolary novel.

In *Man As He Is*, although the ironic narrator is not a character in the story, he is a character in so far as he plays a part through most of the novel. In his addresses to the reader and comments upon the action, he poses as a sceptic painfully aware of the frailty of man's will, somewhat misogynistic and politically conservative. In chapter ten of volume four, for example, he praises the Burkean sentiments expressed by Miss Zaporo in a conversation with the hero and Mr Bardoe. The narrator claims to agree with these 'liberal and enlarged sentiments', and proceeds to praise without naming it 'a book which has lately enchanted all kings, all queens, all bishops', namely, Burke's *Reflections on the Revolution in France*. Then, he relates a conversation he had on the subject with a friend of his, and reports the friend's vehement rebuttal of Burke's thesis, before concluding 'I did not invite my friend to dinner'.[39] Thus, the distance created is not between the reader and the narrative through the mediation of the narrator, but between the reader and the narrator through the mediation of the characters who turn out to be better mouthpieces for the author's opinion than the narrator. The narrator is thus lowered to the level of the villains in the story, the dividing line between character and narrator once more blurred, and the reader invited to realise how biased the voice of the narrator can be and how questionable his moral authority.

In retrospective first person narratives, moral authority is usually vested in the narrator who, in retracing the adventures of his younger self, is able to commend his good actions and condemn his bad ones. The authority of the narrator rests on his being accomplished, perfected, so to speak. Unlike his inexperienced younger self, he has finally come to the true light which enables him to see things as they are. In the case of Moll Flanders or Robinson Crusoe, this is the light of religious faith; what fundamentally separates the narrator from the character is that he or she has found God. In Smollett's *Roderick Random* the hero's restoration to his original social status at the end of the book works as a kind of conversion; the social stability he finds entails, in Smollett's fictional world, a corresponding stability of character: Roderick has reached a perfected state and will henceforth be a 'gentleman', in both the social and moral sense of the word, and it is from this moral standpoint that he can judge his younger self.

But in the works of Godwin and Holcroft, the clear separation of character and narrator is undermined by the authors' belief in man's perfectibility, which forbids them to think of the life of man as consisting of two parts, a pre-conversion imperfect state and a post-conversion perfected state. Life, instead, is a linear development that ends only with death, in which there can be progress towards perfection, but no definite, final perfection. The mind of man is always susceptible of receiving new impressions and forming new opinions accordingly.

The two consequences of this doctrine of perfectibility on the plan of narrative are, first, that their novels are somewhat open-ended: the heroes, we are made to feel, have travelled a long way but have not reached completion. In *Hugh Trevor*, the hero's search for a suitable career is interrupted by his sudden accession to wealth upon his reunion with a long-lost uncle; but the event is, and is presented by himself as, a temporary respite more than a conclusion:

'How long I shall be able to persevere in this eccentric conduct time must tell.'[40] In Godwin's *St Leon: A Tale of the Sixteenth-Century* (1799), the ending is even more obviously open-ended, since the hero's immortality forbids there ever being an end to the development of his character.

The second consequence of the doctrine of perfectibility is the imperfect separation of character and narrator, since the narrator tells his retrospective story without having reached the completion of his story or character. And this insufficient difference between narrator and character blurs their two voices, so that it is often difficult to decide, especially in Godwin's *Fleetwood*, whether the thoughts expressed in the narrative are those of the narrator or those of the character whose 'tone of mind',[41] to use a Godwinian phrase, is retrospectively reconstructed by the narrator. The narrator thus tends to lose his role of moral authority, all the more so as Godwin and Holcroft's interest in the progress of mind inclines them less to blame a character's actions than trace in external impressions the motives for these actions.

The eviction of an authoritative voice entrusted with the moral of the novel, like the promotion of a resolutely prosaic style, has obvious transformational tendencies, to the extent that they not only promote, but effectively exercise in the reader, the faculties of private judgement and free enquiry prized by rational dissenters and political radicals. By adopting a relatively unadorned style, the three novelists seek to address the reader's understanding rather than his fancy or aesthetic judgement, and thus to convince his reason instead of confusing his senses.

Of course, one could argue that novel writing is in itself a decorative mode of writing, however bare the style in which it is written, since it is an image-based means of expressing ideas through characters and stories. But the inconsistency does not seem to have troubled radical novelists, for whom the clear distinction between art and non-art, which romanticism tended to make afterwards, did not exist as yet. For them, the novel was a convenient vehicle for the radical ideals they sought to disseminate, which complemented rather than contradicted the rival medium of the treatise or the essay, and mostly differed from them in so far as it was easier to read and could therefore reach a wider audience.

Leaving the readers to make their own decisions about the moral of the story allows them to use their rational faculty, and forces them to assess the respective merits and reliability of the characters and narrators in the story, as well as form their own judgement instead of receiving it from an omniscient author. But teaching the reader to distrust, or do without, traditional authorities, and encouraging self-reliance on his part instead, has also more politically thorough-going implications. Like the inversion of the traditional hierarchy of characters and plots, it is a way to oppose the social and political hierarchies of eighteenth-century Britain, and make a plea for the equality of men – a plea that is not only proposed to the reader as an ideal, but forced, so to speak, on his mindset and thinking habits as he reads by the very structure of the novels.

There are only few texts in which Godwin, Holcroft and Bage reflect on their novel writing, so it is difficult to establish to what extent the unconventional literary devices we find in their works come from conscious choices. However, the radical ideals that the three authors shared drove them, consciously or unconsciously, to challenge well-established novelistic norms and recast the novelistic mould through which they expressed their opposition to the conventional political and moral ideals of their time.

Notes

1 G. Kelly, *The English Jacobin Novel, 1780–1805* (Oxford: Clarendon Press, 1976).
2 M. Butler, *Jane Austen and the War of Ideas* (Oxford: Clarendon Press, 1975).
3 See, for example, D. E. White, *Early Romanticism and Religious Dissent* (Cambridge: Cambridge University Press, 2006), and Mark Philp's study of the influence of Godwin's dissenting education on the formation of his political thought: M. Philp, *Godwin's Political Justice* (London: Duckworth, 1986). For the influence of the French *philosophes* on British radicals, see Chapter 5.
4 See J. M. S. Tompkins, *The Popular Novel in England, 1770–1800* (London: Methuen & Co, 4th edn, 1969), pp. 194, 296. Tompkins uses 'speculative' for the novels of Godwin and Holcroft, and describes those of Bage as 'novels of opinion'.
5 R. Paulson, *Representations of Revolution, 1789–1802* (New Haven, C.T.; London: Yale University Press, 1983), p. 227.
6 P. M. Spacks, *Novel Beginnings. Experiments in Eighteenth-Century English Fiction* (New Haven, C.T.; London: Yale University Press, 2006), pp. 222–53.

7 P. Clemit, *The Rational Fictions of Godwin, Brockden Brown, Mary Shelley* (Oxford: Clarendon Press, 1993).
8 'If the author shall have taught a valuable lesson, without subtracting from the interest and passion by which a performance of this sort ought to be characterised, he will have reason to congratulate himself upon the vehicle he has chosen.' W. Godwin in his Preface to *Things As They Are; or, The Adventures of Caleb Williams*, 1794, ed. David McCracken (Oxford: Oxford University Press, 1970), p. 1. In the original edition, the novel was published without the preface Godwin had written for it: the novel appeared at the time of the Treason Trials and the publisher feared that the overtly political tone of the preface might do him and Godwin harm and prevent the book from selling well.
9 Tompkins, *Popular Novel*, p. 296.
10 Clemit, *Rational Fictions*, p. 45.
11 W. Godwin, *An Enquiry Concerning the Principles of Political Justice and Its Influence on General Virtue and Happiness*, ed. Isaac Kramnick (London: Penguin Books, 1985), pp. 335–60.
12 Thomas Holcroft, Preface to *Alwyn: or The Gentleman Comedian* (London, 1780), vol. 1, p. vi.
13 F. Robertson, 'Novels', in I. McCalman (ed.), *An Oxford Companion to the Romantic Age, British Culture 1776–1832* (Oxford: Oxford University Press, 1999), p. 287.
14 See chapter titled 'On Fable and Romance', in J. Beattie, *Dissertations Moral and Critical* (Dublin, 1783), vol. 2, p. 312.
15 *Barham Downs: Monthly Review* 71 (September 1796), pp. 223–4, cited in R. Bage, *Hermsprong; or Man As He Is Not*, 1796, ed. Pamela Perkins (Peterborough: Broadview Press, 2002), p. 348.
16 R. Bage, *James Wallace* (London, 1788), vol. 3, p. 264.
17 R. Bage, *Mount Henneth* (London, 2nd edn, 1788), vol. 1, p. 27.
18 Holcroft, *Alwyn*, vol. 1, p. viii.
19 W. Godwin, *The Enquirer. Reflections on Education, Manners and Literature. In a Series of Essays* (London, 1797), pp. 370–3.
20 W. Godwin, 'Of History and Romance', in Pamela Clemit (ed.), *The Philosophical Writings of William Godwin* (London: Pickering, 1993), vol. 5: *Educational and Literary Writings*, p. 298.
21 See, for example, Willam Beckford's *Modern Writing* (1796) and *Azemia* (1797).
22 Godwin, *The Enquirer*, p. 371.
23 Godwin, *Caleb Williams*, p. 5.
24 Godwin, *Caleb Williams*, pp. 10–11.
25 The word 'romantic' rather than 'sentimental' has been chosen here to describe such a plot so as to distinguish it from the conventional plot of the sentimental novels – or novels of sentiment – of the second

half of the eighteenth century, the most famous of which are Sterne's *Sentimental Journey* and Mackenzie's *Man of Feeling*: their story of a sensitive hero's sensitive response to the world in a series of disconnected episodes is different from the tale of love impeded and love triumphant as discussed here. Patricia Spacks stresses the 'disjunctive pattern' of such novels: see Spacks, *Novels Beginnings*, pp. 127–59.

26 See, for example, Clemit, *Rational Fictions*, p. 55, and R. Paulson, 'Gothic fiction and the French Revolution', *English Literary History*, 48:3 (1981), 537–9.

27 The word 'levelling', it may be argued, describes better than 'equalisation' the placing on an equal footing of characters, plots and voices studied here. Radical novelists, however, do not use the word themselves: they prefer the eighteenth-century idiom of 'equality' to the more polemical 'levelling' which would have branded them straight away as rabid destroyers of property, an image that the Anti-Jacobin press and the Association for Preserving Liberty and Property against Republicans and Levellers, founded in 1792, were keen to propagate. Furthermore, in spite of similarities between the claims of seventeenth-century Levellers and eighteenth-century English radicals, the novelists' view of Civil War Levellers – Godwin's at least – seems less sympathetic than one would think. For Levellers and eighteenth-century English radicals, see E. P. Thompson, *The Making of the English Working-Class* (London: Gollancz, 1965), pp. 17–25. In his *History of the Commonwealth of England*, for example, Godwin criticises the 1649 Burford army mutiny and the 'party ... instigated and goaded forward by Lilburne [that] received from their contemporaries, and are known in history by, the name of the Levellers', for their failure to see Cromwell's greater purpose, and readiness to drag the country to its 'ruin'. W. Godwin, *History of the Commonwealth of England. From its Commencement, to the Restoration of Charles the Second* (London, 1824–7), vol. 3, pp. 79–81. On the Levellers, see Chapter 1 and the Introduction in this volume; on the appropriation of Leveller language and/or imagery by eighteenth-century radicals, see Chapters 2 and 7.

28 W. Godwin, *Cloudesley. A Tale* (London, 2nd edn, 1830), vol. 3, pp. 39–40.

29 M. McKeon, *The Origins of the English Novel, 1600–1740* (Baltimore, M.D.: Johns Hopkins University Press, 1987), p. 287.

30 James Wallace and Paulina are discovered to be brother and sister and the long-lost nephews of two of the other characters in the novel, Lady Moreton and Captain Islay. Hermsprong reveals his true origin at the end of the novel: he is Charles Campinet, the rightful heir of the Grondale estate and the cousin of Miss Caroline Campinet with whom he has fallen in love.

31 On the subject of Sterne's influence on Bage, see P. Perkins, Introduction to *Hermpsrong*, pp. 17–23; and W. C. Booth, *The Rhetoric of Fiction* (Chicago, I.L.: University of Chicago Press, 1983), pp. 234–40.

32 W. Godwin, *Fleetwood; or, The New Man of Feeling*, 1805, ed. Gary Handwerk & A. A. Markley (Peterborough.: Broadview Press, 2001).

33 'I conclude with adding that in my opinion, all well written books, that discuss the actions of men, are in reality so many histories of the progress of mind; and, if what I now suppose be truth, it is highly advantageous to the reader to be aware of this truth.' T. Holcroft, Preface, to *The Adventures of Hugh Trevor*, ed. Seamus Deane (London: Oxford University Press, 1974), p. 4.

34 Godwin, *Political Justice*, pp. 96–115.

35 P. Falkner, *Robert Bage* (Boston, M.A.: Twayne Publishers, 1979), p. 90.

36 Bage, *James Wallace*, pp. 507–8.

37 R. Paulson, *Satire and the Novel in Eighteenth-Century England* (New Haven, C.T.; London: Yale University Press, 1967), p. 105.

38 Bage, *Hermsprong*, p. 96.

39 Bage, *Man As He Is*, vol. 4, pp. 62–6.

40 Holcroft, *Hugh Trevor*, vol. 4, p. 494.

41 Godwin, *Fleetwood*, vol. 1, p. 54.

10

~

'The insane enthusiasm of the time': remembering the regicides in eighteenth- and nineteenth-century Britain and North America

Edward Vallance

Through the Act of Indemnity and Oblivion passed in 1660, the restored monarchy sought not only 'to bury all seeds of future discords' but also to suppress 'all remembrance of the former'.[1,2] As George Southcombe and Grant Tapsell have recently put it, remembering itself became an act of rebellion.[3] However, the complete erasure of the memory of the civil wars and revolution was impossible. This was nowhere clearer than in the punishment of the regicides, men implicated – directly or indirectly – in the trial and execution of Charles I. In all thirteen were executed for their part in the King's death. Two others, Isaac Dorislaus and John Lisle, were killed by royalist assassins. Posthumous vengeance was wreaked on the corpses of Oliver Cromwell, Henry Ireton and John Bradshaw.[4] A sense of national guilt for the sin of regicide was encouraged by keeping 30 January, the date of Charles I's execution, as a day of fasting and 'humiliation'.[5] Histories and collective biographies detailing the wicked lives of the 'king killers', and graphic political prints vividly depicting the gruesome punishments reserved for traitors, ensured that this event would not be forgotten.[6] On into the eighteenth century, the regicide was employed by loyalist writers and artists to smear English radicals and to outline the dangerous consequences of arguments for political reform.[7]

However, as Andrew Lacey has noted, there was a paradox at the heart of the solemn commemoration of Charles I's execution – the cult of the royal martyr simultaneously 'kept alive the names and principles of those "bloodthirsty men" whom the Office sought to excoriate. The State Prayers ensured that each year the nation was reminded of the fact of rebellion and regicide, and that it was possible to "turn the world upside down"'.[8] As Timothy Morton and Nigel Smith have reminded us, the history of the Civil Wars and Interregnum could be invoked both to legitimate radical action and to warn of its consequences.[9] In this way, the attempt to contain the radical potential of remembrance was always fraught with the danger that such efforts might instead stimulate its resurgence. Even ostensibly uncontroversial observances of the solemnities of 30 January ensured at least that the regicide could not simply be forgotten. Repetition, as Patrick H. Hutton has argued, is vital to the incorporation of historic moments in collective memory.[10] While symbolic repetition could also take on a critical aspect – witness the alleged celebrations of the 'Calves Head Club' – ceremony that remained staunchly orthodox could also sustain more controversial invocations and recreations of the regicide.[11]

The persistence of the memory of the regicide was more, though, than a consequence of its official commemoration. Much recent historiography is critical of the notion of a clearly definable early modern English 'radicalism' and of the idea of a singular English radical tradition.[12] However, as problematic as those concepts are, positive representations of the regicide were arguably also sustained by what Morton and Smith have identified as fundamental continuities in the content and contexts of radical writing across the seventeenth and eighteenth centuries.[13] In the case of the recuperation of the lives of the King's judges the common strands were the assertion of the right of resistance, a core element of Whig political thought, and the connections between English religious dissent and the period of the Civil Wars and Interregnum. While the dominant narrative was that the execution of the regicides was an act both of justice and divine retribution, an alternative interpretation developed in which the King's judges were not murderers but martyrs themselves. *Speeches and Prayers of some of the late King's Judges* appeared in December 1660. Emerging out of radical post-Restoration print networks, the pamphlet's presentation of the King's judges as men who died bravely and unrepentantly had an enduring influence on later presentations of the regicides.[14] Further weight was added to this radical reading of the regicide by the publication of Edmund Ludlow's *Memoirs* in the 1690s.[15] While Ludlow's editor, usually identified as the freethinker John Toland, may have stripped away the religious significance attached to the regicides' deaths in the original manuscript, the positive presentation of these men was clear in the published text.[16] Later editions of Ludlow also included material from other regicides, notably Charles I's prosecutor, John Cook.[17] Moreover, while the *Memoirs* only implied the justice of the King's execution, Catharine Macaulay's history of the event, drawn from Ludlow, made the righteousness of 1649 explicit.[18] Some Whig politicians were even prepared to defend not just the 1688 Revolution, but also the regicide, as a legitimate act of resistance against royal tyranny, a highly charged comparison given contemporary concern with the excesses of George III's government. Charles James Fox, in his incomplete, posthumously published history of the reign of James II, declared the execution of Charles I an 'exemplary act of substantial justice'.[19]

The regicide, then, remained deeply divisive, enduring as a trigger for political and religious controversy across the eighteenth century. This chapter explores the contested memory of three regicides – John Dixwell, William Goffe and Edward Whalley – who all escaped to New England in the 1660s and spent the remainder of their lives in exile. As will be shown, historical presentations of these men in the eighteenth century split along political lines. However, in the case of the loyalist historian, biographer and antiquary Mark Noble, his predictably hostile depiction of the regicides was tempered by expressions of sympathy for the fate of the New England exiles in particular. In this way, it will be argued, Noble's works represent a significant loyalist contribution to the debate over the politics of sensibility in the late eighteenth century. His treatment of Goffe and Whalley as men subject to powerful delusions resonated both with loyalist arguments about the radical imagination and with contemporary cases of treason in which insanity pleas were integral to the defendants' acquittal. This emphasis upon sympathy and sensibility was also a feature of the literary treatments of these regicides in the early nineteenth century. It will be argued that the literary interest in the story of Dixwell, Goffe and Whalley was the product of the synergy between the story of their lives in exile and the Romantic aesthetic. The Romantic fascination with the passions and extreme emotion in particular supported the reconceptualisation of regicide not as a mortal sin or capital crime but as an act of madness warranting understanding. While that reconfiguring of treason opened the way for narratives of the lives of the King's judges which moved beyond either hagiography or total condemnation, it also diminished the political significance of regicide, turning it instead into a sentimental melodrama.

As will be shown later, the fate of Dixwell, Goffe and Whalley was long shrouded in mystery. The research of Philip Major and Jason Peacey, among others, has now revealed much about the flight and subsequent American exile of these regicides. Edward Whalley, cousin of Oliver Cromwell, Major-General and Cromwellian peer, and his son-in-law and fellow Major-General William Goffe, an MP in the Protectoral Parliaments, sailed from Gravesend to Boston on 12 May 1660. The two men knew that they would receive a warm welcome there, having already been sent an invitation from the reverend John Davenport to come to New England. When they landed in Massachusetts ten weeks later, a loyalist informer, the appropriately named John Crown, reported that the two regicides were received as 'men dropt down from heaven'.[20] Goffe and Whalley initially settled in Cambridge, and for a short time they appear to have enjoyed relative freedom in their exile, attending sermons and participating in local debates. However, royal agents were soon sent out to arrest them, necessitating their movement in 1661 to New Haven, Connecticut. During this period the two men had to seek refuge from their pursuers in what later became known as 'The Judges' Cave' atop West Rock, a hollow created between several massive boulders that Goffe and Whalley made their home for – depending on the account – anywhere from one month to three years. Finally, the two regicides moved to remote Hadley, Massachusetts, where they were given sanctuary in the Reverend John Russell's house. William Goffe continued to write letters to his wife in England and from these it appears that Edward Whalley died around 1675. Goffe's last letter was sent in April 1679 and it is usually assumed that he died in that same year.

Their fellow regicide, John Dixwell, appears to have enjoyed a slightly more comfortable exile, largely as a result of the Restoration authorities never having realised that he had escaped to North America: Dixwell had initially fled to Hanau in Germany with other regicides after the Restoration and it was wrongly assumed that he had remained there. At some point in the early 1660s, however, he sailed to America and by 1665 he was in Hadley with Goffe and Whalley. His stay with his fellow regicides appears to have been brief and Dixwell eventually settled in New Haven under the assumed name of James Davids. Here he married twice, first to Joanna Ling in 1673, who died soon after they were wed, and then in 1677 to Bathsheba How, with whom he had three children. Although Dixwell's exile was certainly less confined than that of Goffe and Whalley, he nonetheless led, in the words of one contemporary, a 'modest and obscure life'. Dixwell died in March 1689, too soon to receive news of the 1688 Revolution from radical associates in England, such as John Wildman, who counselled him to return to England.[21]

Dixwell, Goffe and Whalley's experiences in exile remained largely unknown, at least outside of local folk memory, until the late eighteenth century. *The History of King-Killers; or, The Fanatick Martyrology*, a work published in 1720 which attempted to find a dead regicide for every day of the year, said only of Dixwell that he 'fled to save his scandalous Life, and what became of him afterwards, when or where he dy'd is not known'.[22] *A Brief Account of the Martyrdom of Charles I* published in 1756 stated that Goffe and Whalley had both fled to Lucerne after the Restoration with Goffe then 'wandering about in foreign parts many years after like a vagabond'.[23] Other English accounts of the regicide, such as *England's Black Tribunal*, first published in 1680, were more interested in creating martyrologies of royalist 'sufferers' than in rehearsing the lives of the regicides.[24] The neglect of Dixwell, Goffe and Whalley was a result not only of a lack of information or interest in the King's judges but also of the continuing political sensitivity of the regicide as a topic. Authors who stressed the justice of 1649 faced considerable public opprobrium: Macaulay's later volumes, tackling the regicide and the English republic, were markedly less well received than those covering the early 1640s.[25] The controversial nature of the regicide was also reflected in the content of many 30 January sermons, especially after the 1688 Revolution. While some preachers did court controversy, most preferred to devote themselves to promoting abstract religious and political principles – the power of providence, the duty of obedience – rather than engage with historical events.[26] Indeed, while the office for 30 January was the most well observed of the annual parliamentary politico-religious holidays, this was more a result of the fit of this fast with the parliamentary calendar than the strength of the cult of the royal martyr.[27] Even more politically sympathetic histories of the Commonwealth, such as the biography of Oliver Cromwell usually attributed to the

General Baptist minister Isaac Kimber, preferred to skirt around the King's trial and execution rather than explore it in detail. Kimber largely conceded that the regicide represented a terrible blot on his character:

> To do his character justice two actions sully it in general, namely, cutting off the king, and setting himself up as head of the commonwealth; in the first he dipped his hands in a cold murder on the person of his sovereign; and in the second he darkened all the glory of his gallantry, and the great things he had done in the field, shewing that it was all with a secret aim to gratify his private ambition.[28]

Though Kimber's biography was much expanded in later editions, the regicide was still treated as a shameful episode which it was the biographer's duty to minimise Cromwell's role in rather than to justify.[29] Kimber's biography reflected the general unease of dissenting historians in tackling the regicide, a discomfort which was understandable given the connections still being drawn between nonconformity and republicanism by their High Church critics.[30]

This reticence about discussing the regicide was, however, less evident in a North American context, especially in the decade immediately prior to the American Revolution.[31] In part, this difference in the case of Dixwell, Goffe and Whalley was a result of the greater availability of relevant source material in America. Thomas Hutchinson's *History of the Colony of Massachusetts Bay*, published in 1764, employed original papers, including Goffe's diary and letters, to construct an account of the regicides' North American exile. As Hutchinson himself declared, 'the story of these persons has never yet been published to the world'.[32] Yet it was the perceived relevance of the regicides' experiences to contemporary political struggles which made their story worth telling. Hutchinson was a political loyalist who would be forced into exile at the American Revolution.[33] He had little interest in celebrating the regicides' political ideals and he presented their religious outlook as too excessive to be fit for the tastes of an eighteenth-century audience.[34] Hutchinson recounted the tale of Dixwell, Goffe and Whalley only, he said, as an 'entertainment to the curious'.[35] However, Mark Sargent has persuasively suggested that Hutchinson's treatment of their 'miserable' lives was meant to hint at something more: to offer a warning of the dire consequences of insurrection in a history published at the height of the Stamp Act crisis.[36]

The greater interest in the history of the regicides exiled to New England was also, arguably, a consequence of their persistent presence in public memory. Hutchinson had claimed that the tale of Dixwell, Goffe and Whalley had previously 'never been known in New England' prior to the publication of his history.[37] However, as A. F. Young noted, within four years the names Goffe and Whalley were being used as postscripts to insurrectionary letters in the *Boston Gazette*. These pseudonyms were part of a wider trend identified by Young of opponents of the British colonial authorities employing the memory of the English Civil Wars in support of their own acts of resistance against royal power.[38] The use of the names Goffe and Whalley might have been a sweeping appropriation of Hutchinson's *History*, but it seems more likely that the use of these appellations was a product of already established local folk traditions concerning the three regicides.

These traditions were later recorded in the most extensive and influential treatment of the story of Dixwell, Goffe and Whalley: Ezra Stiles's *A history of three of the Judges of Charles I* published in Hartford in 1794. Stiles's approach in this text was certainly unusual and not, in the eyes of some critics, entirely successful.[39] His book combined archival research, topographical surveys (the work included maps of the regicides' escape route), oral history and radical political polemic. The last one hundred pages or so of Stiles's account took the story of Dixwell, Goffe and Whalley as the starting point for a prophetic and utopian vision of the imminent downfall of monarchy across the world: the 'Scottish martyrs', Thomas Muir, Thomas Fyshe Palmer and Joseph Gerrald, transported for sedition in 1793, were compared to Cromwell, Fairfax and Whalley; the Jacobin clubs were described as 'the salvation of France' and 'bulwarks of liberty'; and the oppression of monarchy would be replaced by the freedom of annual parliaments elected on the basis of universal male suffrage.[40]

Although Stiles was not alone in urging the positive commemoration of the three regicides – in 1792, the Whig chief justice of South Carolina, Adaenus Burke, had called for a monument to Dixwell, Goffe and Whalley to honour their struggle against royal tyranny – the conclusion to his book clearly placed him well beyond the mainstream of contemporary American political opinion.[41] In terms of its subsequent influence, more important than the revolutionary tirade that closed the book, were the oral traditions concerning the judges that Stiles gathered and preserved. The tales Stiles collected were various: Goffe in disguise beating a braggart fencing master with no more than a shield made of cheese and an old broom;[42] Dixwell evading the clutches of Governor Andros, the epitome of Stuart absolutism in North America.[43] But in all of these stories, the regicides were presented as heroic defenders of freedom, righters of wrongs and enemies of the overbearing and prideful, whether a royal governor or a local fencing master. They were also portrayed as men with a seemingly supernatural ability to cheat death, as shown by a number of popular stories of them surviving well into the 1690s.[44] Here Stiles connected myths about Dixwell, Goffe and Whalley to those surrounding other regicides such as John Bradshaw, President of the High Court of Justice. One account had Bradshaw, not dying in 1659 in England and then suffering the ignominy of posthumous disinterment, but escaping post-Restoration to the Caribbean.[45] This story appears to have had considerable currency. According to reports in the English press, the revolutionary epitaph to Bradshaw engraved on a canon in Martha Bay, Jamaica, was 'pasted up in the Houses of North America' during the War of American Independence.[46]

By far the most enduring of these stories, though, was that of the 'Angel of Hadley'. According to this legend, relegated to a footnote by Hutchinson but placed centre stage by Stiles, the people of Hadley, Massachusetts, had come under a surprise Indian attack in 1675 while the townspeople were at prayer. Thrown into disarray by the assault, they had threatened to succumb to the marauders only for an old man, dressed in strange, antique clothing, suddenly to appear and rally them against their foe. With the attack thwarted, the elderly figure vanished as miraculously as he had appeared, never to be seen again. Both Hutchinson and Stiles accepted that the so-called 'Angel of Hadley' was, in fact, none other than the former Major-General William Goffe.[47]

As noted by G. Harrison Oriens, the myth of the 'Angel of Hadley' had been identified in American literary magazines as a potentially fruitful source for authors of fiction as early as 1815.[48] Seven years later, the leading historical novelist of the age, Sir Walter Scott, influenced by Stiles's account, incorporated the legend into his *Peveril of the Peak*.[49] Aside from Scott, the story was retold by John McHenry in *The Spectre of the Forest* (1823), James Fenimore Cooper in *The Wept of Wish-ton-Wish* (1829), Delia

Bacon in 'The Regicides' (published in her *Tales of the Puritans*, 1831) and Nathaniel Hawthorne in 'The Grey Champion' (published in his *Twice Told-Tales*, 1837). Besides prose treatments, Robert Southey in his unfinished *Oliver Newman* (published in 1845) and Ebenezer Elliott, 'the corn-law rhymer', in his *Kerhonah* (1835) also produced poetic dramas based on the story. Sargent has calculated that overall, between the publication of *Peveril of the Peak* and the outbreak of the American Civil War, there were more than a dozen literary productions featuring the story.[50]

What provoked this flurry of literary interest in Goffe, Dixwell and Whalley? Certainly, a direct political connection, as has been inferred by Sargent as being behind the histories of Hutchinson and Stiles, seems hard to sustain. The political outlooks of these nine-teenth-century authors appear too disparate to identify a common ideological thread – what, after all, connects the Tory Scott to the popular radical Elliott?[51] Southey had passed through a radical phase as a young man and had written a poem in honour of the republican and regicide Henry Marten, but by the time he came to compose *Oliver Newman* he was an avowed conservative in both politics and religion.[52] In broader terms, there was more than a passing similarity between Scott's sentiment, as articulated by the Presbyterian Major Bridgenorth, that 'perhaps his [Goffe's] voice may be heard in the field once more, should England need one of her noblest hearts'[53] and Hawthorne's 'Grey Champion' who embodies the 'hereditary spirit' of New England and could reappear whenever tyranny threatened.[54] Both authors return us to the popular champion encapsulated in the stories collected by Stiles. However, they did not in any sense support the Jacobin political vision he had subsequently built upon these tales, nor was it the case that regicide was becoming any less of a sensitive political topic in the early nineteenth century. Letters to the loyalist periodical *John Bull* might contain complaints that the solemnities of 30 January were no longer being widely observed, but its news pages remained filled with stories of the threats posed by bloodthirsty regicides to the July Monarchy in France and the danger presented by their radical equivalents in England.[55] Positive reflections on the regicide from contemporary radicals seem to have been equally rare.[56] Largely, they appear to have been the preserve of a small number of English republicans, such as the London Corresponding Society member and printer Daniel Eaton and the Chartist book illustrator and poet William Linton.[57]

Instead, the fit between the story of Dixwell, Goffe and Whalley and the Romantic sensibility seems to offer the main explanation for the growth in interest in these three regicides. Their history combined central elements of the Romantic aesthetic: the supernatural (the myth of the Angel of Hadley), gothic horror (the regicide itself and then Goffe and Whalley's captivity in Hadley), untamed nature (the judges' cave), exoticism (encounters with Native Americans), a fascination with religious 'enthusiasm' (Goffe's millenarian expectation) and powerful emotional content (the impact on Goffe's wife in England as revealed in his letters).[58] In some literary representations, such as McHenry's *Spectre of the Forest*, the supernatural and Gothic elements were heightened further by the intertwining of the story of the regicides with accounts of the Salem witch trials.[59] In others, such as Delia Bacon's 'The Regicides', the masculine republicanism of Stiles's history was subverted by making the hero of the story Goffe's wife.[60]

The Romantic engagement with the story of Dixwell, Goffe and Whalley required that its literary audience should sympathise with the plight of these regicides if not with the political actions which had placed them in this situation. However, while many of these authors were reliant on Stiles for their source material, or upon other histories which were themselves based on Stiles's account, his history had presented Dixwell, Goffe and Whalley as figures due heroic adoration rather than sympathy.[61] The first empathetic treatment of the regicides can be found not in Stiles but in one of his own sources, Mark Noble's *Memoirs of the Protectorate-House of Cromwell*, first published in 1784.[62] While Noble claimed in the preface to his work that his history was free from 'party prejudice', it was nonetheless, as contemporary critics noted, clearly hostile to anything that smacked of puritanical 'enthusiasm' or 'fanaticism'.[63] As Stiles also observed, in the first edition of this work, Noble was unaware that Cromwell's kinsman Edward Whalley and his son-in-law William Goffe had fled to New England.[64] Even so, Noble's appraisal of Whalley, while denouncing his religious outlook as 'wild and enthusiastic', also applauded his 'valor, and military knowledge' and stated that he had carried out his public offices with 'honesty' and 'propriety'.[65]

These sympathetic aspects of Whalley's personality were drawn out further in the second and third editions of Noble's *Memoirs*, both published in 1787. Noble here offered a detailed narrative of

Goffe and Whalley's exile which was clearly drawn very closely from that offered in Hutchinson's *History*. Noble, however, put a sentimental spin upon Hutchinson's materials, especially the letters he had reprinted from Goffe and his wife. Noble's *Memoirs* urged sympathy for Frances Goffe: 'Whatever might be the criminality of them respecting the king's violent death, humanity will strongly plead in commiseration of her undeserved and most acute misfortunes.'[66] Yet, Noble demanded his readers should empathise not only with Goffe's abandoned spouse but also with the regicides themselves. The hardships experienced by Goffe and Whalley must, Noble said,

> hurt the feelings of any, how much soever they may dislike their political sentiments, and they must pity the condition of two gentlemen, who had held the rank of nobles, and possessed very great power, being obliged for many years to live in constant fear, often in a cavern, and almost constantly confined to a private wretched apartment, depending upon precarious remittances and benefactions, deprived of the comforts of associating with their families, friends, and almost debarred human converse.[67]

Noble's emphasis here on the emotional toll exacted on the regicides by separation from their families seems to presage later loyalist representations of sensibility, notably Edmund Burke's vision of the family unit as the centre of human feeling.[68]

This sympathetic treatment of Goffe and Whalley was maintained and expanded in Noble's *The Lives of the English Regicides*, published in 1798.[69] Noble's work was a clear piece of loyalist history, dedicated to the regicides of France as warning of the grisly fate that would soon befall them.[70] Nonetheless, Noble was also keen to distinguish his book from earlier hostile treatments of the regicide which had privileged condemnation over explanation and factual accuracy. But, as critical reviewers noted at the time, Noble's claim that he would separate 'the man from the crime' was spurious given that the work was clearly directed at the 'rigid condemnation of regicidal doctrines'.[71]

Despite its obvious bias, Noble's *Lives of the English Regicides* did attempt to make its readers find sympathy for those of the King's judges who suffered for sincerely held, if erroneous, beliefs. This came through clearly in Noble's biography of Whalley:

> They had hid themselves in a wild solitude, where they lived very many years literally buried alive in a cave; and when they died their

wretched remains were deposited in the cellar of a house in which they sometimes ventured to inhabit, or rather to secrete themselves. Even royalty itself must feel commiseration for the humiliating and apprehensive torture in which they lingered out their existence, in a vain and wild visionary expectation that God would manifest his approbation of their cause.

Whalley was, Noble said, a 'wild enthusiast' but he had never been given to any of those 'private wickednesses' which disgraced the lives of other regicides: 'He was under powerful delusions, and neither the dreadful corrections of himself, the constant detestation of his vast crime could make him see the enormity of it.'[72]

Noble's biography of Whalley represented an important development of that offered in his memoirs of the Cromwell family in that it clearly suggested the regicide's actions were the product of a form of insanity. This argument was made explicit in his account of John Carew. Noble suggested that in another era Carew's fate – he was executed in October 1660 – might have been avoided: 'In times of peace and domestic harmony such a character would have been judged religiously mad, and shut up in a place proper for the reception of such unhappy creatures, and with due care he might have been restored to reason; if not, he would have been prevented outraging the dearest rights of society.'[73]

While ostensibly sympathetic, Noble's treatment of Goffe and Whalley also performed a number of other functions. It continued the presentation of religious dissent as the source of political extremism; by demonstrating the miserable lives of those who evaded justice, it also showed that providential judgement was inescapable; and by imagining the sympathetic feelings of monarchy for Goffe and Whalley's plight, Noble engaged with contemporary sentimentalised representations of royalty, especially the 'murdered' kings Charles I and Louis XVI.[74] In this way, Noble's presentation of the regicides provided a response to Macaulay's view that the execution of the King's judges demonstrated a lack of 'sympathising tenderness' on the part of Charles II.[75] Yet Noble's reading of regicidal actions as a form of insanity also resonated with contemporary British regicide cases and with loyalist treatments of the radical political imagination in general. As John Barrell has demonstrated, in the late eighteenth century, the radical political imagination came to be characterised as 'deranged' or 'perverted'. In the context of discussions of treason, the idea of 'imagining' the monarch's death moved away from older understandings meaning to design or plan and came to be associated with being the product of such 'wicked' or 'evil' imaginations. Regicide became an act born of warped imagining.[76]

It was seemingly just such an act of madness which led Margaret Nicholson to attempt to stab George III on 2 August 1786 as the King alighted from his carriage at St James' Palace. The King himself viewed this feeble attempt on his life – her weapon was a flimsy dessert knife – as the product of insanity. Nicholson was brought before the Privy Council and on the evidence of two physicians judged to be mad. She was committed to Bethlem Hospital and remained there for the rest of her life, dying in 1828.[77] A similar but more legally significant case was that of James Hadfield, who fired a pistol at George III at the Drury Lane Theatre on 15 May 1800. Hadfield, influenced by a millenarian cult, had become convinced that the death of the King would usher in the second coming of Christ. Placed on trial for treason, Hadfield's defence lawyer, Thomas Erskine, successfully argued for a reinterpretation of insanity from being 'lost to all sense', which Hadfield's ability to plan the assassination seemed to speak against, to the idea that the individual was suffering from an overpowering delusion linked to his millenarian beliefs. Erskine, backed by medical evidence that Hadfield's war injuries had caused brain damage, secured his client's acquittal, with the result that Hadfield was not executed but, like Nicholson, spent the rest of his life in Bethlem Hospital.[78]

These cases had already inspired British Romantic literary efforts: while still an undergraduate at Oxford, Percy Bysshe Shelley, with Thomas Jefferson Hogg, had printed a set of poems ostensibly produced in Bedlam by Margaret Nicholson.[79] Behind the cover of a hoax publication – Nicholson was still alive when these supposed 'posthumous fragments' were published – lay some deeply politically subversive poetry.[80] The lines 'Kings are but dust – the last eventful day/Will level all and make them lose their sway;' offered a similar image to Stiles's vision of a final 'war of kings', but the political threat conveyed in this prophecy was mitigated by the sense of this as a revelation to which only 'enthusiast ears' were attuned.[81]

This combination of regicide and madness was also a feature of some of the British fictional works built on the story of Dixwell, Goffe and Whalley. In Ebenezer Elliott's *Kerhonah*, John Dixwell is portrayed as being mentally tortured by his direct role in the King's death. Elliott recasts Dixwell as not only being Charles's judge but also his executioner.[82] In aiding the Indian chief Kerhonah, Dixwell sees a chance for redemption: 'My deed that shall be! – they though late, may yet/Snatch my redemption from relenting fate,/And win a smile severe from seraph lips./Perchance a sufferer's tear, where all is spotless,/Shed o'er the record of my many crimes,/May wash them out.'[83] Southey's *Oliver Newman* has as its eponymous hero the son of William Goffe, who travels to New England in search of his father. Although Southey portrays Goffe's son as a sympathetic character, a pious Puritan but one whose faith is not inflexible or fanatical, his regicide father is painted as an unbending zealot, one who endures a 'living martyrdom' in the belief that God will call him again to 'fight the battles of the good old cause'. While Southey had deliberately drawn Oliver as a figure who would adjust his principles when they were proved wrong, William's 'malady' was presented as too 'deep-rooted' to be shaken from him.[84] Nonetheless, Southey clearly wanted his audience to pity the deluded regicide as well as identify with Oliver.[85] However, as in Noble's histories, sympathising with the fate of the regicides did not involve endorsing either their political or religious views, or the act of regicide itself. Even Scott's original rendering of the Angel of Hadley story, seemingly an unqualified tale of Puritan heroism, was delivered through an unreliable narrator, Major Bridgenorth, whose judgement was elsewhere described in the novel as being impaired by the 'insane enthusiasm of the time'.[86]

The first significant treatments of the exiled regicides in New England were the products of politically motivated historians, the loyalists Hutchinson and Noble, and the radical Stiles. While the histories of Hutchinson and Stiles were undoubtedly the most significant in uncovering the detail of Dixwell, Goffe and Whalley's exile in New Haven and Hadley, it was Noble whose account of the regicides had the greatest affinity with the Romantic literary representations of these figures in the nineteenth century. Noble's work represents an interesting historical intervention in the debate over the politics of sensibility which scholars now see as a central part of literary discourse in the 1790s.[87] While encouraging his readers to make an emotional connection with radical figures, Noble nonetheless placed himself firmly in the Burkeian camp by emphasising the deleterious impact of Goffe and Whalley's actions on the appropriate object of loyal sentiment – the family. Not only had the regicides slain the nation's 'father', Charles I, but they had also broken apart their own households, abandoning wives and daughters by fleeing into exile. So, though Noble lingered over the emotional strain on Frances Goffe to elicit sympathy from his audience, he also did so to provide a clear warning of the affective cost of misdirected passions, however sincerely held they might be.

British authors and poets of the nineteenth century, like Noble, cast the three regicides as figures whose plight could be empathised with, even if the King's execution itself continued to be portrayed as a national tragedy rather than an act of justice. By presenting the regicides' fate as, like their eighteenth-century equivalents Nicholson and Hadfield, a product of a sincerely held delusion, these authors encouraged a sympathetic, emotional engagement with their lives. Yet at the same time, by presenting the regicide as an act of madness, these writers ultimately diminished its political threat. For British authors, the geographical distance of Dixwell, Goffe and Whalley's exile also afforded an equivalent intellectual distance from the terrible act of 1649. Like the liminal, phantom presence of the King's judges in 30 January sermons, the cave and basement hiding places of Goffe and Whalley were apt metaphors for the dark recesses of the radical imagination in which the barely suppressed memory of the regicide still lurked.[88]

Notes

1 The author would like to thank the editors of this volume, as well as Prof. Ian Haywood and Dr John Seed for their comments on this chapter.

2 'Charles II, 1660: An Act of Free and Generall Pardon Indempnity and Oblivion', *Statutes of the Realm: volume 5: 1628–80* (1819), pp. 226–234; http://www.british-history.ac.uk/statutes-realm/vol5/pp226-234 (accessed 29 August 2015).

3 G. Southcombe and G. Tapsell, *Restoration Politics, Religion and Culture: Britain and Ireland, 1660–1714* (Basingstoke: Palgrave, 2010), p. 9.

4 H. Nenner, 'Regicides (*act.* 1649)', *Oxford Dictionary of National Biography* (hereafter *ODNB*) (Oxford: Oxford University Press, 2004); H. Nenner, 'The trial of the regicides: retribution and treason in 1660', in H. Nenner (ed.), *Politics and the Political Imagination in Later Stuart Britain: Essays Presented to Lois Green Schwoerer* (Woodbridge: University of Rochester Press, 1997), ch. 2.

5 A. Lacey, *The Cult of King Charles the Martyr* (Woodbridge: Boydell, 2003), pp. 136–46; P. Ihalainen, *Protestant Nations Redefined: Changing Perceptions of National identity in the Rhetoric of the English, Dutch and Swedish Public Churches, 1685–1772* (Leiden; Boston, M.A.: Brill, 2005), pp. 31–49.

6 On the visual aspects of anti-regicide literature, see L. Bowen, 'Reviling regicides: the king killers in popular culture, 1649–62', *Cromwelliana: The Journal of the Cromwell Association*, Series 2, no. 8 (2011), 36–51.

7 J. Seed, *Dissenting Histories: Religious Division and the Politics of Memory in Eighteenth-Century England* (Edinburgh: Edinburgh University Press, 2008), pp. 157–8.

8 Lacey, *Cult of King Charles*, p. 143.

9 T. Morton and N. Smith, 'Introduction', in T. Morton and N. Smith (eds), *Radicalism in British Literary Culture, 1650–1850: From Revolution to Revolution* (Cambridge: Cambridge University Press, 2002), pp. 1–26.

10 P. H. Hutton, *History as an Art of Memory* (Hanover, N.H.: University Press of New England, 1993), pp. xx–xxi.

11 N. Smith, 'Radicalism and repetition', in Morton and Smith (eds), *Radicalism*, pp. 45–64. The Calves Head Club has tended to be seen as a creation of Tory propaganda rather than a republican reality: see M. Orihel, '"Treacherous Memories": the Calves Head Club in the age of Anne', *The Historian*, 73:3 (2011), 435–62.

12 See, for example, A. Hessayon and D. Finnegan, 'Introduction: reappraising early modern radicals and radicalism', in A. Hessayon and D. Finnegan (eds), *Varieties of Seventeenth- and Early Eighteenth-Century English Radicalism in Context* (Farnham: Ashgate, 2011), pp. 1–29.

13 Morton and Smith, 'Introduction', in Morton and Smith (eds), *Radicalism*, pp. 8–13. A similar argument about the political continuities of seventeenth- and eighteenth-century English radicalism sustaining the memory of the Leveller John Lilburne has been made in E. Vallance, 'Reborn John? The Eighteenth-Century Afterlife of John Lilburne', *History Workshop Journal*, 74 (2012), 1–26. See also the Introduction in this volume.

14 On this pamphlet, see J. B. Williams [J. G. Muddiman], 'The forged "speeches and prayers" of the Regicides', *Notes & Queries*, series 11, vii (1913), 301–2, 341–2, 383, 442, 502–3; viii (1913), 22–3, 81, 122–4, 164–5, 202–3, 242–3, 361–2; R. Greaves, *Deliver Us From Evil: The Radical Underground in Britain, 1660–63* (New York, N.Y: Oxford University Press, 1986), pp. 218–19; M. Jenkinson, *Culture and Politics at the Court of Charles II, 1660–1685* (Woodbridge: Boydell and Brewer, 2010), pp. 38–42. For recognition of its seventeenth-century

influence, see *Regicides No Saints Nor Martyrs: Freely Expostulated With the Publishers of Ludlow's Third Volume, as to the Truth of Things and Characters* (London, 1700), pp. 63–4.

15 Edmund Ludlow, *A Voyce from the Watch Tower Part Five: 1660–1662*, ed. A. B. Worden (London: Royal Historical Society, 1978); B. Worden, *Roundhead Reputations: The English Civil Wars and the Passions of Posterity* (London: Allen Lane, 2001), ch. 2–4; J. Champion, *Republican Learning: John Toland and the Crisis of Christian Culture, 1696–1722* (Manchester: Manchester University Press, 2003), ch. 4.

16 Worden, *Roundhead Reputations*, pp. 52–4, 83–4.

17 E. Ludlow, *Memoirs of Edmund Ludlow, Esq: … with a Collection of Original Papers, Serving to Confirm and Illustrate many important Passages contained in the Memoirs. To which is now added, The Case of King Charles the First* (London, 1751).

18 C. Macaulay, *The History of England From the Accession of James I to that of the Brunswick Line* (London, 1769), vol. 4, pp. 396–421; vol. 6 published in 1781 recounts the deaths of the regicides, pp. 12–26, 112–15.

19 C. J. Fox, *A History of the early part of the reign of James the Second; with an introductory chapter* (London, 1808), p. 14, and for the regicide in general, pp. 14–18; see also W. Godwin, *History of the Commonwealth of England, from its Commencement to the Restoration of Charles the Second* (London, 1826), vol. 2, pp. 688–90.

20 P. Major, '"A poor exile stranger": William Goffe in New England', in P. Major (ed.), *Literatures of Exile in the English Revolution and its Aftermath, 1640–1690* (Farnham and Burlington, V.T.: Ashgate, 2010), pp. 153–66.

21 J. Peacey, 'John Dixwell', *ODNB*; J. Peacey, '"The good old cause for which I suffer"; the life of a regicide in exile', in Major (ed.) *Literatures of Exile*, p. 169. For more discussions of the lives of these three regicides in exile, see M. P. Schofield, 'The three judges of New Haven', *History Today*, 12 (1962), 346–53; C. Durston, 'William Goffe' and 'Edward Whalley', *ODNB*. The story of the regicides' flight to New England remains a source of popular historical interest, see D. Jordan and M. Walsh, *The King's Revenge: Charles II and the Greatest Manhunt in British History* (London: Little, Brown and Co., 2012); C. Pagliuco, *The Great Escape of Edward Whalley and William Goffe: Smuggled Through Connecticut* (Charleston, S.C.: The History Press, 2012).

22 *The History of King-Killers; or, The Fanatick Martyrology, containing the Lives of Three Hundred Sixty Five Hellish Saints of that Crew, Infamous for Treason, Rebellion, Perjury, Rapine, Murder, &c. being one for every Day in the Year* (London, 1720), vol. 2, p. 22 (but organised by date – see October 7).

23 *A brief account of the martyrdom of Charles I. Of Blessed Memory* (London, 1756), p. 7 (Whalley), pp. 13–14 (Goffe). Of Dixwell (p. 26) it simply says that he went overseas.

24 *England's Black Tribunal* (London, 7th edn, 1744), pp. 52–184 are devoted to cataloguing the sufferings of Royalists.

25 B. Hill, *The Republican Virago: The Life and Times of Catharine Macaulay, Historian* (Oxford: Clarendon Press, 1992), p. 33.

26 Lacey, *Cult of King Charles*, p. 249; Ihalainen, *Protestant Nations*, pp. 38–9, 45–9; Seed, *Dissenting Histories*, pp. 90–3.

27 J. Caudle, 'Preaching in Parliament: patronage, publicity and politics in Britain, 1701–60', in L. A. Ferrell and P. McCullough (eds), *The English Sermon Revised: Religion, Literature and History 1600–1750* (Manchester: Manchester University Press, 2000), pp. 240–1.

28 [Isaac Kimber], *The Life of Oliver Cromwell, Lord Protector of the Commonwealth* (London, 1st edn, 1724), preface.

29 See fourth edition 1741, pp. 107–9. For a similar approach, see W. Harris, *An Historical and Critical Account of the life of Oliver Cromwell* (London, 1762), p. 208.

30 Seed, *Dissenting Histories*, pp. 48–50, 100–2.

31 H. T. Colbourn, *The Lamp of Experience: Whig History and the Intellectual Origins of the American Revolution* (Chapel Hill, N.C.: University of North Carolina Press, 1965), pp. 60–68.

32 T. Hutchinson, *The History of the Colony (Province) of Massachusetts Bay* (Boston, M.A., 1764), vol. 1, p. 214.

33 W. Pencak, 'Thomas Hutchinson', *ODNB*.

34 Hutchinson, *History*, vol. 1, p. 217, talking of the content of Goffe's letters to his wife.

35 Hutchinson, *History*, vol. 1, p. 214.

36 'Their lives were miserable and constant burdens': Hutchinson, *History*, vol. 1, p. 215; M. L. Sargent, 'Thomas Hutchinson, Ezra Stiles and the legend of the regicides', *William and Mary Quarterly*, 49:3 (1992), 431–48; Hutchinson's house and papers were destroyed by a mob inspired by seditious sermonising: see Colbourn, *Lamp of Experience*, p. 63.

37 Hutchinson, *History*, vol. 1, p. 214.

38 A. F. Young, 'English plebeian culture and eighteenth-century American radicalism', in M. and J. Jacob (eds), *The Origins of Anglo-American Radicalism* (London: Allen & Unwin, 1984), p. 199; P. Karsten, *Patriot-Heroes in England and America: Political Symbolism and Changing Values over Three Centuries* (London: University of Wisconsin Press, 1978).

39 E. S. Morgan, *The Gentle Puritan: A Life of Ezra Stiles, 1727–1795*

(New Haven, C.T.: Yale University Press, 1962), p. 458; 'The Cave of the Regicides', *Blackwood's Magazine*, vol. 61, no. 177 (March 1847), pp. 333–49.

40 E. Stiles, *A History of Three of the Judges of King Charles I* (Hartford, 1794), pp. 272, 284–5, 289.

41 Morgan, *Gentle Puritan*, p. 458.

42 Stiles, *History of the Judges*, p. 33.

43 Stiles, *History of the Judges*, pp. 130–1; a story revived by Nathaniel Hawthorne in his 'The Grey Champion', in *Twice Told Tales* (Halifax, 1853), pp. 24–5.

44 Stiles, *History of the Judges*, p. 344, on the rumour that one 'Theophilus Whale' who died when 104 years old was really Edward Whalley. This legend continued to be given credence in the late nineteenth century: see R. P. Robins, 'Edward Whalley, the Regicide', *Pennsylvania Magazine of History and Biography*, 1 (1877), 55–66.

45 Stiles, *History of the Judges*, p. 107; a similar story reappeared in the *Leak Times*, 3 December 1892: see Sean Kelsey, 'John Bradshaw', *ODNB*. John Cook was also rumoured to have avoided death by escaping to Staten Island: Stiles, *History of the Judges*, p. 353, although here Stiles was clear that the written record showed that Cook had been executed.

46 *Public Advertiser* no. 14242 (1 June 1780); *Courier and Evening Gazette* no. 1602 (22 September 1797). For a report of similar invocations of the English regicides in a European context, see *St James' Chronicle* no. 4742 (16–18 August 1791).

47 Stiles, *History of the Judges*, p. 29; Hutchinson, *History*, vol. 1, p. 219.

48 G. Harrison Oriens, 'Literary origins of the Angel of Hadley', *American Literature*, 4 (1932), 257–69.

49 G. Dekker, 'Sir Walter Scott, the Angel of Hadley and American Historical Fiction', *Journal of American Studies*, 17:2 (1983), 211–27.

50 M. L. Sargent, 'The Witches of Salem, the Angel of Hadley and the Friends of Philadelphia', *American Studies*, 34:1 (1993), 105–20.

51 Scott made his condemnation of the regicides clear in his role as editor of the nineteenth-century edition of Somers' tracts: see *A Collection of Scarce and Valuable Tracts ... Revised by Sir Walter Scott* (London, 2nd edn, 1811), vol. 5, p. 214, for his comments on John Cook's *King Charles His Case*.

52 W. A. Speck, *Robert Southey, Entire Man of Letters* (New Haven, C.T.: Yale University Press, 2006), p. 70.

53 Walter Scott, *Peveril of the Peak* (Paris, 1823), vol. 2, p. 39.

54 Quoted in Dekker, 'Historical Fiction', p. 222; Hawthorne, 'Grey Champion', p. 26.

55 For France, see *John Bull* no. 545 (23 May 1831), p. 165; for connecting

supporters of political reform with regicide, *John Bull* no. 1121 (4 June 1842), p. 272; for reports of the decline of observation of 30 January, *John Bull* no. 964 (2 June 1839), p. 258.

56 For an example, see the use of the regicide in arguing for an inquiry into the Peterloo massacre of 1819: *Bell's Life in London and Sporting Chronicle* no. 521 (18 March 1832).

57 Eaton produced an edition of John Cook's *Monarchy no creature of God's making* in 1794 with a four-page editor's addendum linking Cook to the Painite radicalism of the 1790s. Linton, like Southey, produced a poem on Henry Marten, 'Harry Marten's Dungeon Thoughts', in *Claribel and Other Poems* (London, 1865), pp. 67–74; see S. Barber, *A Revolutionary Rogue: Henry Marten and the English Republic* (Stroud: Sutton, 2000), pp. 168–9. The author thanks Ian Haywood for bringing Linton's poetry to his attention.

58 On the connections between the regicides' story and Romanticism in an American context, see P. Gould, *Covenant and Republic: Historical Romance and the Politics of Puritanism* (Cambridge: Cambridge University Press, 1996), ch. 3–5, and V. C. Hopkins, *Prodigal Puritan: A Life of Delia Bacon* (Cambridge, M.A.: Belknap Press, 1959), pp. 39–40.

59 Sargent, 'Witches of Salem', pp. 109–16.

60 Gould, *Covenant and Republic*, p. 120.

61 See Robert Southey, *Oliver Newman: A New England Tale (unfinished) with other poetical remains* (London, 1845), p. 83. He revealed that his inspiration was reviewing Abiel Holmes, *A Chronological History of America* (Cambridge, M.A., 1805), a history which recounted in volume 1 the story of the regicides from a combination of Hutchinson and Stiles, pp. 424–5. For Bacon, see Hopkins, *Prodigal Puritan*, p. 43. On Scott's possible use of Stiles, see Dekker, 'Historical Fiction', pp. 214–15, and for Fenimore Cooper *ibid.*, p. 219.

62 Stiles, *History of the Judges*, pp. 8, 11–13, 182, 355.

63 M. Noble, *Memoirs of the protectorate-house of Cromwell* (Birmingham, 1784), vol. 1, p. vi. While noting Oliver Cromwell's care for the nation's liberty, Noble describes him as a 'flaming, puritanic bigot' in religion, *ibid.*, p. 137; William Richards, *A review of the Memoirs of the Protectoral-house of Cromwell* (Lynn, 1787), pp. 69, 72, 74.

64 Stiles, *History of the Judges*, p. 11; Noble, *Memoirs of the protectorate-house*, vol. 2, p. 184.

65 Noble, *Memoirs of the protectorate-house*, vol. 2, pp. 184–5.

66 M. Noble, *Memoirs of the protectoral-house of Cromwell* (London, 3rd edn, 1787), vol. 1, p. 425. The letter was taken from Hutchinson, *History*, vol. 1, pp. 532–3.

67 Noble, *Memoirs of the protectoral-house*, vol. 2, p. 151.
68 C. Jones, *Radical Sensibility: Literature and Ideas in the 1790s* (Routledge: London, 1993), pp. 85–6. See Burke's comments on Louis XVI: 'As a man, it became him to feel for his wife and his children, and the faithful guards of his person, that were massacred in cold blood about him; as a prince, it became him to feel for the strange and frightful transformation of his civilized subjects.' *Reflections on the Revolution in France* (1790), p. 111.
69 M. Noble, *The Lives of the English Regicides, and other Commissioners of the Pretended High Court of Justice* (London, 1798).
70 Noble, *Lives of the Regicides*, vol. 1, p. iv.
71 Noble, *Lives of the Regicides*, vol. 1, p. ix; *The Gentleman's Magazine* no. 84 (1798), p. 596. Noble's work was also error-strewn: Noble, *Lives of the English Regicides*, vol. 1, p. 162, date of Cromwell's death wrong; pp. 230–1, completely fallacious story about 7th Lord Fairfax of Cameron; p. 303, confuses Sir James Harrington with the author of *Oceana*.
72 Noble, *Lives of the Regicides*, vol. 2, pp. 328–9.
73 Noble, *Lives of the Regicides*, vol. 1, pp. 134–5.
74 On which, see J. Barrell, *Imagining the King's Death: Figurative Treason, Fantasies of Regicide 1793–1796* (Oxford: Oxford University Press, 2000), pp. 68–79.
75 Macaulay, *History*, vol. 6, p. 21.
76 Barrell, *Imagining the King's Death*, pp. 22–3, 30–3.
77 J. P. Egen, 'Margaret Nicholson', *ODNB*, and for a detailed discussion of public reaction to the case and Nicholson's treatment, see S. Poole, *The Politics of Regicide in England, 1760–1850* (Manchester: Manchester University Press, 2000), ch. 4. There were other, similar cases in the 1790s: see Barrell, *Imagining the King's Death*, ch. 15.
78 J. P. Egen, 'James Hadfield', *ODNB*.
79 [P. B. Shelley], *Posthumous Fragments of Margaret Nicholson; Being Poems Found Amongst the Papers of that Noted Female Who Attempted the Life of the King in 1786*, edited by John Fitzvictor (Oxford, 1810).
80 See *Shelley and His Circle 1773–1822*, ed. Kenneth N. Cameron (Cambridge, M.A.: Harvard University Press; London: Oxford University Press, 1961), vol. 1, pp. 34–8.
81 [Shelley], *Posthumous Fragments*, pp. 9–10.
82 E. Elliott, *Kerhonah, the Vernal Walk, Win Hill, and Other Poems* (London, 1835), p. 13.
83 Elliott, *Kerhonah*, p. 29.
84 Southey, *Oliver Newman*, p. 51, and for Southey's description of Oliver's religion, p. 87.

85 For a later example of a politically unsympathetic narrator empathising with the plight of the regicides, see 'Cave of the Regicides', pp. 348–9.

86 Scott, *Peveril of the Peak*, vol. 4, p. 137; Dekker, 'Historical Fiction', p. 221. As Dekker notes, American authors were able to accommodate seventeenth-century Puritanism into a heroic narrative with greater ease: see Hawthorne, 'Grey Champion', p. 21. Joel Hawes, of whose strict Independent church Delia Bacon was a member, saw American democracy as the unequivocal legacy of the Pilgrim fathers: Hawes, *A Tribute to the Memory of the Pilgrims, and A Vindication of the Congregational Churches of New-England* (Hartford, C.T.,1830), pp. 62–3; Hopkins, *Prodigal Puritan*, p. 25; see also Gould, *Covenant and Republic*, ch. 4.

87 An overview of recent scholarship in this area is provided by E. O'Brian, 'Sentimentalism and 1790s Radical Novels', *Literature Compass*, 7:11 (2010), 990–8.

88 Seed neatly describes them as having a 'wraith-like' presence: *Dissenting Histories*, p. 89.

Select bibliography

Owing to their sheer number and range, we deemed it unnecessary to include primary sources in the bibliography. We refer the reader to individual chapters.

Aldridge, A. O. 'Thomas Paine and the New York Public Advertiser'. *New York Historical Society Quarterly*, 37 (1953).

Ashcraft, R. *Revolutionary Politics and Locke's Two Treatises on Government*. Princeton, N.J.: Princeton University Press, 1986.

Bailyn, B. 'The Most Uncommon Pamphlet of the American Revolution: *Common Sense*'. *American Heritage*, 25:1 (1973).

Barber, S. *A Revolutionary Rogue: Henry Marten and the English Republic*. Stroud: Sutton, 2000.

Barbour, H. *The Quakers in Puritan England*. New Haven, C.T.; London: Yale University Press, 1964.

Barrell, J. *Imagining the King's Death: Figurative Treason, Fantasies of Regicide: 1793–1796*. Oxford: Oxford University Press, 2000.

Bauman, R. *Let Your Words Be Few: Symbolism of Speaking and Silence Among Seventeenth-Century Quakers*. London: Quaker Home Service, 1998.

Beiser, F. C. *The Sovereignty of Reason: The Defence of Rationality in the Early English Enlightenment*. Princeton, N.J.: Princeton University Press, 1996.

Belchem, J. 'Republicanism, popular constitutionalism and the radical platform in early nineteenth-century England'. *Social History*, 6 (1981).

Bindman, D. *The Shadow of the Guillotine: Britain and the French Revolution*. London: British Museum Publications, 1989.

Blakemore, S. *Intertextual War, Edmund Burke and the French Revolution*

251

in the Writings of Mary Wollstonecraft, Thomas Paine, and James Mackintosh. London: Associated University Presses, 1997.

Blom, H. W. 'Popularising government: democratic tendencies in Anglo-Dutch republicanism', in G. Mahlberg and D. Wiemann (eds), *European Contexts for English Republicanism – Politics and Culture in Europe, 1650–1750*. Farnham: Ashgate, 2013.

Booth, W. C. *The Rhetoric of Fiction*. Chicago, I.L.: University of Chicago Press, 1983.

Borot, L. 'Richard Overton and radicalism: the new intertext of the civic ethos in mid seventeenth-century England', in G. Burgess and M. Festenstein (eds), *English Radicalism 1550–1850*. Cambridge: Cambridge University Press, 2007.

— '"Vive le Roi!" ou "Mort au tyran!"'? Le procès et l'exécution de Charles Ier dans la presse d'information de novembre 1648 à février 1649', in F. Laroque and F. Lessay (eds), *Figures de la royauté en Angleterre de Shakespeare à la Glorieuse Révolution*. Paris: Presses de la Sorbonne Nouvelle, 1999.

Boulton, J. T. *The Language of Politics in the Age of Wilkes and Burke*. Westport, C.T.: Greenwood Press, 1975.

Bourdieu, P. *Language and Symbolic Power*. Trans. G. Raymond and M. Adamson. Cambridge: Polity Press, 1991.

Bowen, L. 'Reviling regicides: the king killers in popular culture, 1649–62'. *Cromwelliana: The Journal of the Cromwell Association*, Series 2, no. 8 (2011).

Brace, L. *The Idea of Property in Seventeenth-Century England: Tithes and the Individual*. Manchester: Manchester University Press, 1998.

Brailsford, H. *The Levellers and the English Revolution*. 2nd edn. Nottingham: Spokesman, 1983.

Brewer, J. *Party Ideology and Popular Politics at the Accession of George III*. Cambridge: Cambridge University Press, 1976.

Brims, J. D. 'The Scottish Democratic Movement in the Age of the French Revolution'. PhD dissertation. University of Edinburgh, 1983.

Burgess, G. 'A matter of context: "Radicalism" and the English Revolution', in M. Caricchio and G. Tarantino (eds), *Cromohs Virtual Seminars: Recent Historiographical Trends of British Studies (17th–18th Centuries)* (2006–7). www.cromohs.unifi.it/seminari/.

— 'Common Law, Norman Yoke and political "radicalism"', in P. Lurbe (ed.), *Le Joug normand, La Conquête normande et son interprétation dans l'historiographie et la pensée anglaises (XVIIe et XVIIIe siècles)*. Caen: Presses Universitaires de Caen, 2004.

— 'On revisionism: an analysis of early Stuart historiography in the 1970s and 1980s'. *Historical Journal* 33 (1990).

— 'Radicalism and the English Revolution', in G. Burgess and M. Festenstein (eds), *English Radicalism, 1550–1850*. Cambridge: Cambridge University Press, 2007.

Burgess, G. and M. Festenstein (eds). *English Radicalism 1550–1850*. Cambridge: Cambridge University Press, 2007.

Burns, W. E. 'A Whig Apocalypse: astrology, millenarianism, and politics in England during the Restoration crisis, 1678–1683', in J. E. Force and R. H. Popkin (eds), *Millenarianism and Messianism in Early Modern European Culture*. 4 vols. Dordrecht: Kluwer Academic Publications, 2001, vol. 3: *The Millenarian Turn: Millenarian Contexts of Science, Politics, and Everyday Anglo-American Life in the Seventeenth and Eighteenth Centuries*.

Burr, W. H. *Thomas Paine: Was He Junius?* San Fransisco, C.A.: The Freethought Publishing Co., 1890.

Butler, M. *Jane Austen and the War of Ideas*. Oxford: Clarendon Press, 1975.

Campbell, G. and T. N. Corns. *John Milton: Life, Work, and Thought*. Oxford: Oxford University Press, 2012.

Caricchio, M. 'News for the new Jerusalem: Giles Calvert and the radical experience', in A. Hessayon (ed.), *Varieties of Seventeenth- and Early Eighteenth-Century Radicalism in Context*. Farnham: Ashgate, 2011.

Carretta, V. *George III and the Satirists from Hogarth to Byron*. Athens, G.A.; London: University of Georgia Press, 1990.

Carter, P. *Men and the Emergence of Polite Society: 1660–1800*. Harlow: Longman, 2000.

Cash, A. H. *John Wilkes: The Scandalous Father of Civil Liberty*. London: Yale University Press, 2006.

— 'Wilkes, Baxter and d'Holbach at Leiden and Utrecht: An answer to G.S. Rousseau'. *The Age of Johnson*, 7 (1996).

Caudle, J. 'Preaching in Parliament: patronage, publicity and politics in Britain, 1701–60', in L. A. Ferrell and P. McCullough (eds), *The English Sermon Revised: Religion, Literature and History 1600–1750*. Manchester: Manchester University Press, 2000.

Champion, J. *The Pillars of Priestcraft Shaken: The Church of England and Its Enemies, 1660–1730*. Cambridge: Cambridge University Press, 1992.

— *Republican Learning: John Toland and the Crisis of Christian Culture, 1696–1722*. Manchester and New York: Manchester University Press, 2003.

— '"May the last king be strangled in the bowels of the last priest": irreligion and the English Enlightenment, 1649–1789', in T. Morton and N. Smith (eds), *Radicalism in British Literary Culture, 1650–1830 – From Revolution to Revolution*. Cambridge: Cambridge University Press, 2002.

Claeys, G. *The French Revolution Debate in Britain: The Origins of Modern Politics*. Basingstoke: Palgrave Macmillan, 2007.

—*Thomas Paine: Social and Political Thought*. Boston: Unwin Hyman, 1989.

Clark, A. *The Struggle for the Breeches: Gender and the Making of the British Working Class*. Berkeley, C.A.: University of California Press, 1995.

Clark, J. C. D. *Our Shadowed Present: Modernism, Postmodernism and History*. London: Atlantic, 2003.

—'Religion and the origins of radicalism in nineteenth-century Britain', in G. Burgess and M. Festenstein (eds), *English Radicalism 1550–1850*. Cambridge: Cambridge University Press, 2007.

Clemit, P. *The Rational Fictions of Godwin, Brockden Brown, Mary Shelley*. Oxford: Clarendon Press, 1993.

—(ed.). *The Cambridge Companion to British Literature of the French Revolution in the 1790s*. Cambridge: Cambridge University Press, 2011.

Colbourn, H. T. *The Lamp of Experience: Whig History and the Intellectual Origins of the American Revolution*. Chapel Hill, N.C.: University of North Carolina Press, 1965.

Cole, A. 'The Quakers and the English Revolution'. *Past & Present*, 10 (1956).

Colley, L. *Captives: Britain, Empire and the World, 1600–1850*. London: Jonathan Cape, 2002.

Condren, C. *The Language of Politics in Seventeenth-Century England*. Basingstoke: Macmillan, 1994.

—'Afterword: Radicalism revisited', in G. Burgess and M. Festenstein (eds), *English Radicalism 1550–1850*. Cambridge: Cambridge University Press, 2007.

—'Radicals, Conservatives and Moderates in early modern political thought: a case of the Sandwich Islands Syndrome?'. *History of Political Thought*, 10 (1989).

Conway, M. D. *The Life of Thomas Paine*. London: Routledge/Thoemmes Press, 1996.

Cooper, T. 'Hodgson, William (1745–1851)', *Oxford Dictionary of National Biography*. Oxford University Press, 2004.

Cotlar, S. *Tom Paine's America: The Rise and Fall of Transatlantic Radicalism in the Early American Republic*. Charlottesville, V.A.: University of Virginia Press, 2011.

Cotton, A. N. B. 'John Dillingham, journalist of the Middle Group'. *The English Historical Review* 93 (1978).

Cowie, L. W. 'Parr, Samuel (1747–1825)'. *Oxford Dictionary of National Biography*. Oxford: Oxford University Press, 2004.

Cragg, G. R. *Freedom and Authority: A Study in English Thought in the Early Seventeenth Century.* Philadelphia, P.A.: The Westminster Press, 1975.

Curelly, L. 'The Diggers and the Ranters: eccentric bedfellows?', in S. Aymes-Stokes and L. Mellet (eds), *In and Out: Eccentricity in Britain.* Newcastle upon Tyne: Cambridge Scholars Publishing, 2012.

— '"Do look on the other side of the water": de la politique étrangère de Cromwell à l'égard de la France'. *E-rea*, 11:2 (2014).

— '"The French, those monkies of mankind": the Fronde as seen by the newsbook *Mercurius Politicus*'. *Revue de la Société d'Études Anglo-Américaines des XVIIe et XVIIIe siècles*, 69 (2012).

Curran, M. *Atheism, Religion and Enlightenment in Pre-Revolutionary Europe.* Woodbridge: Boydell Press and the Royal Historical Society, 2012.

Cushing, M. P. 'Baron d'Holbach: A Study of Eighteenth-Century Radicalism in France'. PhD dissertation. New York, 1914.

Darnton, R. *The Literary Underground of the Old Regime.* London: Harvard University Press, 1985.

— 'The life cycle of a book: a publishing history of d'Holbach's *Système de la Nature*', in C. Armbruster (ed.), *Publishing and Readership in Revolutionary France and America.* Westport, C.T.: Greenwood Press, 1993.

Davies, A. 'Levelling Quakers?', in A. Davies, *The Quakers in English Society, 1655–1725.* Oxford: Clarendon Press, 2000.

Davis, J. C. *Fear, Myth, and History: The Ranters and the Historians.* Cambridge: Cambridge University Press, 1986.

— 'Afterword: reassessing radicalism in a traditional society: two questions', in G. Burgess and M. Festenstein (eds), *English Radicalism 1550–1850.* Cambridge: Cambridge University Press, 2007.

— 'Puritanism and revolution: themes, categories, methods and conclusions'. *Historical Journal*, 33 (1990).

— 'Radicalism in a traditional society: the evaluation of radical thought in the English Commonwealth 1649–1660'. *History of Political Thought*, 3 (1982).

Davis, M. T. 'The Mob Club? The London Corresponding Society and the politics of civility in the 1790s', in M. T. Davis and P. A. Pickering (eds), *Unrespectable Radicals?: Popular Politics in the Age of Reform.* Aldershot; Burlington, V.T.: Ashgate, 2008.

Dawson, R. L. *Confiscations at Customs: Banned Books and the French Booktrade during the Last Years of the Ancien Régime.* Oxford: Voltaire Foundation, 2006.

Deane, S. *The French Revolution and Enlightenment in England, 1789–1832.* London: Harvard University Press, 1988.

Dekker, G. 'Sir Walter Scott, the Angel of Hadley and American Historical Fiction'. *Journal of American Studies*, 17:2 (1983).

De Miranda, M. L. 'The Moral, Social and Political Thought of the Third Earl of Shaftesbury, 1671-1713: Unbelief and Whig Republicanism in the Early Enlightenment'. PhD. Dissertation. University of Cambridge, 1995.

De Negroni, B. *Lectures interdites: le travail des censeurs au XVIIIe siècle: 1723–1774*. Paris: Albin Michel, 1995.

Dickinson, H. T. *Liberty and Property: Political Ideology in Eighteenth-Century Britain*. Oxford: Blackwell, 1985.

— 'The eighteenth-century debate on the "Glorious Revolution"'. *History*, 61 (1976).

Diethe, J. 'The *Moderate*: politics and allegiances of a revolutionary newspaper'. *History of Political Thought*, 4 (1988).

Downie, J. A. 'William Stephens and the Letter to the Author of the Memorial of the State of England Reconsidered'. *Bulletin of the Institute of Historical Research*, 50:122 (1977).

Duff, D. 'Burke and Paine: contrasts', in P. Clemit (ed.), *The Cambridge Companion to British Literature of the French Revolution*. Cambridge: Cambridge University Press, 2011.

Duprat, A. 'Introduction', in *The Mediterranean Corsairs in Narrative: Territories, Corpus and Series*, online publication of the CORSO project, November 2010, p. 3, www.oroc-crlc.paris-sorbonne.fr/.

Durey, M. *Transatlantic Radicals and the Early American Republic*. Lawrence, K.S.: University Press of Kansas, 1997.

Durston, C. 'Edward Whalley'. *Oxford Dictionary of National Biography*. Oxford: Oxford University Press, 2004.

— 'William Goffe'. *Oxford Dictionary of National Biography*. Oxford: Oxford University Press, 2004.

Duthille, R. 'Célébrer 1688 après 1789: le discours de la *Revolution Society* et sa réception en France et en Angleterre', in T. Coignard, P. Davis and A. C. Montoya (eds), *Lumières et histoire/Enlightenment and History*. Paris: Honoré Champion, 2010.

Egen, J. P. 'James Hadfield'. *Oxford Dictionary of National Biography*. Oxford: Oxford University Press, 2004.

— 'Margaret Nicholson'. *Oxford Dictionary of National Biography*. Oxford: Oxford University Press, 2004.

Ellis, R. J. 'Radical Lockeanism in American political culture'. *The Western Political Quarterly*, 45:4 (1992).

Epstein, J. *In Practice: Studies in the Language and Culture of Popular Politics in Modern Britain*. Stanford, C.A.: Stanford University Press, 2003.

— *Radical Expression: Political Language, Ritual, and Symbol in England, 1790–1850*. Oxford: Oxford University Press, 1994.

—'"Equality and No King": sociability and sedition: the case of John Frost', in G. Russell and C. Tuite (eds), *Romantic Sociability: Social Networks and Literary Culture in Britain 1770–1840*. Cambridge: Cambridge University Press, 2002.

Epstein, J. and D. Karr. 'Playing at revolution: British "Jacobin" performance'. *Journal of Modern History*, 79:3 (2007).

Ezell, M. *Writing Women's Literary History*. Baltimore, M.D.; London: The Johns Hopkins University Press, 1993.

Falkner, P. *Robert Bage*. Boston, M.A.: Twayne Publishers, 1979.

Fate Norton, D. and M. J. Norton (eds). *The David Hume Library*. Edinburgh: Edinburgh Bibliographical Society in association with the National Library of Scotland, 1996.

Fish, S. 'Marvell and the art of disappearance', in S. Fish, *Versions of Antihumanism: Milton and Others*. Cambridge: Cambridge University Press, 2012.

Foner, E. 'Thomas Paine's republic: radical ideology and social change', in A. Young (ed.), *Explorations in the History of American Radicalism. The American Revolution*. DeKalb, I.L.: Northern Illinois University Press, 1976.

Foxley, R. *The Levellers: Radical Political Thought in the English Revolution*. Manchester: Manchester University Press, 2013.

—'John Lilburne and the Citizenship of "Free-Born Englishmen"'. *Historical Journal*, 47:4 (2004).

—'The Levellers: John Lilburne, Richard Overton, and William Walwyn', in L. L. Knoppers (ed.), *The Oxford Handbook of Literature and the English Revolution*. Oxford: Oxford University Press, 2012.

Freedman, J. *Books without Borders in Enlightenment Europe: French Cosmopolitanism and German Literary Markets*. Philadelphia, P.A.: University of Pennsylvania Press, 2012.

Fruchtman, J. *Thomas Paine: Apostle of Freedom*. New York, N.Y.: Four Walls Eight Windows, 1994.

Fulcher, J. 'Gender, politics and class in the early nineteenth-century English reform movement'. *Historical Research*, 67:162 (1994).

Gentles, I. *The English Revolution and the Wars of the Three Kingdoms, 1638–1652*. Harlow: Pearson Education, 2007.

—*The New Model Army in England, Ireland, and Scotland, 1645–1653*. Oxford; Cambridge, M.A.: Blackwell Publishers, 1992.

—'The *Agreements of the People* and their political contexts, 1647–1649', in M. Mendle (ed.), *The Putney Debates of 1647 – the Army, the Levellers and the English State*. Cambridge: Cambridge University Press, 2001.

Gilmartin, K. *Writing against Revolution: Literary Conservatism in Britain, 1790–1832*. Cambridge: Cambridge University Press, 2007.

Giry-Deloison, C. 'Le rôle de l'Angleterre dans les événements de la Fronde bordelaise 1649–1653', in A.-M. Cocula and M. Boisson-Gabarron (eds), *Adhésions et résistances à l'État en France et en Espagne 1620–1660*. Bordeaux: Presses Universitaires de Bordeaux, 2001.

Goldie, M. 'The civil religion of James Harrington', in Anthony Pagden (ed.), *The Languages of Political Theory in Early-Modern Europe*. Cambridge: Cambridge University Press, 1990.

Goubert, P. *Mazarin*. Paris: Fayard, 1990.

Gould, P. *Covenant and Republic: Historical Romance and the Politics of Puritanism*. Cambridge: Cambridge University Press, 1996.

Greaves, R. L. *Deliver Us From Evil: The Radical Underground in Britain, 1660–3*. New York, N.Y.: Oxford University Press, 1986.

— 'The early Quakers as advocates of educational reform'. *Quaker History*, 58:1 (1969).

Greenberg, J. 'The confessor's laws and the radical face of the Ancient Constitution'. *English Historical Review*, 104:412 (1989).

Gregg, P. *Free-Born John*. London: George Harrap, 1961.

Habermas, J. *The Structural Transformation of the Public Sphere*. Trans. T. Burger. Cambridge, M.A.: Massachusetts Institute of Technology, 1991.

— *Theory and Practice*. Trans. J. Viertel. Boston, M.A.: Beacon Press, 1973.

Hammersley, R. *The English Republican Tradition and Eighteenth-Century France: Between the Ancients and the Moderns*. Manchester: Manchester University Press, 2010.

Hampsher-Monk, I. 'The political theory of the Levellers: Putney, property and Professor Macpherson'. *Political Studies*, 24 (1976).

Harris, T. *London Crowds in the Reign of Charles II: Propaganda and Politics from the Restoration until the Exclusion Crisis*. Cambridge: Cambridge University Press, 1987.

— *Revolution: The Great Crisis of the British Monarchy, 1685–1720*. Harmondsworth: Penguin, 2007.

Harrison Oriens, G. 'Literary origins of the Angel of Hadley'. *American Literature*, 4 (1932).

Harvey, K. 'Ritual encounters: punch parties and masculinity in the eighteenth century'. *Past and Present*, 214:1 (2012).

Henley, D. 'Thomas Paine: an emerging portrait', in J. Chumbley and L. Zonneveld (eds), *Thomas Paine in Search of the Common Good. Proceedings of a Colloquium Held at the United Nations in New York on December 10, 1987*. Nottingham: Spokesman Books, 2009.

Hessayon, A. 'Calvert, Giles, (bap. 1616, d. 1663), bookseller', in *Oxford Dictionary of National Biography*. Oxford: Oxford University Press, 2004.

—'Early modern communism. The Diggers and community of goods'. *Journal for the Study of Radicalism*, 3:2 (2009).

—'Fabricating radical traditions', in M. Caricchio and G. Tarantino (eds), *Cromohs Virtual Seminars: Recent Historiographical Trends of British Studies (17th–18th Centuries)* (2006–7).

—'Jacob Boehme's writings during the English Revolution', in Hessayon and Apetrei (eds), *An Introduction to Jacob Boehme: Four Centuries of Thought and Reception*. New York, N.Y.; Abingdon: Routledge, 2014.

--'Reappraising early modern radicals and radicalisms', in A. Hessayon and D. Finnegan (eds), *Varieties of Seventeenth- and Early Eighteenth-Century English Radicalism in Context*. Farnham: Ashgate, 2011.

Hessayon, A. and S. Apetrei (eds), *An Introduction to Jacob Boehme: Four Centuries of Thought and Reception*. New York, N.Y.; Abingdon: Routledge, 2014.

Hill, B. *The Republican Virago: The Life and Times of Catharine Macaulay, Historian*. Oxford: Clarendon Press, 1992.

Hill, C. *A Turbulent, Seditious and Factious People: John Bunyan and his Church*. Oxford: Clarendon Press, 1988.

—*Intellectual Origins of the English Revolution Revisited*. Oxford: Clarendon Press, 1997.

—*Puritanism and Revolution, Studies in Interpretation of the English Revolution of the Seventeenth Century*. London: Secker and Warburg, 1958.

—*The World Turned Upside Down: Radical Ideas During the English Revolution*. London: Maurice Temple Smith, 1972.

—'From Lollards to Levellers', in M. Cornforth (ed.), *Rebels and their Causes: Essays in Honour of A. L. Morton*. London: Lawrence and Wishart, 1978.

—'Winstanley and freedom', in R. Richardson, G. Ridden (eds), *Freedom and the English Revolution*. Manchester: Manchester University Press, 1986.

Hinds, H. *George Fox and Early Quaker Culture*. Manchester: Manchester University Press, 2001.

Hirst, D. 'A happier man: the refashioning of William Walwyn'. *The Seventeenth Century*, 27:1 (2012).

—'Making contact'. *Journal of British Studies*, 45 (2006).

Hobby, E. '"Oh Oxford thou art full of filth": the prophetical writings of Hester Biddle, 1629(?)–1696', in S. Sellers *et al.* (eds), *Feminist Criticism: Theory and Practice*. Toronto: University of Toronto Press, 1991.

Hodson, J. *Language and Revolution in Burke, Wollstonecraft, Paine and Godwin*. Aldershot: Ashgate, 2007.

Holstun, J. *Ehud's Dagger: Class Struggle in the English Revolution*. London; New York, N.Y.: Verso, 2000.

Hopkins, V. C. *Prodigal Puritan: A Life of Delia Bacon*. Cambridge, M.A.: Belknap Press, 1959.

Horwitz, H. *Parliament, Policy and Politics in the Reign of William III*. Manchester: Manchester University Press, 1977.

Hutton, P. H. *History as an Art of Memory*. Hanover, N.H.: University Press of New England, 1993.

Ihalainen, P. *Protestant Nations Redefined: Changing Perceptions of National Identity in the Rhetoric of the English, Dutch and Swedish Public Churches, 1685–1772*. Leiden; Boston, M.A.: Brill, 2005.

Israel, J. *A Revolution of the Mind: Radical Enlightenment and the Intellectual Origins of Modern Democracy*. Princeton, N J.: Princeton University Press, 2010.

—*Radical Enlightenment: Philosophy and the Making of Modernity 1650–1750*. Oxford: Oxford University Press, 2001.

Jacob, M. C. 'The nature of early eighteenth-century religious radicalism'. *Republics of Letters: A Journal for the Study of Knowledge, Politics, and the Arts*, 1 (2009).

Jacob, M. and J. (eds). *The Origins of Anglo-American Radicalism*. London: Allen & Unwin, 1984.

Jenkinson, M. *Culture and Politics at the Court of Charles II, 1660–1685*. Woodbridge: Boydell and Brewer, 2010.

Jones, C. *Radical Sensibility: Literature and Ideas in the 1790s*. Routledge: London, 1993.

Jones, R. M. *Spiritual Reformers in the Sixteenth and Seventeenth Centuries*. London: Macmillan, 1914.

Jordan, D. and M. Walsh, *The King's Revenge: Charles II and the Greatest Manhunt in British History*. London: Little, Brown and Co., 2012.

Karsten, P. *Patriot-Heroes in England and America: Political Symbolism and Changing Values over Three Centuries*. London: University of Wisconsin Press, 1978.

Kaye, H. *The Education of Desire: Marxists and the Writing of History*. New York, N.Y.; London: Routledge, 1992.

Keane, J. *Tom Paine: A Political Life*. London: Bloomsbury, 1995.

Keeble, N. H. *The Literary Culture of Nonconformity in Later Seventeenth-Century England*. Athens, G.A.: University of Georgia Press, 1987.

—(ed.). *The Cambridge Companion to Writing of the English Revolution*. Cambridge: Cambridge University Press, 2001.

Kelly, G. *The English Jacobin Novel, 1780–1805*. Oxford: Clarendon Press, 1976.

Kelsey, S. 'John Bradshaw'. *Oxford Dictionary of National Biography*. Oxford: Oxford University Press, 2004.

Kerr, P. *Dark Matter: The Private Life of Sir Isaac Newton*. New York, N.Y.: Three Rivers Press, 2002.

Key, N. E. '"High feeding and smart drinking": associating Hedge-Lane Lords in Exclusion Crisis London', in J. McElligott (ed.), *Fear, Exclusion and Revolution: Roger Morrice and Britain in the 1680s*. Aldershot: Ashgate, 2006.

Killeen, K. *Biblical Scholarship, Science and Politics in Early Modern England: Thomas Browne and the Thorny Place of Knowledge.* Farnham: Ashgate, 2009.

Kitson, P. J. '"Not a reforming patriot but an ambitious tyrant": representations of Cromwell and the English Republic in the late eighteenth and early nineteenth centuries', in T. Morton and N. Smith (eds), *Radicalism in British Literary Culture, 1650–1830: From Revolution to Revolution.* Cambridge: Cambridge University Press, 2002.

Klein, L. E. *Shaftesbury and the Culture of Politeness: Moral Discourse and Cultural Politics in Early Eighteenth-Century England.* Cambridge; New York, N.Y.: Cambridge University Press, 1994.

Knachel, P. *England and the Fronde – The Impact of the English Civil War and Revolution on France.* Ithaca, N.Y.: Cornell University Press, 1967.

Knoppers, L. L. (ed.). *The Oxford Handbook of Literature and the English Revolution.* Oxford: Oxford University Press, 2012.

Kors, A. C. *D'Holbach's Coterie: An Enlightenment in Paris.* Princeton, N.J.: Princeton University Press, 1976.

Kötting, H. *Die Ormée 1651–1653.* Münster: Aschendorff, 1983.

Kramnick, I. *Republicanism and Bourgeois Radicalism: Political Ideology in Late Eighteenth-Century England and America.* Ithaca, N.Y.: Cornell University Press, 1990.

Lacey, A. *The Cult of King Charles the Martyr.* Woodbridge: Boydell, 2003.

Lessay, J. *Thomas Paine: professeur de révolutions, député du Pas-de-Calais.* Paris: Perrin, 1987.

Levillain, C.-E. 'William III's military and political career in neo-roman context, 1672–1702'. *Historical Journal*, 48:2 (2005).

Lewis, E. *Medieval Political Ideas.* London: Routledge & Paul, 1954.

Lounissi, C. *La Pensée politique de Thomas Paine en contexte: théorie et pratique.* Paris: H. Champion, 2012.

Lovejoy, D. *The Glorious Revolution in America.* Hanover, N.H.: University Press of New England, 1972.

Lutaud, O. *Des révolutions d'Angleterre à la Révolution française – Le tyrannicide et Killing No Murder.* The Hague: Martinus Nijhoff, 1973.

Lynch, B. 'Ponder, Nathaniel (1640–1699), bookseller', in *Oxford Dictionary of National Biography*. Oxford: Oxford University Press, 2004.

Lynd, S. *Intellectual Origins of American Radicalism*. Cambridge; New York, N.Y.: Cambridge University Press, 2009.

Mahlberg, G. 'Les Juges Jugez, Se Justifians (1663) and Edmund Ludlow's protestant network in seventeenth-century Switzerland'. *Historical Journal*, 57:2 (2014).

Mahlberg, G. and D. Wiemann (eds). *European Contexts for English Republicanism – Politics and Culture in Europe, 1650–1750*. Farnham: Ashgate, 2013.

Major, P. '"A poor exile stranger": William Goffe in New England', in P. Major (ed.), *Literatures of Exile in the English Revolution and its Aftermath, 1640–1690*. Farnham ; Burlington, V.T.: Ashgate, 2010.

Marcil-Lacoste, L. 'A propos de la philosophie de Thomas Paine: sens commun et droits fondamentaux'. *Canadian Human Rights Yearbook*, 6 (1989–90).

Martin, C. G. *Milton among the Puritans: The Case for Historical Revisionism*. Farnham: Ashgate, 2010.

Matar, N. 'English accounts of captivity in North Africa and the Middle East, 1577–1625'. *Renaissance Quarterly*, 54:2 (2001).

McCalman, I. *Radical Underworld: Prophets, Revolutionaries, and Pornographers in London, 1795–1840*. Cambridge: Cambridge University Press, 1988.

McCormack, M. *The Independent Man: Citizenship and Gender Politics in Georgian England*. Manchester: Manchester University Press, 2005.

— 'Rethinking "loyalty" in eighteenth-century Britain'. *Journal for Eighteenth-Century Studies*, 35 (2012).

McDowell, N. *The English Radical Imagination: Culture, Religion, and Revolution, 1630–1660*. Oxford: Clarendon Press, 2004.

— 'Writing the literary and cultural history of radicalism in the English revolution', in M. Caricchio and G. Tarantino (eds), *Cromohs Virtual Seminars: Recent Historiographical Trends of British Studies (17th–18th Centuries)* (2006–7). www.cromohs.unifi.it/seminari/.

McElligott, J. *Censorship and the Press, 1640–1660*. London: Pickering & Chatto, 2009.

— *Royalism, Print and Censorship in Revolutionary England*. Woodbridge: Boydell, 2007.

— 'The book trade, licensing, and censorship', in L. L. Knoppers (ed.), *The Oxford Handbook of Literature and the English Revolution*. Oxford: Oxford University Press, 2012.

McGregor, J. F., B. Capp, N. Smith, B. J. Gibbons. 'Fear, myth and furore: reappraising the "Ranters"', *Past and Present*, 140 (1993).

McKeon, M. *The Origins of the English Novel, 1600–1740*. Baltimore, M.D.: Johns Hopkins University Press, 1987.

Mee, J. 'The strange career of Richard "Citizen" Lee: poetry, popular radicalism and enthusiasm in the 1790s', in T. Morton and N. Smith (eds), *Radicalism in British Literary Culture, 1650–1830 – From Revolution to Revolution*. Cambridge: Cambridge University Press, 2002.

Monod, P. K. *Jacobitism and the English People, 1688–1788*. Cambridge: Cambridge University Press, 1993.

Moore, R. *The Light in their Consciences: Early Quakers in Britain 1646–1666*. University Park, P.A.: Pennsylvania State University Press, 2000.

Morgan, E. S. *The Gentle Puritan: A life of Ezra Stiles, 1727–1795*. New Haven, C.T.: Yale University Press, 1962.

Morgan, J. *Godly Learning: Puritan Attitudes Towards Reason, Learning, and Education, 1560–1640*. Cambridge: Cambridge University Press, 1986.

Morrill, J. *The Nature of the English Revolution*. London: Longman, 1993.

— 'John Philipps Kenyon'. *Proceedings of the British Academy*, 101 (1999).

Morrill, J. and P. Baker. 'The case of the armie truly re-stated', in Mendle (ed.), *The Putney Debates of 1647– the Army, the Levellers and the English State*. Cambridge: Cambridge University Press, 2001.

Morton, L. *The World of the Ranters: Religious Radicalism in the English Revolution*. London: Lawrence & Wishart, 1970.

Morton, T. and N. Smith (eds). *Radicalism in British Literary Culture, 1650–1830 – From Revolution to Revolution*. Cambridge: Cambridge University Press, 2002.

Mott Harrison, F. 'Nathaniel Ponder', *The Library*, 15:3 (1934).

Müller, P. '"The able Designer, who feigns in behalf of Truth": Shaftesbury's philosophical poetics', in P. Müller and C. Jackson-Holzberg (eds), *'New Ages, New Opinions': Shaftesbury in his World and Today*. Frankfurt: Peter Lang, 2014.

— 'Rewriting the divine right theory for the Whigs: the political implications of Shaftesbury's attack on the doctrine of futurity in his *Characteristicks*', in M. Hansen and J. Klein (eds), *Great Expectations: Futurity in the Long Eighteenth Century*. Frankfurt: Peter Lang, 2012.

Munby, A. N. L. and L. Coral (eds), *British Book Sale Catalogues, 1676–1800: A Union List*. London: Mansell, 1977.

Navickas, K. *Loyalism and Radicalism in Lancashire, 1798–1815*. Oxford: Oxford University Press, 2009.

Nenner, H. 'Regicides (*act.* 1649)'. *Oxford Dictionary of National Biography*. Oxford: Oxford University Press, 2004.

— 'The trial of the regicides: retribution and treason in 1660', in H. Nenner (ed.), *Politics and the Political Imagination in Later Stuart Britain: Essays Presented to Lois Green Schwoerer*. Woodbridge: University of Rochester Press, 1997.

Norris, J. M. *Shelburne and Reform*. London: Macmillan, 1963.

Nuttall, G. *The Holy Spirit in Puritan Faith and Experience*. 2nd edn. Chicago, I.L.; London: University of Chicago Press, 1992.

O'Brian, E. 'Sentimentalism and 1790s Radical Novels'. *Literature Compass*, 7:11 (2010).

O'Gorman, F. 'Campaign rituals and ceremonies: the social meaning of elections in England'. *Past and Present*, 135 (1992).

— 'Political ritual in eighteenth-century Britain', in J. Neuheiser and M. Schaich (eds), *Political Rituals in Great Britain 1700–2000*. Augsburg: Wissner, 2006.

Ordahl Kuppermann, K. *Providence Island, 1630–1641: The Other Puritan Colony*. Cambridge: Cambridge University Press, 1995.

Orihel, M. '"Treacherous Memories": the Calves Head Club in the age of Anne'. *The Historian*, 73:3 (2011).

Page, A. *John Jebb and the Enlightenment Origins of British Radicalism*. London: Praeger, 2003.

Pagliuco, C. *The Great Escape of Edward Whalley and William Goffe: Smuggled Through Connecticut*. Charleston, S.C.: The History Press, 2012.

Patrides, C. A. 'Introduction', in *The Cambridge Platonists*, ed. C. A. Patrides. London: Edward Arnold, 1969.

Paulson, R. *The Beautiful, Novel, and Strange: Aesthetics and Heterodoxy*. Baltimore, M.D.: The Johns Hopkins University Press, 1996.

— *Representations of Revolution, 1789–1802*. New Haven, C.T.; London: Yale University Press, 1983.

— *Satire and the Novel in Eighteenth-Century England*. New Haven, C.T.; London: Yale University Press, 1967.

— 'Gothic fiction and the French Revolution'. *English Literary History*, 48:3 (1981).

Paxson Grundy, M. 'Learning to be Quaker: spiritual formation and religious education among early Friends'. *Quaker Studies*, 11:2 (2007).

Peacey, J. *Politicians and Pamphleteers: Propaganda during the English Civil Wars and Interregnum*. Aldershot: Ashagte, 2004.

— *Print and Public Politics in the English Revolution*. Cambridge: Cambridge University Press, 2013.

— '"The good old cause for which I suffer"; the life of a regicide in exile', in P. Major (ed.), *Literatures of Exile in the English Revolution and its Aftermath, 1640–1690*. Farnham and Burlington, V.T.: Ashgate, 2010.

— 'John Dixwell'. *Oxford Dictionary of National Biography*. Oxford: Oxford University Press, 2004.

— 'News, Pamphlets, and Public Opinion', in L. L. Knoppers (ed.) *The Oxford Handbook of Literature and the English Revolution*. Oxford: Oxford University Press, 2012.

Pencak, W. 'Thomas Hutchinson'. *Oxford Dictionary of National Biography.* Oxford: Oxford University Press, 2004.

Pettet, E. C. 'Coriolanus and the Midlands insurrection of 1607', in C. M. S. Alexander, S. Wells, T. Hawkes and P. Holland (eds), *The Cambridge Shakespeare Library. Vol I: Shakespeare's Times, Texts, and Stages.* Cambridge: Cambridge University Press, 2003.

Pettit, P. *Republicanism: A Theory of Freedom and Government.* Oxford: Oxford University Press, 1997.

Philp, M. *Godwin's Political Justice.* London: Duckworth, 1986.

—'The fragmented ideology of reform', in M. Philp (ed.), *The French Revolution and British Popular Politics.* Cambridge: Cambridge University Press, 1991.

Pierson, C. *Just Property: A History in the Latin West.* Oxford: Oxford University Press, 2013.

Pincus, S. 'The State and civil society in early modern England: capitalism, causation and Habermas's bourgeois public sphere', in P. Lake and S. Pincus (eds), *The Politics of the Public Sphere in Early Modern England.* Manchester: Manchester University Press, 2007.

Poole, S. *The Politics of Regicide in England, 1760–1850.* Manchester: Manchester University Press, 2000.

Raymond, J. *The Invention of the Newspaper: English Newsbooks, 1641– 1649.* Oxford: Clarendon Press, 1996.

—*Pamphlets and Pamphleteering in Early Modern Britain.* Cambridge: Cambridge University Press, 2003.

—'The newspaper, public opinion and the public sphere in the seventeenth century', in J. Raymond (ed.), *News, Newspapers and Society in Early Modern Britain.* London, Frank Cass, 1999.

—(ed.). *The Oxford History of Popular Print Culture – Volume One: Cheap Print in Britain and Ireland to 1660.* Oxford: Oxford University Press, 2011.

Reay, B. 'The World Turned Upside Down: a retrospect', in J. Eley and W. Hunt (eds), *Reviving the English Revolution.* London: Verso, 1988.

Reid, L. *Charles James Fox: a Man for the People.* London: Longman, 1965.

Remer, G. *Humanism and the Rhetoric of Toleration.* University Park, P.A.: The Penn State University Press, 1996.

Ricoeur, P. *Histoire et vérité.* Paris: Seuil, 1967.

Robbins, C. *The Eighteenth-Century Commonwealthman: Studies in the Transmission, Development, and Circumstance of English Liberal Thought from the Restoration of Charles II until the War with the Thirteen Colonies.* Cambridge, M.A.: Harvard University Press, 1959.

Robertson, F. 'Novels', in I. McCalman (ed.), *An Oxford Companion to the Romantic Age, British Culture 1776–1832.* Oxford: Oxford University Press, 1999.

Rodway, A. E. *Godwin and the Age of Transition*. London: Harrap, 1952.

Rosenfeld, S. 'Thomas Paine's common sense and ours'. *William and Mary Quarterly*, 55:4 (2008).

Rousseau, G. S. *Perilous Enlightenment: Pre and Post-Modern Discourses, Sexual, Historical*. Manchester: Manchester University Press, 1991.

Rykwert, J. *The First Moderns: The Architects of the Eighteenth Century*. Cambridge M.A.; London: The MIT Press, 1980.

Sargent, M. L. 'Thomas Hutchinson, Ezra Stiles and the legend of the regicides'. *William and Mary Quarterly*, 49:3 (1992).

— 'The Witches of Salem, the Angel of Hadley and the Friends of Philadelphia', *American Studies*, 34:1 (1993).

Schofield, M. P. 'The three judges of New Haven'. *History Today*, 12 (1962).

Schofield, R. E. *The Enlightened Joseph Priestley*. University Park, P.A.: Pennsylvania State University Press, 2004.

Scott, J. *England's Troubles – Seventeenth-Century English Political Instability in European Context*. Cambridge: Cambridge University Press, 2000.

Seed, J. *Dissenting Histories: Religious Division and the Politics of Memory in Eighteenth-Century England*. Edinburgh: Edinburgh University Press, 2008.

Sharp, A. 'John Lilburne and the Long Parliament's Book of Declarations: a radical's exploitation of the words of authorities'. *History of Political Thought*, 9:1 (1988).

Shepard, A. '"Swil-bols and tos-pots": drink culture and male bonding in England, c.1560–1640', in L. Gowing, M. Hunter and M. Rubin (eds), *Love, Friendship and Faith in Europe, 1300–1800*. Basingstoke; New York, N.Y.: Palgrave-Macmillan, 2003.

Skipp, J. 'Masculinity and social stratification in eighteenth-century erotic literature, 1700–1821'. *Journal for Eighteenth-Century Studies*, 29:2 (2006).

Smith, E. E. and E. Greenwell Smith. *William Godwin*. New York, N.Y.: Twayne, 1965.

Smith, N. *Andrew Marvell: The Chameleon*. New Haven, N.J.; London: Yale University Press, 2012.

— *Perfection Proclaimed: Language and Literature in English Radical Religion, 1640–1660*. Oxford: Clarendon, 1989.

— 'England, Europe, and the English Revolution', in L. L. Knoppers (ed.) *The Oxford Handbook of Literature and the English Revolution*. Oxford: Oxford University Press, 2012.

— 'Radicalism and repetition', in T. Morton and N. Smith (eds), *Radicalism in British Literary Culture, 1650–1830 – From Revolution to Revolution*. Cambridge: Cambridge University Press, 2002.

Smith, O. *The Politics of Language, 1791–1819*. Oxford: Clarendon Press, 1984.

Smyth, A. (ed.). *A Pleasing Sinne: Drink and Conviviality in Seventeenth-Century England*. Cambridge: D. S. Brewer, 2004.

Southcombe, G. and G. Tapsell. *Restoration Politics, Religion and Culture: Britain and Ireland, 1660–1714*. Basingstoke: Palgrave, 2010.

Spacks, P. M. *Novel Beginnings. Experiments in Eighteenth-century English Fiction*. New Haven, C.T.; London: Yale University Press, 2006.

Speck, W. A. *Robert Southey, Entire Man of Letters*. New Haven, C.T.: Yale University Press, 2006.

Tapper, A. 'The beginnings of Priestley's materialism'. *Enlightenment and Dissent*, 1 (1982).

Thomas, D. O. *Ymateb i Chwyldro: Response to Revolution*. Cardiff: University of Wales Press, 1989.

Thomson, A. *Bodies of Thought: Science, Religion, and the Soul in the Early Enlightenment*. Oxford: Oxford University Press, 2008.

Thomson, A., S. Burrows and E. Dziembowski (eds). *Cultural Transfers: France and Britain in the Long Eighteenth Century*. Oxford: Voltaire Foundation, 2010.

Thompson, E. P. *The Making of the English Working Class*. Harmondsworth: Penguin, 1963.

Tompkins, J. M. S. *The Popular Novel in England, 1770–1800*. 4th edn. London: Methuen & Co, 1969.

Torrey, N. L. *Voltaire and the English Deists*. London: Yale University Press, 1930.

Turner, J. 'Burke, Paine, and the nature of language'. *The Yearbook of English Studies: The French Revolution in English Literature and Art*, 19 (1989).

Underdown, D. 'Puritanism, revolution and Christopher Hill', in G. Eley and W. Hunt (eds), *Reviving the English Revolution*. London: Verso, 1988.

Underwood, T. L. *Primitivism, Radicalism, and the Lamb's War: Baptist-Quaker Conflict in Seventeenth-Century England*. New York, N.Y.; Oxford: Oxford University Press, 1997.

Vallance, E. 'Reborn John? The Eighteenth-Century Afterlife of John Lilburne'. *Historical Workshop Journal*, 74:1 (2012).

Van Leeuwen, H. G. *The Problem of Certainty in English Thought: 1630–1690*. The Hague: Martinus Nijhoff, 1963.

Vaughan, A. T. 'John Smith satirized: the legend of Captaine Jones'. *The William and Mary Quarterly*, 3rd Series, 45:4 (1988).

Venning, T. *Cromwellian Foreign Policy*. London: Macmillan; New York, N.Y.: St Martin's Press, 1999.

Vercruysse, J. *Bibliographie descriptive des écrits du Baron d'Holbach*. Paris: Minard, 1971.

Vicherd, C. 'La "République" dans les mazarinades: à propos des événements anglais contemporains de la Fronde', in Y.-C. Zarka (ed.), *Monarchie et république au XVIIᵉ siècle*. Paris: Presses Universitaires de France, 2007.

Vitkus, D. 'Barbary captivity narratives from early modern England: truth claims and the (re)construction of authority', in *La guerre de course en récits (XVIe-XVIIIes)*. *Terrains, corpus, series*. Online publication of the CORSO project. November 2010. www.oroc-crlc.paris-sorbonne.fr/.

Voitle, R. B. *The Third Earl of Shaftesbury, 1671–1713*. Baton Rouge, L.A.; London: Louisiana State University Press, 1984.

Watkins, O. C. *The Puritan Experience: Studies in Spiritual Autobiography*. London: Routledge and Kegan Paul, 1972.

Westrich, S. *The Ormée of Bordeaux: a Revolution during the Fronde*. Baltimore, M.D.: Johns Hopkins University Press, 1972.

Weststeijn, A. 'Why the Dutch didn't read Harrington: Anglo-Dutch republican exchanges, c. 1650–1670', in G. Mahlberg and D. Wiemann (eds), *European Contexts for English Republicanism – Politics and Culture in Europe, 1650–1750*. Farnham: Ashgate, 2013.

White, D. E. *Early Romanticism and Religious Dissent*. Cambridge: Cambridge University Press, 2006.

Wickwar, W. H. *Baron d'Holbach: A Prelude to the French Revolution* (1935). New York, N.Y.: A.M. Kelley, 1968.

William, J. B. *A History of English Journalism to the Foundation of the Gazette*. London; New York, N.Y.: Longmans, Green, & Co, 1908.

— 'The forged "speeches and prayers" of the Regicides'. *Notes & Queries*, series 11, vii (1913).

Williams, R. *Marxism and Literature*. Oxford; New York, N.Y.: Oxford University Press, 1977.

Williamson, A. *Thomas Paine: his Life, Work and Time*. London: Allen and Unwin, 1973.

Wilson, K. 'Inventing revolution: 1688 and eighteenth-century popular politics'. *Journal of British Studies*, 28 (1989).

Woodcock, B. 'Writing the revolution: aspects of Thomas Paine's prose'. *Prose Studies*, 15:2 (1992).

Woolrych, A. 'The debates from the perspective of the army', in M. Mendle (ed.), *The Putney Debates of 1647– The Army, the Levellers and the English State*. Cambridge: Cambridge University Press, 2001.

Wootton, D. 'The republican tradition: from Commonwealth to *Common Sense*', in D. Wootton, *Republicanism, Liberty and Commercial Society, 1649–1776*. Stanford, C.A.: Stanford University Press, 1994.

Worden, B. *Roundhead Reputations: The English Civil Wars and the Passions of Posterity*. London: Allen Lane, 2001.

Wright, L. M. *The Literary Life of the Early Friends, 1650–1725*. New York, N.Y.: Columbia University Press, 1935.

Young, A. F. 'English plebeian culture and eighteenth-century American radicalism', in M. and J. Jacob (eds), *The Origins of Anglo-American Radicalism*. London: Allen & Unwin, 1984.

Zaret, D. *Origins of Democratic Culture: Printing, Petitions and the Public Sphere in Early Modern England*. Princeton, N.J.: Princeton University Press, 2000.

Index

absolutism 103, 108, 110, 113–16,
129, 137, 236
Agreement of the People 19–23,
51
America 60, 62, 66, 69–71, 128,
173–4, 176, 232, 234–8
American Revolution 66, 69,
234
Anglicanism *see* Church of England
Antinomianism 3, 45, 86
atheism 114, 125–6, 129, 132,
135, 137–40

Bage, Robert 135, 211, 213–14,
217, 219–22, 225
Bateman, Susanna 89–91
Bible 25, 65, 80, 86–9, 91, 205
see also Scripture
Biddle, Hester 87, 89
Burke, Edmund 64, 66–7, 71, 171,
177–8, 215–16, 222, 239, 242

Calvert, Giles 13, 19, 162
Catholicism 20, 30, 103, 105–6,
108, 116, 137, 160, 195, 199
censorship 13, 52, 70, 193,
199–200
Charles I 6, 174, 229, 231, 233,
235, 240, 243

Charles II 26, 108, 172, 240
Church of England 5, 136, 193,
195, 198
clubs 63, 71, 103, 136, 172, 230,
235
see also coffee houses
coffee houses 63, 181, 196, 202
see also clubs
Commonwealth (1649–53) 16,
18–22, 83, 161, 163, 173–4,
233–4
conservative 61, 112, 117, 176,
178, 216, 222, 237
Coppe, Abiezer 3, 41, 43, 46–7,
53
Cromwell, Oliver 19, 21, 23, 151,
177, 197, 229, 232–5, 238,
240
cultural transfer 17–18, 23, 126,
136, 140

Deist 114, 135, 141
democracy 4, 60, 64–5, 67
Diggers 3, 9, 16, 18, 24–5, 43–6,
48, 53–4, 65, 67–8
see also Winstanley, Gerrard
dissent 8, 195–6, 199, 211, 216,
230, 240
see also nonconformity

dissenter 126, 173, 177, 193, 195, 224
see also nonconformist
Dutch see Netherlands

education 80–4, 86–9, 93, 211, 216
see also knowledge; learning
Enlightenment 60, 65, 73, 114, 125, 131
equality 44–9, 54, 64–7, 211, 213, 225

fiction 1, 27, 29, 217, 222–3, 236, 241
Fox, George 82, 85–6, 89, 91
France 8, 18–19, 21–3, 25, 63, 109, 125, 129–30, 140–1, 175–7, 182, 222, 235, 237, 239
freedom 44–50, 173, 176, 181, 193, 195, 205–6, 232, 235–6
see also liberty
French Revolution 1, 17, 64, 69, 177, 211, 216

George III 66, 180, 182, 231, 241
Glorious Revolution 104, 106, 111, 173–4, 176, 231, 233
Godwin, William 126, 134–6, 141, 211–18, 220, 223
Caleb Williams 135, 212, 215–18

Harrington, James 9, 108–9, 111–12, 115–16
heterodoxy see dissent; nonconformity
Hill, Christopher 2, 4, 24, 41, 52, 152–4, 195–6
historiography 4, 11, 17, 112, 153, 155, 230
Marxist historiography 4, 7, 9, 41–2, 153
see also Hill, Christopher
revisionist historiography 4, 41–2, 153–4

Hobbes, Thomas 44–5, 82, 116
Hodgson, William 127, 134, 139–40, 181–2
Holbach, Baron d'– 125–47
Système de la nature 125–31, 133–6, 138–40
Système social 131, 134–5
Holcroft, Thomas 211–14, 217, 220, 223–5
Hume, David 126–7, 131–4, 138
Hutchinson, Thomas 234–7, 239, 242

Independents 5–6, 16, 20, 81, 193, 196
Ireton, Henry 6, 16, 50–1, 229

Jacobin 140, 211–12, 214, 235, 237
Jacobite 23, 30, 106, 109, 170, 181
Jebb John 126, 134, 136–7, 141, 174

knowledge 80–3, 86–8, 91, 93–5, 174, 204, 213, 238
see also education; learning

learning 80–8, 90, 92–5
see also education; knowledge
Levellers 2–3, 6, 9–10, 13, 15–16, 19–23, 41, 43, 45–6, 48–52, 54, 65, 67, 151–2, 160, 162–5
see also Lilburne, John; Walwyn, William
liberty 20, 22, 44, 46–7, 51, 53, 103–4, 107, 109–10, 114, 173–4, 176, 196, 206, 227, 235
see also freedom
Lilburne, John 3, 10, 67, 160, 162–4
see also Levellers; Walwyn, William
Locke, John 60, 105, 174
London Corresponding Society 127, 139, 172, 178, 182, 237

Loyalist 71, 172, 175, 177–82, 184, 229, 231–2, 234, 237, 239–40, 242

Macaulay, Catharine 179, 231, 233, 240
Marvell, Andrew 11, 90, 174, 193–4, 196–7, 199–206
materialism 82, 125, 132, 135–9
millenarianism 17–18, 41, 44, 47, 114–15, 238, 241
monarchy 6, 21, 64–70, 72–3, 109–12, 115, 229, 235, 237, 240

narration 213, 216, 221–2
narrator 194, 203, 213, 216, 220–5, 242
Netherlands 18, 132, 201
networks 13, 17–18, 25–6, 126, 131, 133–5, 140, 154–5, 173, 230
New England 17, 231–2, 235, 237–8, 242
nonconformist 193, 196, 198–200, 205–6
   see also dissenter
nonconformity 193, 195, 234
   see also dissent
Norman Yoke 48, 65, 67

Paine, Thomas 60–79, 171, 174–5, 179–80
   Common Sense 61–2, 64–5, 67–8, 70, 73
   Rights of Man 61, 63, 67, 69–72, 74
Paris 17, 19, 127, 131, 133–4, 138, 178
   see also France
participatory politics 155, 157, 163–5
petitioning 10, 12–13, 151–2, 155–6, 158, 161, 163
Ponder, Nathaniel 13, 193, 195–6, 198–9, 206

Presbyterian 5–6, 8, 15–16, 84–5, 193, 237
Price, Richard 67, 173, 177, 179, 211
Priestley, Joseph 126, 130, 133–4, 137–9, 141, 177, 211
print culture 4, 12–13, 17, 153–6
property 9, 41–52, 54, 112, 193
Protestant 20, 28, 80, 105–7, 109–10, 193, 195, 199–200
public sphere 13, 42, 53, 64, 140, 152, 155
Puritan 9, 83, 88, 95, 153, 196–8, 216, 237–8, 242
Putney debates 6, 10, 21, 23, 50–1

Quakers 3, 9, 43, 49, 53–4, 80–100, 193

Ranters 3, 4, 7, 9, 18, 43, 45–6, 48, 52–4, 89
   see also Coppe, Abiezer
republicanism 18, 60, 107–8, 115, 175, 178, 234, 238
Restoration 8, 23, 25, 28, 105, 116, 230, 232–3, 236

Scripture 53, 89, 91, 199–200
   see also Bible
Shaftesbury, 3rd Earl of 103–24
   Characteristicks 104, 110, 112, 116, 118
   Danger of Mercenary Parliaments, The 108
   Miscellaneous Reflections 112–13, 115
   Paradoxes of State 109–10
   Second Characters 104, 116
Sidney, Algernon 71, 108, 174
style 19, 61, 67, 73, 176, 199, 202–3, 213–17, 224

Toland, John 107–11, 115–16, 127, 230
toleration 5, 20, 114, 173, 195

Trenchard, John 65, 67, 108–9, 127

tyranny 49, 64–5, 69–70, 73, 112, 114, 160, 173, 194, 205, 231, 235, 237

United States of America *see* America

universal suffrage 23, 49, 51, 60, 235

Walwyn, William 3, 10, 51–2

Whig 4, 13, 65, 104–10, 112, 114–16, 181, 183, 230–1, 235

Wilkes, John 126–7, 131–3, 136, 170, 174, 179

Winstanley, Gerrard 9, 16, 41, 43–7, 52–3, 65, 68
see also Diggers

Wollstonecraft, Mary 134–5, 179, 211

EU authorised representative for GPSR:
Easy Access System Europe, Mustamäe tee 50,
10621 Tallinn, Estonia
gpsr.requests@easproject.com

www.ingramcontent.com/pod-product-compliance
Lightning Source LLC
Chambersburg PA
CBHW050633280326
41932CB00015B/2622